ALIENS

FOREWORD AND SCREENPLAY BY JAMES CAMERON

Edited and with an Introduction
by Paul M. Sammon

ORION

First published in Great Britain in 2001 by
Orion Books Ltd
Orion House
5 Upper St Martin's Lane
London WC2H 9EA

Design and layout by Essential Books

A CIP catalogue record for this book is available
from the British Library

Printed and bound in Italy by Printer Trento S.r.l.

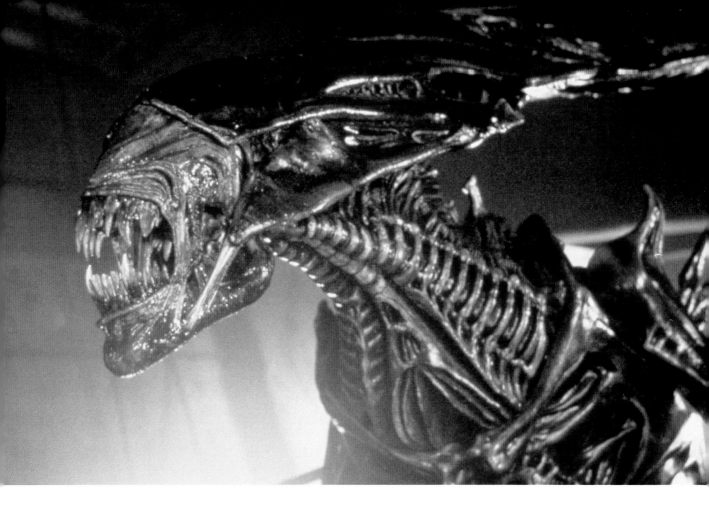

CONTENTS

FOREWORD BY JAMES CAMERON

I have always been an avid fan of science fiction, both in literature and films. So when I first saw *Alien* on its opening night, in 1979, it had a great effect on me.

The first thing that struck me about Ridley Scott's new film was its heightened sense of realism – virtually a first for a science-fiction film that dealt with a completely separate environment. *Alien* created a very realistic milieu, with real characters that spoke like real people, instead of running around in silver jumpsuits and speaking dialogue that we all know wouldn't be that way. I was also attracted to Ripley, the *Alien* character played by Sigourney Weaver. I tend to like strong female characters; they interest me dramatically. But back in 1979, a strong female character hadn't been done that much. Particularly one like Ripley, who displayed a balance between femininity and strength.

Then there was *Alien*'s graphic sense. By 1979, there had been a recent, tremendous explosion of new film ideas and design parameters, and *Alien* managed to create this great lens that focused that energy down into one movie. Of course, that design synthesis was the product of Ridley Scott; Scott had hired the French artist Moebius, the Swiss artist Giger, and the American artist Ron Cobb to work on *Alien*, then put their styles together in this incredible minestrone. This gave *Alien* an overall look and feel that was distinctive to Scott's own photographic style.

All of its distinctive traits meant that, for me, *Alien* was one of those totally seminal moments that occasionally happen in film and science fiction. It created such a high benchmark for visual design in SF, as well as photography, acting, sound and editing – all the things that one did not necessarily associate with science fiction. In other words, it was a classic. In fact, in the sense that the first film had created such a benchmark, all the *Alien* sequels – mine included – have been standing on the back of a giant.

That's why I was very excited when Walter Hill and David Giler (two of *Alien*'s producers) hired me to write and direct the first *Alien* sequel in 1984. Of course, I then had to map out a way of continuing the story from the first film, while making the second *Alien* my own.

This strategy raised a number of problems. The most obvious was, 'How can I do a proper homage to the original film without becoming a mindless fan? How can I create something that is a piece of entertainment and a story in its own right?' Because just doing a reprise of all the elements from *Alien* would have been pointless. Yet certain elements were necessary for the story's continuation, and I had to come up with an entertaining way of having that story evolve *beyond* what we had seen before; that way, people would have an expectation of going beyond a horizon that they already knew.

So I quickly made a number of decisions about what I would and would not do to *Aliens*. The first was the fact that I could not make a more terrifying film about shadows and slime than Ridley had in *Alien*. This is why I decided to place *Aliens* in an entirely different emotional arena, with more of

ALIENS

an emphasis on character, dialogue and action. Next, I decided that my screenplay should feature many of the full-grown creatures you'd seen a single example of in *Alien*, instead of just one. Further, I felt that I should present the aliens in a more matter-of-fact way than the first film had, showcasing them almost as a force of nature. Finally, I chose to have *Aliens* focus on the character of Ripley. *Aliens* would be *her* story and, as such, an opportunity to do something that was dimensionally more intricate, from both a character *and* a dramatic standpoint.

Over all of these decisions hung the realisation that I had to create my own stylistic territory to surprise the audience during *Aliens*, while also being true to the first film. But the real trick is finding the right kind of surprise; one that works. The Alien Queen was a nice surprise within *Aliens*, but I think the larger surprises were for people to see Ripley used in a different way and for the military to be brought into the *Alien* universe.

In any event, these were the foundations I laid when I first began my *Aliens* script. Much more information about the process of writing that document can be found in 'Mothers With Guns', the remarkable essay *Aliens* expert Paul M. Sammon has provided for this book. For now, suffice it to say that I have always been proud of what I achieved with *Aliens* – and that I hope you enjoy reading the *Aliens* script.

James Cameron and
Sigourney Weaver on set

The Colonial Marines' Hypersleep Capsules aboard the Sulaco

MOTHERS WITH GUNS
BY PAUL M. SAMMON

The image: A standing woman – tall, dishevelled, defiant. In the crook of one arm she cradles a frightened girl; in the other, a futuristic firearm.

The tagline: 'This time it's war.'

The title: *Aliens.*

These three components comprise the 'one-sheet' (advertising poster) for James Cameron's *Aliens* (1986), the first sequel to 1979's *Alien. Alien* had been an astonishingly designed, immensely influential sci-fi/horror fusion directed by Ridley Scott. Fans of the film, therefore, had waited seven years to see which direction Cameron's sequel would take. Yet *Aliens* managed to avoid the pitfalls associated with raging 'sequelitis' by *not* offering the same, simplistic bill of fare viewers had come to expect from most Hollywood follow-ups. Instead, *Aliens* delivered an unusually affecting, high-octane blend of combat, maternalism and monsters – the same three elements suggested by

Pre-production design painting by James Cameron showing Ripley
(inside a 'Power Loader') battling the Alien Queen

the film's one-sheet.

Audiences responded. By year's end, *Aliens* was considered one of 1986's most popular pictures. It also exceeded the box-office grosses of its illustrious forebear, and turned Sigourney Weaver into a star (*Alien* had only introduced her). Moreover, *Aliens* cemented James Cameron's reputation as a supremely successful A-level director of intelligent transgeneric hybrids.

Yet while the broad outlines of *Aliens*' cultural impact have been rehashed *ad infinitum* – how *Aliens* earned Sigourney Weaver a Best Actress Oscar nomination, for example, or how the general public seemed to prefer *Aliens* over director Ridley Scott's original film – little has been written about the most crucial ingredient of James Cameron's hit. That, of course, was his *Aliens* screenplay. This was the first, and so far only, *Alien*-related project to be written by the person that directed it. But what was the genesis of that script? How did Cameron, a then-fledgling film-maker, arrive at *Aliens*' unusual mix of action film tropes, science-fiction technology and war-movie conventions?

To uncover the answers to those questions, I interviewed Cameron himself during a wet, chilly afternoon in early January 1998, at his Lightstorm Entertainment complex in Santa Monica,

Ripley levels her Pulse Rifle at oncoming Aliens

But first, before the interview, some backstories.

Alien had related the harrowing tale of the deep-space tugboat *Nostromo* – an enormous, mostly automated vessel – whose small crew is almost totally wiped out by a vicious, shapeshifting extraterrestrial. The sole survivor of that crew, Ripley (played with take-charge authority by Sigourney Weaver), then blows up the *Nostromo*, escapes in a 'lifeboat', and destroys its hitch-hiking alien, before settling into a state of artificially induced hibernation ('hypersleep') to await rescue.

Aliens begins with the revelation that the sleeping Ripley had drifted through space for *57 years* before finally being discovered and brought back to Earth. Circumstances then force her to return to the same mysterious planet where the *Nostromo* first encountered *Alien*'s single, extremely dangerous extraterrestrial. However, this time Ripley is accompanied by a group of heavily armed 'Colonial Marines', who encounter *hordes* of the homicidal ETs, plus a gigantic Alien Queen.

The adrenalised admixture of action and science-fiction elements found in *Aliens* first took root in the mind of its writer/director/designer, James Cameron. Born 14 August 1954, in Kapuskasing, Ontario, Canada, Cameron's youthful passions included super 8mm film-making, science-fiction literature and engineering. He also loved figurative art (illustration and design), as well as comic books. In fact, *Aliens*' creator used the latter to teach himself to draw, by imitating the panels found in *Marvel* comic books.

ALIENS

Early design of the Alien Queen's egg-laying ovipositor;
pre-production painting by James Cameron

In 1971, Cameron's family relocated to Brea, California. After a stint at Fullerton College (where he studied physics and literature 'and devoured every technically oriented movie book and magazine I could get my hands on'), Cameron made a twelve-minute, 35mm science-fiction short to help raise funds for a feature-length film he had co-written with friend William Wisher. However, his 1978 effort – on which Cameron served as producer, director, co-writer, editor, miniature builder, cinematographer and special-effects supervisor – did not lead to the full-length feature assignment for which Cameron had hoped. Therefore, after examining the way he was currently earning his living (as a truck driver and machinist; Cameron also harboured vague hopes of becoming a science-fiction novelist), the budding auteur decided to apply for employment within the motion

James Cameron on the miniature Egg Chamber set

picture industry. In 1979, that decision led to a job at a company named New World Pictures.

New World had been founded by Roger Corman, a legendary B-movie producer/director, who was involved in the production of a *Star Wars* knock-off titled *Battle Beyond the Stars*. Cameron was handed an entry-level position as a model-maker on this film. However, he was soon also providing miniatures and matte paintings for *Battle*, before eventually becoming appointed the head of that film's visual-effects department and its primary art director. Then Cameron began learning film-making Corman-style, working at a furious pace and jumping from project to project in a variety of capacities. One of these was a stint as a production designer and then second unit director for a separate Corman rip-off (this one, ironically, of *Alien*) entitled *Galaxy of Terror* (1980).

Galaxy proved a key moment in Cameron's career by introducing him to Italian producer Ovidio G. Assonitis, who then hired Cameron to direct his first feature, *Piranha II: The Spawning* (1982). However, this mostly unsuccessful, Italian-based sequel to 1978's *Piranha* (a low-budget hit) proved an extremely unpleasant experience for James Cameron. In fact, his relationship with Assonitis deteriorated so badly that, during production, Cameron amused himself by concocting a complicated revenge fantasy. This involved a sophisticated killing machine travelling back from the future to slay *PII*'s producer. Yet Cameron soon realised that the central concept had potential beyond any fantasised revenge, so he expanded that concept into a feature-length script Cameron intended to direct. Its title? *The Terminator*.

It was now 1982. *The Terminator*, Cameron was certain, would help establish him as a film-maker with his own unique identity. But a lean, year-long period of trying to assemble a production deal followed. To help the process along, Cameron paired himself with aspiring producer (and former New World alumnus) Gale Anne Hurd, a talented young woman Cameron first met when Hurd was working as Roger Corman's executive assistant. Hurd then shopped Cameron's *Terminator* script throughout Hollywood, and a deal was finally put together in 1983.

Two production companies – Hemdale and HBO – would finance this project, while Orion Pictures would distribute it. However, Cameron and Hurd were then told that the actor they wanted to star in *The Terminator*, Arnold Schwarzenegger, would be delayed while the Austrian bodybuilder-turned-movie star finished filming producer Dino De Laurentiis' sword and sorcery fantasy *Conan the Destroyer*. Whereupon, as Cameron himself recalls, 'The story behind my *Aliens* script really began.'

SCRIPTING ALIENS

It was now the autumn of 1983. Schwarzenegger's delay had, in Cameron's words, 'left me in a six-month hole with no income and a film (*Terminator*) that was fully prepared and ready to go. So I had very little to do.' Therefore, Cameron instructed his agent to circulate his *Terminator* script again throughout Hollywood, this time as a writing sample, in the hope that Cameron might receive a screenwriting assignment to keep him busy until Schwarzenegger became available.

The *Terminator* script now passed through various production companies. One was Brandywine, which essentially consisted of producers Walter Hill, David Giler (already established screenwriters/directors themselves) and Gordon Carroll. These same three men had previously produced *Alien*. Interestingly, Brandywine had been discussing the possibility of doing a sequel to that film since its initial release. But star Sigourney Weaver had expressed a pronounced reluctance towards even the *idea* of an *Alien* follow-up, fearing an inferior sequel would diminish the power of Scott's original. Additionally, Hill and Giler had been unable to come up with the script for an acceptable sequel on their own.

'Walter Hill, who I have a great deal of respect for as a writer and director, does not have a mind that goes into science fiction,' Cameron adds, explaining why it took Brandywine seven years to create their first *Alien* sequel. 'He doesn't know the lore of it. And David Giler would just as soon be doing anything else but science fiction. So that's why there was no sequel to *Alien* until I came aboard; *Alien* had been such a specific type of science-fiction film that Brandywine didn't know where to go with it.'

Indeed, by the fall of 1983, the year Cameron first talked to Giler and Hill, Brandywine was focused on developing non-*Alien*-related projects. One was a science-fiction version of *The Great Escape* (ultimately unproduced); another was a sci-fi remake of *Spartacus* (also never made). Yet it was precisely because of this *Spartacus* 'update' that James Cameron had been asked to meet with Giler and Hill in the first place.

'My *Terminator* script had gotten a good response at Brandywine,' Cameron says, 'so I was called in to pitch my ideas on their *Spartacus*-in-space project. But it quickly became clear that David Giler wanted a swords and sandals-type film set in outer space – with *literal* swords and sandals. That was a concept I found pretty idiotic. It certainly didn't jibe with the pitch I'd come up with for my own take on their remake, so I basically told them this wasn't going to work and got up to leave the meeting. But Giler insisted that he still wanted to do something with me. I asked him if he had anything specific in mind. Giler replied, "Well, there's always the next *Alien*."'

'Now, picture my brain at that moment,' Cameron continues. 'It was like a pinball machine going off. I hadn't known Giler had been involved with *Alien*. I told him, "You guys have the rights to *Alien*?!?"'

Cameron's sudden enthusiasm was due to the fact that he'd long been a fan of Scott's film. '*Alien* was a watershed in science-fiction film-making,' says Cameron. 'A truly seminal moment. In fact, along with *2001*, *Alien* is my favourite science-fiction film.' Therefore, when Giler responded that Brandywine did indeed control *Alien*, Cameron excitedly offered to write a treatment for a possible sequel to the film. 'It wasn't going to be called *Aliens* at this point, though,' Cameron explains. 'Brandywine had another name for the project, and that was *Alien II*.'

After then enquiring whether Brandywine had any ideas for an *Alien* sequel, Cameron was handed a typed, one-paragraph story outline by David Giler. 'That outline,' Cameron explains, 'said something like, "Ripley gets rescued and goes back to the planet with a bunch of soldiers. They are attacked and eaten." That was pretty much it. Except that – and I'll never forget this – the outline concluded with this sentence; "And then some other bullshit happens." Which I thought trivialised the entire process of actually figuring out what the story should be.'

Still, fired up by the possibility of creating a companion piece to one of his favourite films, Cameron returned home and started work on the *Alien II* treatment. This was completed within a single week. The resulting 42-page document included all of what were to become *Aliens*' main characters – Ripley, Newt, Hicks, Hudson, Vasquez, Drake – as well as such soon-to-be-famous *Aliens* inventions as the Power Loader, Drop Ship, and deserted human colony to which Ripley and the Colonial Marines travel for their rescue attempt (called, in Cameron's script, 'Hadley's Hope'). The *Alien II* treatment also featured the final confrontation between Ripley and the Alien Queen aboard the *Sulaco*, the Marines' spacecraft, plus a 'complicating factor concerning a surviving android character from the colony that I eventually took out of my screenplay'.

'Basically,' Cameron continues, 'my *Alien II* treatment had everything that later showed up in the film, except the dialogue.' What Brandywine did not know was that Cameron had actually based his quickly written *Alien II* treatment on a *pre-existing* story, one Cameron had created years earlier for his own amusement. 'Right after my meeting with Brandywine, I pulled something out of my files that had been inspired by *Alien*,' Cameron continues. 'I'd written it years earlier; it was originally titled *ET*. But when I found out that a guy named Spielberg was making his own movie called *ET*, I changed the title of my *ET* to *Mother*. And *Mother* already had most of the structure, characters and key scenes that would later show up in *Aliens*. I didn't tell Brandywine that, though. I simply added

ALIENS

the character of Ripley, changed the title from *Mother* to *Alien II*, and came back to Brandywine a week later with a 42-page story outline.'

Mother, like *Aliens*, was set in the future. Its story took place on the planet Venus, and concerned an off-world mining operation. 'But *Mother* also featured a character very much like Ripley, had its own type of Alien Queen, and ended with a final battle between the protagonist and 'Mother' while the main character was encased in what I'd later call a Power Loader,' Cameron adds. 'Also, at the end, the entire Venus-based complex where the humans were based in *Mother* started falling apart, just like the Atmosphere Processor does at the end of *Aliens*. Except that in *Mother*'s case, the structure was being wrecked by super-heated gases boiling up from Venus's interior.'

In any event, after turning in his reworked *Mother/Alien II* treatment to Brandywine, the production company offered Cameron a verbal agreement to write an *Alien II* script – at which point certain troubles began. Ironically, however, these problems did not take place during principal photography. For although it's become fashionable to report that the production phase of most Cameron films is best described as 'tense', *Aliens* principal photography period was actually a relatively tranquil one. Instead, it was the film's pre-production process which was far from sedate. For instance, Cameron would discover that Giler and Hill had put their own names on his *Alien II* treatment. They then received payment for 'story rights' – monies Cameron would have no share in. 'Walter and David got a cheque for my treatment, and I got nothing,' Cameron recalls. 'I was pretty pissed off about that one.'

Despite such aggravations, Cameron soldiered on. He now informed 20th Century Fox that the prime condition for his writing the *Alien II* screenplay would be an agreement allowing him to direct the film as well. Fox said 'Yes', and Cameron then began determining how large a fictional mirror he would need to build, in order to reflect certain elements from the first film.

'I saw *Alien* on its opening night in 1979,' Cameron begins. 'And it had a great effect on me: Scott's film was just one of those totally seminal moments. But for a film-maker to go into the territory created by another film-maker is dangerous ground. So I knew that I had to create my own stylistic territory in *Alien II*, to surprise the audience while also being true to the first film.'

In order to maintain that connection between *Alien I* and *Alien II*, Cameron opened his script with the discovery of the *Narcissus*, the lifeboat jettisoned from the *Nostromo* at *Alien*'s climax. Cameron also retained the first film's character of Jones the Cat, plus *Alien*'s Chestburster, Facehugger and adult creature. Yet, at the same time, Cameron was inventing new components for the *Alien* Saga. For example, where conventional thinking would have invested *Alien II* with more of the claustrophobic Gothic nastiness typifying *Alien* (which primarily took place aboard a single, cramped spacecraft), Cameron decided to *expand* the scope of his own story, playing it out within a variety of spacious settings. The director also skirted the original's hard-core horror elements, focusing instead on action, character and suspense (with a particular emphasis on action). Furthermore, Cameron invented new nomenclatures and morphologies for the *Alien* Saga.

Among these were Cameron's decision to call *Alien*'s heretofore unnamed adult creature a

'Xenomorph' (literally, 'a strange variant on an animal'), plus his choice to give *two* different names to the (also previously unnamed) celestial body upon which the *Nostromo* crew discovered *Alien*'s lethal eggs. One of these was 'LV-426' ('which I gave to the planet as an official designation for navigational purposes'); Cameron's second name for *Alien/Aliens* storm-lashed planet was 'Acheron'. This particular designation came from Greek mythology, which calls Acheron one of the five rivers flowing through Hades; in this case, the river of woe.

Another interesting Cameronian addition to the *Alien* mythos was his spelling of the manipulative corporation first presented in Ridley Scott's film. *Alien* had identified this company as the '*Weylan*-Yutani' corporation – but the film itself had never presented a graphic displaying the correct spelling of this combine. Perhaps that's why Cameron called *his* company '*Weyland*-Yutani', a spelling variation that has since has become the accepted norm. 'I also tried to straighten out an error concerning LV-426 that appeared in the first film,' Cameron adds. 'You see, in *Alien*, the place they landed on to find the eggs is described as a planetoid. But there's no such thing as a planetoid – you have asteroids, and you have planets. So, for *Aliens*, I officially designated LV-426 a planet.'

Next came Cameron's crucial addition to the extraterrestrial biology so unnervingly portrayed in Ridley Scott's film. 'When I began writing the *Alien II* script, I realised I'd have to slightly tweak the creatures' life-cycle,' Cameron points out. 'Because, at least in the release print of *Alien*, there's no answer as to where the first stage of the creature's life, those alien eggs, came from. *Alien* originally *did* have a scene that dealt with that, but it was cut just before the film came out. That sequence showed Captain Dallas and Brett slowly turning into eggs themselves, after the creature captured them [*Cameron is referring to* Alien's *famous deleted 'Cocoon scene'; see my 1999 book* Alien: The Illustrated Screenplay *for further details*].

'Now, what this suggested was that once an individual was cocooned by an alien, that individual then *became* an alien egg. Which I thought was a stupid concept then, and a stupid concept now. So I went in a totally different direction; I determined that the eggs were actually being laid by a single, more highly evolved alien organism. A Queen, if you will. I specifically had the social and biological aspects of a termite queen in mind while I was doing this. For instance, a termite queen is much larger than worker termites, and she's also equipped with an enormous ovipositor, this egg-laying sack that produces new termites. That biological fact, coupled with the idea of a giant Alien Queen, was, I thought, a lot more interesting as a concept than a captured human becoming an egg.

'I also wanted to present something that hadn't been done before in *Alien*,' Cameron goes on to say. 'The Facehuggers, the Chestbursters, the adult creatures you see in *Aliens*, those were all kind of leftovers from Scott's movie. But the Queen was an opportunity to take a design stand that went beyond the first film, to strike out in a new direction with a new organism. Not one that was *so* new you'd be lost when you saw it, though. I was very careful about that. I wanted to make sure that, when we finally saw the Queen, audiences intuitively understood what she was and what she did. Which was to make new aliens.'

The designer in Cameron, however, knew that his Alien Queen would be better understood by

James Cameron (right) directs the 'Opening of the Marines'
Hypersleep Capsules' scene

Brandywine and Fox if she first appeared in pre-production art. 'That's why I did a few sketches of the Queen very early on, to give everybody an idea of her appearance. Now, that look was obviously inspired by H.R. Giger's approach, at least in terms of how he'd designed the creatures from the first film. I wanted to continue with that design philosophy. I also wanted to get at certain other characteristics, like size and speed and grace, plus certain feminine qualities that the *Alien* warriors wouldn't have. What's funny about all this is that the first full sketch I did of the Queen – who was sort of a cross between a black widow and a dinosaur – was actually remarkably close to what we finally wound up with.'

Having decided on what to retain and what to change from the first film, and having created his initial designs for the Alien Queen, Cameron began attacking his *Aliens* script in earnest. Yet one more pre-production roadblock soon barred his way.

Cameron was now contacted by CarolCo (*Total Recall, Cliffhanger*), a major Hollywood production entity. The company had just received Cameron's *Terminator* script, and liked it. Moreover, CarolCo wanted to offer Cameron *another* writing assignment.

'I actually got offered the writing job on *Aliens* and the writing job from CarolCo on the same day,' Cameron continues. 'CarolCo asked if I'd be interested in writing *Rambo*, the sequel to Stallone's *First Blood* (1982). So I called up David Giler at Brandywine and said, "I don't really know what to do here. I just got offered *First Blood II*, and you guys have offered me *Alien II*. What should I do?" Giler's response was, "Do what I do. Take both jobs, and write real fast." So I said "okay". I took advice from the sage, the person who had gone before me, and agreed to both jobs.'

Unfortunately, Cameron had only 90 days to finish these scripts. 'At first I didn't see a problem there, though,' the director says. 'I'd worked out mathematically how fast I could write a script page, how many hours I had a day to do those pages, and how many days overall I had to finish the scripts. I then realised that if I stuck to my schedule, I could write both screenplays and have a little time left over for a quick polish on the *Terminator* script.'

But Cameron finished only part of the *Alien II* script before his carefully planned schedule began falling apart. 'CarolCo kept asking for more and more rewrites on the *Rambo* project [Rambo *was also heavily rewritten by Sylvester Stallone before filming began*] and eventually, the *Rambo* stuff I was doing – all the revisions and polishes you have to perform – took up all the time I'd planned to use finishing *Alien II*. So I didn't get that script done in time.

'I then called up David Giler and said, "I don't have the *Alien II* screenplay done yet; I only have about 60 pages finished. I also just found out that *The Terminator* is ready to go – Arnold is now free to participate – and I basically have to start that picture tomorrow. So, I'm sorry." And Giler just lost it. He actually said something I never thought I'd ever hear anyone say in Hollywood – "You'll never work in this town again!" But Giler was angry as hell. Then he hung up on me.'

Worried, Cameron now called Larry Wilson, Brandywine's head of development, who counselled the film-maker to remain calm and to send him the 60 pages of the partial *Alien II* script, so that Wilson could pass them on to Walter Hill. 'Which I did,' Cameron continues, 'sweating the whole time. I mean, I was just about to direct my first real studio picture, and I needed every friend I could get.'

But Cameron's fears proved groundless. Walter Hill contacted the writer/director the next day, to inform Cameron that 'he loved my pages. He loved the dialogue, loved the development of the storyline. Then Walter told me they'd had a little conversation over at Brandywine, and decided that they could wait until I was done with *The Terminator* to finish the *Alien II* script. There was only a gentlemen's agreement between us on this, though. Which of course would have gotten kicked aside like a sandcastle in a heartbeat, if Brandywine had had a shot at getting someone of Ridley Scott's stature to do *Alien II* while I was working on *Terminator*. But Walter kept saying, "Don't worry. We'll wait. Then we'll make our movie together." So I thanked him, hung up, and didn't think about *Alien II* again until I was done with my movie with Arnold.'

The Terminator was released nine months later (on 28 October, 1984) to an unexpectedly enthusiastic audience. '*Terminator* was a real sleeper,' says Cameron, 'the hit that came out of nowhere. It was number one at the box office for something like three weeks. Suddenly, I was this hot new director. But I still wanted to do *Alien II*, even though everyone was now telling me, "Don't do *Alien II*. It's a sequel to somebody else's work – do your own stuff instead." But my position was, "I *want* to

ALIENS

On the LV-426 Med Lab set, James Cameron (centre) directs Michael Biehn (right, playing Hicks)

do *Alien II*. It'll be fun. I love the first picture, and I know exactly what to do for the second one." So I call Brandywine again and ask, "Are we still on for *Alien II*? And how about Sigourney? Is she up for this?" David Giler tells me everything's fine; I can go ahead with *Alien II*, and Sigourney Weaver is signed for the second picture. So off I go to finish the script which, in the course of writing, I retitled from *Alien II* to *Aliens*. I was doing this strictly on a promise, you understand. I hadn't really negotiated my deal yet. But I'd told Brandywine I would do it, so I was doing it.'

Since Cameron had previously mapped out *Aliens*' general narrative territory with his treatment, he now had the luxury of inserting subtexts and references to other genres into his script. 'One was the old WWII combat movie,' Cameron explains, 'the type where a small squad of ethnically diverse soldiers find themselves trapped behind enemy lines. I also had *The Alamo* (1960), that old John Wayne film in mind when I wrote *Aliens*. In fact, that's what I told Fox about *Aliens*. That LV-426 was the Alamo, and that Ripley was John Wayne. But they didn't get it.'

Even so, Cameron deepened *Aliens* 'combat movie' undertones by layering it with specific parallels between *Aliens*' heavily armed Colonial Marines and the United States' war in Vietnam. 'While I was doing research for *Rambo*, I'd read every book I could get my hands on about Vietnam. That research was still very much in my head while I was finishing *Aliens*. One day, it just hit me that the basic story I was telling here was the perfect metaphor for America's involvement in Vietnam. In both cases, you had the most technologically advanced army in the world going off to wage battle against an enemy that was working barely above the medieval level. Yet the advanced forces lose. That's exactly what happened to us in 'Nam, so the Vietnam analogy in *Aliens* was absolutely intentional.'

Cameron further laced his script with another militaristic overlay. This was a nod to the classic science-fiction literature of his youth; specifically, to Robert Heinlein's 1959 novel *Starship Troopers*. 'That's a great book,' Cameron says, 'about Earth warring against a race of intelligent insects. So I included a few throwaway references to it in *Aliens*. The term "Drop Ships", the phrase "Bug Hunt" [*spoken by Hudson, Bill Paxton's character*], all those little asides were my salute towards *Starship Troopers*. In fact, when I heard that they were making a film out of Heinlein's novel (1997's *Starship Troopers*, directed by Paul Verhoeven), my first thought was, "Why are they making that movie? I already did it."'

Cameron's final *Aliens* screenplay embellishment – which, to some eyes, was the director's most surprising – was its maternal love story. 'After *Titanic* came out, everybody acted like it was a big surprise that I had done a love story,' Cameron relates. 'Well, *The Terminator* was a love story. *The Abyss* also, definitely was, and to a lesser degree, so was *Aliens*. A mother-daughter love story.'

Indeed, what critics of Cameron's fast-paced oeuvre have often overlooked is how his films reveal *two* James Camerons: one drawn to big-budget action spectacles, the other to passionately felt 'relationship' stories. Furthermore, Cameron frequently feminises his material by telling his stories through women – Sarah Conner in *The Terminator*, Jamie Lee Curtis in *True Lies*, Kate Winslet in *Titanic*. *Aliens* is no different in this respect, since most of it is experienced from Sigourney Weaver's perspective.

However, Cameron also had to grapple with the essential *character* of Ripley, at least in terms of how she'd been presented in *Alien*. 'Ripley didn't have a prior life in the first movie,' the director explains. 'You knew she was a junior officer and an independent thinker capable of courageous acts, but that was about it. Ripley didn't even have a first name in *Alien*. So I made one up for her – Ellen. I intentionally left the larger details of Ripley's life vague, however. For example, *Aliens* tells us that she had a daughter back on Earth, who'd aged and died while Ripley was in hypersleep. But we don't learn the circumstances surrounding that daughter. Maybe Ripley had a husband who was also in the space service. Or maybe she wasn't married, and Ripley decided to have a kid. Sigourney and I would have conversations about this all the time. But I'd purposefully omitted those details. Calling her Ellen and giving her a child was as far as I went with Ripley's backstory.'

Aliens screenplay reveals Ripley's motherhood during a sequence set on Gateway Station, the enormous space station to which Ripley is taken to convalesce after being discovered in hypersleep. Here, Weyland-Yutani man Burke informs Ripley that, during her 57-year hibernation, Amanda McClaren-Ripley, Ripley's daughter, has grown old and died (a scene I have dubbed 'A Virtual Park'

ALIENS

in this book's 'Aliens Script Cuts' chapter). Said sequence was then shot, but later cut, from the film by Cameron himself.

Yet, in many ways, the 'Virtual Park' sequence was vital to the film. This scene not only conveys crucial information about Ripley's past, it implies that Ripley is suffering hidden sorrow and guilt during her LV-426 expedition; dark emotions that will later turn protective when a young girl named Newt is discovered to be the only survivor of Acheron's alien-infested colony.

'A maternal element was already in *Mother*, the earlier story I'd based the *Alien II* treatment on,' Cameron notes. 'I'd felt that that fit like a glove in the development of Ripley's character for *Aliens*. Sigourney seemed to respond well to that, too. I don't think she had any children at that point (1985), but she did talk about wanting to have a baby. So *Aliens* maternal angle keyed right into Sigourney's own personality back then.'

Not surprisingly, *Aliens*' motherhood subtext – which comes to the foreground at the film's end, as Ripley and the Alien Queen battle one another to protect their respective 'children' – ties in with that other recurring Cameron motif. This is his 'empowerment of women' theme, best typified by the strong, assertive females seen in *The Abyss*, both *Terminators*, *Aliens* and *Titanic*. Why, then, does Cameron seem compelled to return to this motif?

'I think my fascination with strong female characters comes from a number of different things, all congealing,' Cameron remarks. 'One is science-fiction literature, which has certainly influenced my writing. Prose science fiction has historically been very egalitarian; the female and male characters have always been on the same playing field there. In fact, if you look beyond the covers of the old SF pulp magazines – which usually show a scantily clad damsel being abducted by an alien – you'll find that the women in the *stories* behind those covers were not only as smart as men, but often the heroes of the piece. That's probably one reason why women are often the centrepiece of my films.

'But,' Cameron continues, 'when you are trying to break into the film business, as I was with *The Terminator* and *Aliens*, and you are trying to make a statement, you also frequently have to do something different. And interesting women were just not being written into science-fiction films back then. I mean, did anyone ever really believe Raquel Welch knew her stuff as a neurosurgeon in *Fantastic Voyage* (1966)? So I suppose my so-called "empowerment of women" theme springs from that too. Plus, I guess I just have a natural proclivity for writing women. Other than that, I don't really know where this comes from.'

With *Aliens* conceptual compass set, Cameron now spent from December of 1984 to February of 1985 completing his script. He then turned that screenplay over to Brandywine on 28 February 1985 – and was almost immediately beset by a new round of problems.

'After I finished the script [*Cameron also did two rewrites, dated 28 May and 23 September 1985*], I finally made my deal as a writer/director on *Aliens*. Then I brought Gale [Anne Hurd] into the mix. But Fox initially didn't want to take her on as *Aliens*' producer, because they weren't that familiar with Gale. Now, by this time Gale and I had become close – we'd decided to get married at this point – but my insistence on Gale as *Aliens* producer was strictly business. I told Fox, "Gale is an excellent producer, and she must work with me on this film. We are a team. You either hire her and me together, or I don't do *Aliens*." Fox saw the kind of movie they could make with me, and it looked like we also could do *Aliens* for cheap. So eventually it made sense to them, and Gale came aboard.'

Yet this incident was still not the end of *Aliens* pre-production woes. As previously noted, before he'd completed his screenplay, James Cameron had been reassured that Sigourney Weaver was committed to his film. But once *Aliens*' script was delivered, Cameron abruptly learned she was not. 'All of a sudden I'm asking, "Sigourney *doesn't* know about *Aliens*?" Brandywine told me, "Well, we wanted to wait until we got the script. Then we were going to call her." That infuriated me. So I got Sigourney's number, called her, and said, "Look. You don't know me from Adam, but I just wrote this script I'm calling *Aliens*. And now I'm in an embarrassing situation. I've been working on this film for some time, but now I'm being told you know nothing about it. So – can I send you the script? Have you read it? Then we can meet to talk about it." Sigourney said sure. So I sent her the script, and we got together and Sigourney was great. She loved the screenplay. But she also confirmed that she still hadn't made her deal, and that she wasn't under option, either.'

By now it was April 1985. Fox had scheduled *Aliens* start date for September of that year. Cameron, however, feared that the new 'Weaver situation' would scuttle the project. 'So at this point I told the studio, "Gale and I are going to Hawaii for our honeymoon. We'll give you until we get back to lock in Sigourney's deal. If it hasn't happened by then, we're out." Then we got back from our honeymoon – and a deal still hadn't been made. So, since Gale and I had created a deadline scenario that we now had to play out, I figured I had only a couple of days to decide what to do. But I really wanted to make this picture. So I came up with a ploy.

'First I called Arnold Schwarzenegger's agent, who worked at the same firm [ICM] as Sigourney's agent. I told him I'd been thinking over this *Aliens* situation and my new place in the Hollywood pecking order. I went on to say that, since I'd done *Terminator,* everybody was telling me that I shouldn't do *Aliens*, because I'd just made my mark with a completely original film. And the more baggage I carried into the sequel from the first film, the more strikes I'd have against me in terms of trying to create my own original vision of *Aliens*. I then told Arnold's agent that, since I had some great original characters in *Aliens*, I'd decided to drop the character of Ripley altogether, and build the story around Newt and the Marines. That way *Aliens* would be 100 per cent mine; this would get me over the stigma of doing a sequel to somebody else's classic picture. I finished by saying I was starting the rewrite today. Then I hung up.

'What I'd done,' Cameron continues, 'was a total ploy. I'd never had any intention of writing Ripley out of the story. But I just *knew* that after I hung up, the next call Arnold's agent's was going to make would be to Sigourney's agent, and that that person would then immediately call Larry Gordon, head of production at Fox, to tell him what I'd said. And you know what? That's exactly what happened. Sigourney's deal was made that day. But it was a close call. People will never know how close *Aliens* came to not happening.'

Yet securing Weaver's services would be only the latest salvo in *Aliens* ongoing prep battle,

ALIENS

since Hurd and Cameron now faced yet another conflict – *Aliens*' budget. Fox originally wanted to price the film at $12 million, only $3 million more than *Alien*'s cost. However, Cameron and Hurd were adamant in informing Fox that the studio had underestimated *Aliens* production floor. A strained give-and-take period followed. Ultimately, though, Fox raised *Aliens*' budget to $15.6 million; final cost for the film was $17.5 million.

Although 1985 had been a stressful year for Cameron and Hurd, *Aliens* was now almost ready to roll. Only a few details were left to attend to. One concerned the film's design team. Cameron had originally considered employing H.R. Giger as *Aliens* production designer (since the Swiss artist had previously designed the derelict ship, alien eggs, Facehugger and adult alien for the first film), but subsequently discovered that Giger was already working on another project, MGM's *Poltergeist II*. So Cameron decided instead to split up *Aliens*' design chores into three different areas handled by three different people. Cameron himself would design the Alien Queen, as well as the Colonial Marines weaponry. American cartoonist/designer Ron Cobb (who'd worked on *Alien* designing the *Nostromo*) would create LV-426's human colony. Former *Blade Runner* designer Syd Mead would then design the *Sulaco* exterior, its Drop Ship Bay, and other *Sulaco* interiors (like its hypersleep capsules).

With this decision, Cameron's pre-production headaches ceased. *Aliens* now began four months of principal photography on 30 September 1985 (Cameron's final draft script was completed 23 September), at England's Pinewood Studios. Cameron looks back on this phase as 'one of my least problematic. Gale and I did run into some scepticism from the British crew, who basically didn't think we had what it took to do the project. Otherwise, *Aliens* was a fairly smooth shoot.'

Then came *Aliens* editing phase, during which Cameron decided to excise three interesting sequences from the film's theatrical print. One was the previously mentioned 'Virtual Park' scene; another took place on LV-426, and showed Newt's family (the Jordens) accidentally stumbling upon the remains of *Alien*'s egg-infested derelict spacecraft (although said discovery is *Aliens*' logical lowpoint; how could humans advanced enough to terraform an entire planet *not* discover an alien ship on the surface of that planet?). A third excised sequence had Ripley discovering Burke, who'd been earlier snatched by the Xenomorphs, 'cocooned' in the bowels of Acheron's Atmosphere Processor. Ripley then hands the imprisoned man a live hand grenade, before walking away.

Two of these deleted scenes (the Virtual Park and Jorden Family segments), were restored to the film by Cameron in 1991, for the laserdisc/home video 'Special Edition' version of *Aliens*. So why did Cameron feel the need for such deletions in the first place?

'I cut the scene at Gateway,' Cameron begins, 'because, when I first watched the movie cut together, I thought, "Oh, how convenient." Burke lets us know that Ripley has lost a daughter, but guess who the one survivor of the entire LV-426 colony is? A little girl. That struck me as real Hollywood story-telling, overly convenient and symmetrical. You also have to remember that *Aliens* took its time revving up, since I was settling down and doing a lot of character at the beginning. Even so, I thought the Gateway sequence slowed things down *too* much. So I cut it out. That's the same reason the Jorden family's expedition was removed – we didn't need it. *Aliens* Theatrical Cut ran 2 hours 17 minutes, and, back in 1986, there had not been many films that were that long for a while. But leaving in the edited sequences would have made *Aliens* even longer; the *Special Edition*, for instance, runs 154 minutes. So both scenes were mainly cut for reasons of pacing and length. That's not the reason I dropped the scene of Ripley handing Burke a hand-grenade to commit suicide, though. I cut that simply because I felt we hadn't done a good job on the scene. I didn't like the way it looked. So I removed it. Permanently, in this case.'

After the final addition of a pounding musical score by composer James Horner, *Aliens* opened (in the USA) on 18 July 1986. Its first wave of patrons seemed genuinely appreciative of Cameron's emphasis on character and action, particularly in view of *Alien*'s insistence on horror and suspense; *Aliens* also attracted a wider audience demographic, pulling in many viewers (such as young women) not normally enticed by a science-fiction film. Cameron's effort then became a bonafide hit, grossing over $180 million worldwide in 1986 alone.

Next came *Aliens* nomination for seven Academy Awards®. These included Weaver's Best Actress nod, although the film would go on to win 'only' two Oscars, for Best Visual Effects and Best Sound Effects. Shortly thereafter NATO, the National Association of Theater Owners, named James Cameron its Director of the Year, while *Time* magazine spotlighted *Aliens* as a featured cover story. And as late as the year 2001, *Aliens* still ranked as one of the highest grossing R-rated films of all time. But why?

DISSECTING ALIENS

Let's begin with Sigourney Weaver. Part of *Aliens*' crossover appeal can surely be ascribed to Weaver's alternately warm and commanding performance. But *Aliens* also *enlarged* Ripley's character, mythologised her, transformed the resourceful (if somewhat callow) young woman from *Alien* into a full-blown cinematic icon – the first female action hero.

Such a coronation was not without attendant ironies, however. For the Ripley of *Aliens* uses her *intellect* as much as her weaponry, commanding our respect for being a serious, sceptical, vulnerable professional, rather than a two-dimensional killing machine. Moreover, Weaver herself has rejected Ripley's action-star status, preferring to describe her character as a stylised fighter battling exaggerated instances of the same sexism and difficult life-choices facing ordinary twentieth-century women (maybe that's why *Aliens*' one-sheet, showing Ripley holding a gun in one hand and a child in the other, resonates so strongly with contemporary female viewers). Yet while there's little doubt that Ripley remains *Aliens*' emotional linchpin, it is this writer's opinion that the overall effectiveness of Cameron's noisy, exciting sequel – whose beautifully realised action setpieces are just as important as Weaver's compelling humanity – can, like the film before it, be squarely laid at its director's feet.

By smoothly melding the gritty conventions of a Hollywood combat movie with extravagant

ALIENS

futuristic sets and a softer, more intimate subtext of maternal loss and love, Cameron wisely steered *his Alien* away from the haunted-house ambience so brilliantly realised by Ridley Scott. Yes, *Aliens* is occasionally 'scary'. But it is also thrilling, sentimental, unrelenting, moving, with a performance by Sigourney Weaver that's so likeable and believable she was nominated for a Best Actress Oscar ...and how many science-fiction films can claim that? Furthermore, James Cameron gave his *Aliens* audience much more than they'd paid for. This is a director who often talks of an unbreakable compact with his viewers; the sincere and, more importantly, *serious* way Cameron goes about fulfilling that contract in *Aliens* definitely connects film-maker to audience.

The most enthralling aspect of this strategy? Cameron's decision to end-load *Aliens*' third act with escalating multiple climaxes. It may be hard to remember now, since that last-act approach has been copied or aped by almost two decades worth of subsequent action films, but terracing the final 45 minutes of a motion picture with so many crises was an unheard-of tactic in 1986. The aliens capture of Newt, Ripley's subsequent rescue attempt, the stowaway Alien Queen, Bishop's mutilation, Ripley's Power Loader battle, her final struggle inside the *Sulaco* airlock – any number of terrifying and/or seemingly hopeless situations are set before the audience during *Aliens* final act, and each crisis tops the one that preceded it. Consequently, by the film's end we're satiated, exhausted, wrung out – an emotional state perfectly in tune with *Aliens*' final shot of *two* Sleeping Beauties, each in their respective hypersleep capsule.

In many respects, then, *Aliens* remains the ultimate Jim Cameron film, his *Titanic* and *Terminator* pictures notwithstanding. This is a grand, supremely well-executed entertainment, deftly mixing multiple genres in sturdy service of a tight, well-constructed script – perhaps Cameron's best. All of which leads us to this essay's penultimate query: what did Ridley Scott, director of the first film, think of *Aliens*?

'Well, obviously, mine was more of a terror film, whereas Cameron's was an action movie,' Scott told me in 1995. 'So we're talking two very different things here. I suppose my main criticism of *Aliens* would be that there were too many of them. You were exposed to too much of the warriors and even the mother Alien, which, by the way, I thought was a very good idea. Therefore, there was no catatonic fear. And you know Sigourney is going to win. So right there you've saddled yourself with a problem. But,' Scott concludes emphatically, 'there's also no question that Cameron made an excellent film with *Aliens*. It really is an achievement.'

Scott's remark seem the perfect segue to one final, oft-argued question – which is the better film, *Alien* or *Aliens*? The easiest way to respond to that query would be to say it's irrelevant; *Aliens*, at bottom, is simply a *different* film than *Alien*, more concerned with action and character than slime and suspense. Of course, that rejoinder doesn't address the 'which film is better?' question so much as avoid it. So, for the record, here is this writer's opinion: while *Aliens* may be the better remembered film today, *Alien* remains the more qualitative and durable work – art, even. However, that belief is not meant to dismiss *Aliens* as an inferior effort, since Cameron's film remains as riveting today as it was fifteen years ago. Moreover, general audiences would probably disagree

Ripley leads a group of high-tech Colonial Marines against the scourge of Aliens

with my assessment, responding that, for them, *Alien*'s sequel remains the better offering.

So how to best finalise the 'which film is better?' debate? Perhaps it's best to answer this way: *Aliens* may be the preferred choice for film-goers, but *Alien* is the favourite of film-*makers*. And James Cameron's view is even more direct: 'All the subsequent *Alien* films – mine included – have been standing on the back of a giant,' Cameron insisted, back in 1998. Which certainly is a refreshingly ego-less statement from a film-maker of his stature, as well as a commendably candid one. Even if Cameron's riveting, marvellously written *Aliens* script might make some doubt the objectivity of his last remark.

Until next time, then.

ALIENS

ALIENS

Revised Final Draft
by James Cameron

23 September 1985

Scene 1 : 'It is the Narcissus, lifeboat of the ill-fated star freighter Nostromo'

FADE IN

SOMETIME IN THE FUTURE – SPACE   1

Silent and endless. The stars shine like the love of God
...cold and remote. Against them drifts a tiny chip of technology.

CLOSER: It is the *Narcissus*, lifeboat of the ill-fated star freighter *Nostromo*. Without interior or running lights it seems devoid of life. The ping of a ranging radar grows louder, closer. A shadow engulfs the Narcissus. Searchlights flash on, playing over the tiny ship, as a massive dark hull descends toward it.

INT. NARCISSUS   2

Dark and dormant as a crypt. The searchlights stream in the dusty windows. Outside, massive metal forms can be seen descending around the shuttle. Like the tolling of a bell, a basso profundo clang reverberates through the hull.

ALIENS

CLOSE ON THE AIRLOCK DOOR: Light glares as a cutting torch bursts through the metal, moving with machine precision, cutting a rectangular path. The torch cuts off. The door falls inward revealing a bizarre multi-armed figure. A robot welder.

Figures enter, back-lit and ominous. Three men in bio-isolation suits, carrying lights and equipment. They approach a sarcophagus-like hypersleep capsule, foreground. The leader's gloved hand wipes at an opaque layer of dust on the canopy.

ANGLE INSIDE CAPSULE: as light stabs in where the dust is wiped away, illuminating a woman, her face in peaceful repose. WARRANT OFFICER RIPLEY sole survivor of the Nostromo. Nestled next to her is JONES, the ship's wayward cat.

> LEADER
> Bio-readouts are all in the green.
> She's alive. Well, there goes our salvage, guys.

DISSOLVE TO:

EXT. SPACE/EARTH ORBIT   2-A

Panning across the serene blue curve of Earth as seen from high orbit onto Gateway Station, a sprawling complex of modular orbital habitats. In foreground a viewing portal opens in a vertical wall of the medical section.

INT. HOSPITAL ROOM   3

Harsh sunlight fills the room as the motorised shield continues to rise. A FEMALE MED-TECH turns from the window controls.

> MED-TECH
> Watch your eyes.

She crosses to a bed in which Ripley lies, looking wan, amid an array of arcane white medical equipment. The tech exudes practiced cheeriness, but Ripley isn't buying it.

> RIPLEY
> When am I going to see someone in authority?

> MED-TECH
> So. Feeling stronger, are we?

> RIPLEY
> We are tired of the runaround. Why won't anybody
> tell me what's going on? How long has it been?

                              MED-TECH
             Well, you've been here at Gateway Station for three
             days. You were pretty groggy at first so –

                              RIPLEY
             Look, I know that part! How long was I in
             hypersleep?

The tech glances up as the door opens os. She smiles, saved by the distraction.

                              MED-TECH
             Looks like you have a visitor.

A MAN crosses the room carrying a familiar large, orange tomcat.

                              RIPLEY
                 Jones!

Ignoring the man she grabs the cat and hugs it to her. Jones seems none the worse for wear and
begins to purr.

                              RIPLEY
             Jonesy. You ugly thing.

The visitor sits beside the bed and Ripley finally notices him. He is thirtyish and handsome, in
a suit that looks executive or legal, the tie loosened with studied casualness. A smile referred to
as 'winning'.

                              MAN
             Nice room. I'm Burke. Carter Burke. I work for the
             Company, but other than that I'm an okay guy. Glad
             to see you're feeling better.

Ripley's gaze turns stony.

                              RIPLEY
             You're with the Company? Then you're the last
             person I want to be talking to.

                              BURKE
                 (genuinely wounded)
             Why is that?

ALIENS

Scene 2: 'INT. NARCISSUS. Dark and dormant as a crypt'

RIPLEY
Because I'm bringing you guys up on charges...
wilful negligence leading to the deaths of my crew,
for starters.

BURKE
Whoa, Ripley. That's not me. Those guys are gone.
There've been some changes. That's what I came
here to tell you about.

RIPLEY
How long was I out there?

BURKE
It's bad, kiddo. It's gonna be a shock.

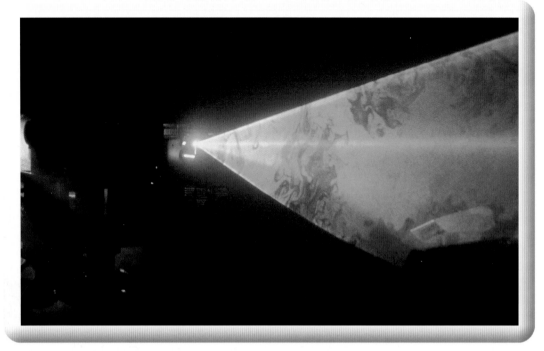

Scene 2: 'The door falls inward revealing a bizarre figure. A robot welder'

She grabs his arm, surprisingly strong.

> RIPLEY
>
> How long?

> BURKE
>
> Fifty-seven years.

Ripley is stunned. She seems to deflate, her expression passing through amazement and shock to realisation of all she has lost. Friends. Family. Her world.

> RIPLEY
>
> Fifty-seven...oh, Christ...

Scene 2: 'INSIDE CAPSULE a WOMAN, her face in peaceful repose'

BURKE
You'd drifted right through the core systems. It's
blind luck that deep-salvage team caught you when
they did. One in a thousand. You're just damn lucky
to be alive...

While Burke is talking we have pushed in to a tight close-up on Jones, who begins to hiss and
struggle in Ripley's arms. We go into subtle slow motion. The cat leaps to the floor, bounding
away. Ripley coughs, suddenly, as if choking. Her expression becomes one of dawning horror.
Burke, unaware of what is coming, hands her a glass of water from the nightstand. She slaps it
away. It shatters with a smash. Jones dives, yowling, under a cabinet.

Ripley grabs her chest, struggling as if she is strangling. The med-tech hits a console button.

MED-TECH
(shouting)
Code Blue! 415. Code Blue! 4-1-5!

Burke and the med-tech are holding Ripley's shoulders as she goes into convulsions. A
DOCTOR and TWO TECHS run in. Ripley's back arches in agony.

RIPLEY
No...nooo!

They try to restrain her as she thrashes, knocking over equipment. Her EKG races like mad.
Jones, under the cabinet, hisses wide-eyed.

DOCTOR
Hold her...Get me an airway, stat! And fifteen ccs
of...Jesus!

Ripley stares at the shape rising under the sheet. Tearing itself out of her. A glimpse of the
chittering horror...it screeches...

Right on Ripley, screaming, snapping up into frame. Alone in the darkened hospital room. She
gasps for breath, clutching pathetically at her chest. There is no demented horror ripping itself
out of her. Her eyes snap about wildly, slowing focusing on the reality of her safety.
Shuddering, bathed in sweat, she kneads her breastbone with the heel of her hand and sobs.

A video monitor beside the bed snaps on. The med-tech's face.

MED-TECH
Bad dreams again? Do you want something to help
you sleep?

RIPLEY
(faint)
No. I've slept enough.

The tech shrugs and switches off. Touching a button on the nightstand Ripley opens the
viewport, revealing Gateway and the turquoise Earth. She hugs Jones to her and rocks with
him like a child, still shattered by the nightmare.

CUT TO:

EXT. PARK   4

Sunlight streams in shafts through a stand of poplars, beyond which a verdant meadow is visible. Jones stalks towards a bird hopping among fallen leaves. He leaps. And smacks into a wall.

                         RIPLEY
              (voice-over)
         That's brilliant, Jones.

WIDER: As Jones steps back confused from the high-resolution environment wall screen, a sort of cinerama video-loop. Ripley sits on a bench in what we now see is an atrium off the medical centre. Burke enters in his usual mode, casual haste.

                         BURKE
         Sorry...I've been running behind all morning.

                         RIPLEY
         Have they located my daughter yet?

                         BURKE
         Well, I was going to wait until after the inquest...

He opens his briefcase, removing a sheet of printer hard copy, including a telestat photo.

                         RIPLEY
              Is she...?

                         BURKE
              (scanning)
         Amanda Ripley-McClaren. Married name, I guess.
         Age: sixty-six...at time of death. Two years ago.
              (looks at her)
         I'm sorry.

Ripley studies the photograph, stunned. The face of a woman in her mid-sixties. It could be anybody. She tries to reconcile the face with the little girl she once knew.

                         RIPLEY
              Amy.

                         BURKE
              (reading)
         Cancer. Hmmmm. They still haven't licked that one.
         Cremated. Interred Westlake Repository, Little Chute,
         Wisconsin. No children.

Ripley gazes off, into the pseudo-landscape, into the past.

> RIPLEY
> No children.
> (a beat, then)
> I promised her I'd be home for her birthday. Her
> eleventh birthday.

> BURKE
> Some promises you just can't keep.

Let's get one thing straight...Ripley can be one tough lady. But the terror, the loss, the emptiness are, in this moment, overwhelming. She cries silently. Burke puts a reassuring hand on her arm.

> BURKE
> The hearing convenes at 09.30. You don't want to be
> late.

INT. CORRIDOR – GATEWAY   5

Elevator doors part and Ripley emerges, in mid-conversation with Burke.

> RIPLEY
> You read my deposition...it's complete and accurate.

> BURKE
> Look, I believe you, but there are going to be some
> heavyweights in there. You got feds, you got
> interstellar commerce commission, you got colonial
> administration, insurance company guys...

> RIPLEY
> I get the picture.

> BURKE
> Just tell them what happened. The important thing
> is to stay cool and unemotional.

INT. CONFERENCE ROOM – ON RIPLEY – GATEWAY   6

Not cool. Not unemotional.

RIPLEY

Do you people have earwax, or what. We have been
here three hours. How many different ways do you
want me to tell the same story?

She faces the EIGHT MEMBERS of the board of inquiry at a long conference table. Grey suits
and grim faces. They aren't buying. Behind Ripley on a large videoscreen, PARKER grins like a
goon from his personnel mugshot. His file prints out next to it. BRETT's face and dossier
replace it, and then the others as the scene continues...KANE, LAMBERT, ASH the android
traitor, DALLAS. VAN LEUWEN, the ICC representative, steeples his fingers and frowns.

VAN LEUWEN

Look at it from our perspective, please. You freely
admit to detonating the engines of, and thereby
destroying, an M-Class star freighter. A rather
expensive piece of hardware...

INSURANCE INVESTIGATOR

Forty-two million in adjusted dollars. That's minus
payload, of course.

VAN LEUWEN

The lifeboat's flight recorder corroborates some
elements of your account. That for reasons unknown
the *Nostromo* set down on LV-426, an unsurveyed
planet at that time. That it resumed its course and
was subsequently set for self-destruct. By you. For
reasons unknown.

RIPLEY

Look, I told you, we set down there on company
orders to get this thing, which destroyed all of us and
your precious ship...

VAN LEUWEN

The recorder did not contain any entries concerning
this hostile organism you allegedly picked up.

RIPLEY

Oh, that's cute. Allegedly. I like that.

Van Leuwen sighs with exasperation.

VAN LEUWEN

The analysis team which went over the lifeboat centimetre by centimetre found no physical evidence of the creature you describe...

RIPLEY

That's because I blew it out the goddamn airlock!
(pause)
Like I said.

INSURANCE MAN
(to the ECA rep)
Are there any species like this 'hostile organism' on LV-426?

ECA REP

No. It's a rock. No indigenous life.

Ripley grits her teeth in frustration.

RIPLEY

What? Did IQs drop sharply while I was gone? I already said it was non-indigenous. There was a derelict spacecraft. An alien ship. It wasn't from there. Get it? We homed on its beacon...

ECA REP

And found something which has never been reported once from over three hundred surveyed worlds...a creature...(she reads from Ripley's statement)...'gestates inside a living human host', these are your words, and has 'concentrated acid for blood'.

RIPLEY

Look, I can see where this is going. But I'm telling you those things exist. Kane, the guy that went in, said he saw thousands of eggs in that ship. Thousands...

VAN LEUWEN

Thank you, Officer Ripley. That will be...

ALIENS

                        RIPLEY
            You're not listening. Just one of those things
            managed to kill my entire crew –

Van Leuwen stands, out of patience.

                      VAN LEUWEN
            Thank you! That will be all.

                        RIPLEY
                   (shouting)
            That's not all, Goddammit! It those things get back
            here, that will be all. Then you can just kiss all this
            goodbye, just kiss it goodbye.

INT. CORRIDOR   7

Ripley kicks the wall next to Burke who is getting coffee and donuts at a vending machine.

                        BURKE
            You had them eating out of your hand, kiddo.

                        RIPLEY
            They had their minds made up before I even went in
            there. They think I'm some kind of headcase.

                        BURKE
                   (cheerfully)
            You are a headcase. Have a donut.

INT. CONFERENCE ROOM – TIGHT ON RIPLEY – LATER   8

Van Leuwen clears his throat.

                      VAN LEUWEN
            It is the finding of this board of inquiry that Warrant
            Officer Ellen Ripley, NOC-14472, has acted with
            questionable judgement and is unfit to hold an ICC
            licence as a commercial flight officer.

Burke watches Ripley taking it on the chin, white-lipped but subdued.

VAN LEUWEN
Said licence is hereby suspended indefinitely. No
criminal charges will be filed at this time and you are
released on own recognisance for a six-month period
of psychometric probation, to include monthly
review by an ICC psychiatric tech...

Ripley's video-dossier fills the screen behind her. At the bottom a new entry prints out: FILE
CLOSED.

INT. CORRIDOR   9

Dolly back as the conference-room door bangs open and Ripley strides through. She shrugs off
Burke's restraining arm and catches up to Van Leuwen walking down the corridor.

RIPLEY
Why won't you just check out LV-426?

VAN LEUWEN
Because I don't have to. There have been people
there for over twenty years and they never reported
any hostile organism.

RIPLEY
What are you talking about? What people?

Van Leuwen steps into an elevator with some others, but Ripley holds the door from closing.

VAN LEUWEN
Terraformers...planet engineers. They go in, set up
these big atmosphere processors to make the air
breathable. Takes decades. It's what we call a shake
'n' bake colony.

The door tries to close again. Ripley slams it back. People are getting annoyed.

RIPLEY
How many are there? How many colonists?

VAN LEUWEN
I don't know. Sixty, maybe seventy families.

RIPLEY
Families...Jesus.

INSURANCE INVESTIGATOR
Do you mind?

Ripley's hand slides off the door, strengthless. It closes in her face.

CUT TO:

EXT. ALIEN LANDSCAPE – DAY   10

Panning slowly across a storm-blasted vista of tortured rock and bleak twilight on to a metal sign which reads:
HADLEY'S HOPE – POP. 159

Some local has added 'have a nice day' with a spray can. Gale-force wind screeches around the corroded sign. In the background is the colony, a squat complex surrounded by an angled storm-barrier wall.

EXT. COLONY COMPLEX   11

Several angles establishing the town, a cluster of bunker-like buildings huddling in the wind. Visible across two kilometres of barren heath, background, is the massive atmosphere processor, looking like an oil refinery bred with an active volcano.

INT. COLONY – MAIN CONCOURSE   12

A wide corridor bustling with routine activity. We see a cross-section of the hardy frontier stock who have come to live in this godforsaken wilderness. Some children race in the corridor on wheeled plastic toys.

INT. OPERATIONS ROOM/CONTROL BLOCK   13

The nerve centre of the colony, jammed with computer terminals, displays, technicians.

Dollying ahead of SIMPSON, the harried operations manager, as he is approached by his assistant, LYDECKER.

SIMPSON
What?

LYDECKER
You remember you sent some wildcatters out to the middle of nowhere last week? Out past the Ilium range.

SIMPSON

Yeah. What?

LYDECKER

One of them's on the horn, mom-and-pop survey team. Says he's on to something and wants to know will his claim be honoured.

SIMPSON

Why wouldn't his claim be honoured?

LYDECKER

Well, because you sent them to that particular middle of nowhere on Company orders, maybe. I don't know.

SIMPSON

Christ. Some honch in a cushy office on Earth says go look at a grid reference, we look. They don't say why, and I don't ask. I don't ask because it takes two weeks to get an answer out here and the answer's always 'don't ask'.

LYDECKER

So what do I tell this guy?

SIMPSON

Tell him, as far as I'm concerned, he finds something it's his.

EXT. ACHERON – THE MIDDLE OF NOWHERE – DAY   14

An eight-wheeled tractor roars across corrugated rock, blasting through soggy drifts of volcanic ash.

INT. TRACTOR   15

At the controls, intent on a pinging scope, is RUSS JORDEN, independent prospector. Beside him is his wife/partner Anne and in the back their two kids are playing among the heavy sampling equipment.

ALIENS

                                 JORDEN
                          (a gloating cackle)
                   Look at this fat, juicy magnetic profile. And it's mine,
                   mine, mine.

                                  ANNE
                   Half mine, dear.

NEWT, their six-year-old daughter, yells from the back...

                                  NEWT
                   And half mine!

                                 JORDEN
                   I got too many partners.

                                  NEWT
                   Daddy, when are we going back to town?

                                 JORDEN
                   When we get rich, Newt.

                                  NEWT
                   You always say that. I wanna go back,
                   Dad, can we?

Her older brother TIM sticks his jeering face close to hers.

                                  TIM
                   Yeah, so you can play 'Monster Maze'.
                   Well, we're not gonna let you play anymore. You
                   cheat!

                                  NEWT
                   Do not!

                                  TIM
                   Do too! You go in places we can't fit.

                                  NEWT
                   So! That's why I'm the best.

                    ANNE
          Knock it off! I catch either of
          you playing in the air ducts again
          I'll tan your hides.

                    NEWT
          Mom. All the kids play it...

                    JORDEN
               (reverently)
          Holy shiiit!

Angle through front canopy: on a bizarre shape looming ahead. An enormous bone-like mass
projecting upwards from the bed of ash. Canted on its side and buckled against a rock
outcropping by the lava flow, it is still recognisable as an extraterrestrial ship. Bio-mechanoid.
Non-human design.

                    JORDEN
          Folks, we have scored big this time!

The tractor moves around the base of the vast enigma, approaching a gash in the hull.

                    ANNE
          Shouldn't we call in?

                    JORDEN
          Let's wait 'til we know what to call it in as.

                    ANNE
               (nervous)
          How about 'big weird thing'?

EXT. TRACTOR   16

Jorden and Anne step down, wearing environment suits. Carrying lights, packs, cameras, test
gear. Their breath clouds in the chill air.

                    ANNE
          You kids stay inside. I mean it: we'll be right back.

They trudge towards the alien derelict.

They pause at the enormous gash in the hull. Blackness inside.

ALIENS

INT./EXT. TRACTOR   17

Newt has her face pressed to the glass, steaming it. Watching her parents enter the strange ship. Tim grabs her from behind. She shrieks.

                              TIM
                    Cheater!

EXT. LANDSCAPE – NIGHT   18

The tractor and the derelict are dark and motionless. The wind howls around them.

INT. TRACTOR   19

Tim is curled up in the driver's seat. Newt shakes him awake, trying hard not to cry.

                             NEWT
                Timmy...they've been gone a long time.

Tim considers the night. The wind. The vast landscape. He bites his lip.

                              TIM
                It'll be okay, Newt. Dad knows what he's doing.

Crash! Newt screams as the door beside her is ripped open. A dark shape lunges inside! Anne, panting and terrified, grabs the dash mike.

                             ANNE
                Mayday! Mayday! This is Alpha Kilo
                Two Four Niner calling Hadley Control.
                Repeat. This is...

As Anne shouts the Mayday Newt looks past her, to the ground. Russ Jorden lies there inert, dragged somehow by Anne from inside the ship. There is something on his face. An appalling multilegged creature, pulsing with obscene life. Newt begins to scream hysterically, competing with the shrieking wind which rises to a crescendo as we:

                                                               CUT TO:

INT. RIPLEY'S APARTMENT – GATEWAY – DAY   20

Silence. Ripley, looking haggard, sits at a table in the dining alcove contemplating the smoke rising from her cigarette. The place is minimal, the bed is unmade, there are dishes in the sink. Jones prowls across the counter. The wallscreen is on, a vapid commercial.

The door buzzes. Ripley jumps like a cat. Jones doesn't.

INT. CORRIDOR   21

Carter Burke stands in the narrow, dingy corridor with LIEUTENANT GORMAN, Colonial Marine Corps. Young and severe in his officer's parade uniform. The door opens slightly.

> BURKE
> Hi, Ripley. This is Lieutenant Gorman of the...

Slam. Burke buzzes again. Talks to the door...

> BURKE
> Ripley, we have to talk. They've lost contact with the colony on LV-426.

The door opens. Ripley considers the ramifications of that. She motions them inside.

INT. RIPLEY'S APARTMENT – A LITTLE LATER   22

Burke and Gorman are seated, nursing coffees. Ripley paces, very tense.

> RIPLEY
> No. There's no way!

> BURKE
> Hear me out...

> RIPLEY
> I can't believe this. You guys throw me to the wolves
> ...and now you want me to go back out there? Forget
> it: it's not my problem.

> BURKE
> Look, we don't know what's going on out there. It
> may just be a down transmitter. But if it's not, I want
> you there...as an adviser. That's all.

> GORMAN
> You wouldn't be going in with the troops. I can
> guarantee your safety.

ALIENS

BURKE

These Colonial Marines are some tough hombres,
and they're packing state-of-the-art firepower.
Nothing they can't handle...right, Lieutenant?

GORMAN

We're trained to deal with these kinds of situations.

RIPLEY

(to Burke)
What about you? Why are you going?

BURKE

Well, the corporation co-financed that colony with
the Colonial Administration, against mineral rights.
We're getting into a lot of terraforming...'Building
Better Worlds'.

RIPLEY

Yeah, yeah. I saw the commercial.

BURKE

I heard you were working in the cargo docks.

RIPLEY

That's right.

BURKE

Running loaders, forklifts, that sort of thing?

RIPLEY

What about it?

BURKE

Look, I know it's all you could get. It's okay, you
gotta stay busy. Nothing wrong with it. But what if I
said I could get you reinstated as a flight officer? And
that the Company has agreed to pick up your
contract?

RIPLEY

If I go.

                              BURKE
              If you go. It's a second chance, kiddo. And it'll be
              the best thing in the world for you to face this fear
              and beat it. You gotta get back on the horse...

                              RIPLEY
              Spare me, Burke. I've had my psych evaluation this
              month.

Burke leans close, a let's-cut-the-crap intimacy.

                              BURKE
              Yeah, and I've read it. You wake up every night,
              sheets soaking, the same nightmare over and over...

                              RIPLEY
              No. The answer is no. Now please go. I'm sorry. Just
              go, would you?

Burke nods to Gorman who rises with him. He slips a translucent card on to the table, and
heads for the door.

                              BURKE
              Think about it.

EXT. ACHERON LANDSCAPE – NIGHT   23

As the wind howls through tormented rock, building in pitch until we:

                                                                CUT TO:

INT. APARTMENT   24

Ripley lunges up into frame with an animal outcry. She clutches her chest, breathing hard.
Bathed in sweat she lights a cigarette with trembling hands.

Tight on phone console: as Ripley's hand inserts Burke's card into a slot. Burke's face, bleary
with sleep, appears.

                              BURKE
              Hello? Oh, Ripley. Hi...

ALIENS

> RIPLEY
> Burke, just tell me one thing. That you're going out
> there to kill them. Not to study. Not to bring back.
> Just to burn them out...clean...for ever.

> BURKE
> That's the plan. My word on it.

CLOSE-UP – RIPLEY: taking a deep slow breath. It's time to look the demon in the eye.

> RIPLEY
> All right. I'm in.

She punches off before Burke replies, before she can change her mind. She turns to Jones sitting on the bed and her tone becomes admonishing...

> RIPLEY
> And you my dear, are staying right here.

Jones blinks, cynical cat-eyes...'count me right out'.

CUT TO:

EXT. DEEP SPACE – THREE WEEKS LATER   25

An empty starfield. Metal spires slice across frame, followed by a mountain of steel. A massive military transport ship, the *Sulaco*. Ugly, battered...functional.

[26 OUT]

INT. CARGO LOCK   27

An enormous chamber, cavernous and dark. Squatting in the shadows are two orbit-to-surface shuttles. Drop Ships.

[28 OUT]

INT. HYPERSLEEP VAULT   29

Blackness, until a bank of indicators lights up. Hydraulics lift a grid of equipment from a row of horizontal hypersleep cylinders. It reaches the ceiling. Locks.

DISSOLVE TO:

Scene 29: 'Hydraulics lift equipment from a row of hypersleep cylinders'

INT. HYPERSLEEP VAULT   30

Lit up, white and sterile.

The canopies of the row of capsules are raised. Ripley sits up. Rubs her arms briskly. Next to
her, Gorman and Burke are stirring and beyond them the troopers, wearing shorts and dog tags.
They are: MASTER SERGEANT APONE, CORPORAL HICKS, CORPORAL DIETRICH (female),
PFC HUDSON, PFC VASQUEZ (female), PRIVATES DRAKE, FROST, WIERZBOWSKI and
CROWE, plus the Drop Ship crew: CORPORAL FERRO (female, pilot) and crew-chief PFC
SPUNKMEYER. In addition there is EXECUTIVE OFFICER BISHOP who supervises planetary
manoeuvering. Groans echo across the chamber.

SPUNKMEYER
Arrgh. I'm getting too old for this shit.

ALIENS

Scene 29: 'The canopies of the row of capsules are raised'

DRAKE
They ain't payin' us enough for this, man.

DIETRICH
Not enough to have to wake up to your face, Drake.

DRAKE
Suck air. Hey, Hicks...you look like I feel.

Hicks just snorts good-naturedly. Sergeant Apone moves down the row of freezers.

APONE
Awright, whattya waitin' for, breakfast in bed? Let's
go. Let's go.

49

HUDSON
Man, this floor's freezing.

APONE
Christ. I never saw such a buncha old women. You
want me to fetch you your slippers, Hudson?

HUDSON
Would you, sir?

Ripley steps back as the troopers shuffle past nodding cursory hellos. She feels isolated by the
camaraderie of this tight-knit group.

Vasquez eyes her coldly as she passes. Her combat-primer was the street in a Los Angeles
barrio, and she is tough even by the standards of this group.

HUDSON
Hey, Vasquez...you ever been mistaken for a man?

VASQUEZ
No. Have you?

She slaps Drake's open palm and it clenches into a greeting which is part contest. Playful but
rough. We sense the bond between them.

FROST
I need some slack, man. How come they send us
straight back out like this, we got some slack comin',
right?

HICKS
You just got three weeks.

FROST
I mean breathing, not this frozen shit.

DIETRICH
Yeah, 'Top'...what about it?

APONE
You know it ain't up to me. Awright! Let's knock off
the grabass. First assembly's in fifteen...let's shag it.

ALIENS

Through the swirling steam Hudson, Vasquez and Ferro are watching Ripley dry off.

> VASQUEZ
> Who's the freshmeat again?

> FERRO
> She's supposed to be some kinda
> consultant...She saw an alien once.

> HUDSON
> Whoooah: no shit? I'm impressed.

> APONE
> Let's go...let's go.

Cycle through:

INT. MESS HALL   32

An unconscious segregation takes place as the troopers assemble at one long table while Gorman, Burke and Ripley sit at another. Everybody is nursing a coffee waiting for eggs from the autochef, served by Bishop.

> HUDSON
> Hey, 'Top'. What's the op?

> APONE
> Rescue mission. There's some juicy colonists'
> daughters we gotta rescue from virginity.

> SPUNKMEYER
> Shee-it. Dumbass colonists. What's this crap
> supposed to be?

> FROST
> Cornbread, I think. Hey, I wouldn't mind getting me
> some more a that Arcturan poontang. Remember
> that time?

> HUDSON
> Hey, Bishop, man. Do the thing with the knife.

BISHOP

Oh, please. Not again.

FROST

Yeah, do it, Bishop. Go on, man. This is great.

Frost tosses Bishop a K-Bar combat knife and Bishop slaps his palm on the table. He proceeds to stab the point down rapidly between his spread fingers, speeding up until the knife is a blur, as the others cheer. Inhumanly fast and precise.

HICKS

(low)
Looks like that new Lieutenant's too good to eat with us grunts.

FROST

Yeah. Got a corn cob up his ass, definitely.

Across the room, at the other table, Gorman sits with his creases perfect...the consummate strack NCO. Bishop takes a seat beside Ripley. He is sucking on one finger, scowling. He examines the tiny cut closely and to Ripley's horror a trickle of white synthetic blood runs down his finger. Ripley spins on Burke, her tone accusing.

RIPLEY

You never said anything about an android being here: why not?

BURKE

Well, it didn't occur to me. It's just policy to have a synthetic on board.

BISHOP

I prefer the term 'artificial person' myself. Is there a problem?

BURKE

A synthetic malfunctioned on her last trip out. Some deaths were involved.

BISHOP

I'm shocked. Was it an older model?

BURKE

Hyperdyne Systems 120-A/2.

ALIENS

Scene 32: 'A trickle of white synthetic blood runs down his finger'

Bishop turns to Ripley, very conciliatory.

> BISHOP
> Well, that explains it. The A/2's were always a bit
> twitchy. That couldn't happen now with our
> behavioural inhibitors. Impossible for me to harm or,
> by omission of action, allow to be harmed a human
> being.
> (smiling)
> More cornbread?

Wham! Ripley knocks the plate out of his hand, halfway across the room.

> RIPLEY
> Just stay away from me, Bishop. You got that
> straight?

Burke and Gorman exchange glances. Frost, at the next table, shrugs and turns back to the other troopers.

> FROST
> She don't like the cornbread either.

INT. READY ROOM – ARMOURY   33

Tight on Apone: bellowing.

> APONE
> Tench-hut!

Wider angle: as the troops snap-to from their lounging among the racks of high-tech weaponry. Gorman enters with Burke and Ripley.

> GORMAN
> At ease. I'm sorry we didn't have time to brief before
> we left Gateway but...

> HUDSON
> Sir?

> GORMAN
> Yes, Hicks?

> HUDSON
> Hudson, sir. He's Hicks.

> GORMAN
> What's the question?

> HUDSON
> Is this going to be a stand-up fight, sir, or another
> bug-hunt?

> GORMAN
> All we know is that there's still no contact with the
> colony and that a Xenomorph may be involved.

> FROST
> A what?

HICKS

It's a bug-hunt.
(louder)
So what are these things?

Gorman nods to Ripley, who stands before the troops.

RIPLEY

I'll tell you what I know. One of our crew members
was brought back in with this thing on his face...like
a parasite. We tried to get it off. We couldn't, but
later it just came off by itself and died. Kane seemed
okay. Then we were all having dinner and...it must
have laid something inside him...down his throat
...we were having dinner, and he just grabbed his
chest and, uh...

VASQUEZ

Look, man, I only need to know one thing...where
they are.

Vasquez coolly points her finger, cocks her thumb, and blows away an imaginary alien.

DRAKE

Yo! Vasquez. Kick ass!

VASQUEZ

Anytime. Anywhere.

HUDSON

Somebody said alien...she thought they said illegal
alien and signed up.

VASQUEZ

Fuck you.

HUDSON

Anytime. Anywhere.

RIPLEY

Are you finished, Hudson? Because you know, none
of us here would like to interfere with your love life.

Hudson settles down, smirking. Ripley locks eyes with Vasquez.

RIPLEY
I hope you're right. I really do.

Gorman stands, clearly taking over.

GORMAN
Okay, right. Thanks. We also have Ripley's report on
disk, and I suggest you study it. Are there any
questions? Hudson?

HUDSON
How do I get out of this chickenshit outfit?

GORMAN
All right: I want this to go smooth and by the
numbers. I want DCS and tactical database
assimilation by 0830.
       (some groans)
Ordnance loading, weapons strip and Drop Ship
prep details will have seven hours...

EXT. SPACE – LV-426   34

They have arrived. From orbit the planet looks serene. The *Sulaco* floats, its manoeuvring jets
firing.

[35 OUT]

INT. LOADING BAY – CARGO LOCK   36

Tight on massive forks: sliding into a heavy ordnance rack with an echoing clang. Pull back,
revealing two powerful hydraulic arms. Spunkmeyer, seated inside a power-loader, swings the
ordnance up into a belly nacelle of the Drop Ship. The loader is a sort of forklift that you wear,
a robotic exo-skeleton with two legs and two arms, powered by hydraulics.

Spunkmeyer's machine swings out from under the Drop Ship and we become aware of the
intense activity throughout the cavernous loading bay. Troopers on foot or driving tow-motors,
overhead loading arms...all in motion. Hicks checks off items on an electronic manifest.

INT. READY ROOM – ARMOURY   37

Frost, Drake and Vasquez are fieldstripping light weapons with precise movements. Around
them, in racks, is an arsenal of advanced personal artillery.

ALIENS

Scene 38: 'I can drive that loader. I've got a Class Two rating'

Vasquez swings one of the smart-guns out on a workstand. It is a computer-aimed, video-targeted automatic weapon.

INT. CARGO LOCK   38

A massive APC, armoured personnel carrier, crosses the loading deck, background, as Ripley approaches Apone and Hicks, standing near the Drop Ship.

> RIPLEY
> Is there anything I can do?

> APONE
> I don't know. Is there anything you can do?

> RIPLEY
> I can drive that loader. I've got a Class Two rating.

Apone turns. A second power-loader sits unused in an equipment bay. Apone and Hicks exchange a skeptical glance, considering.

Tight on power switch: as Ripley's finger punches it on. A rising whine of power. Tight on the hydraulics as the massive machine stirs to life.

Full, as the loader stands.

Ripley spins the wrist servos. The huge claws swing, open...slide smoothly into lifting brackets on a cargo module, nearby. She raises it deftly.

> RIPLEY
> Where you want it?

Hicks looks at Apone, cocks an eyebrow appreciatively.

INT. READY ROOM – ARMOURY   39

The troopers are suiting up for the drop. Strapping on their bulky combat armour.

> APONE
> Let's move it, boys and girls: on the ready-line. Let's
> go, let's go.

INT./EXT. APC   40

Ripley double times into the APC with the line of hulking troopers. They take seats and begin strapping in. A klaxon sounds and the APC drives up a ramp into the Drop Ship.

Hudson prowls the aisle, his movements predatory and exaggerated. Ripley watches him working his way towards her.

> HUDSON
> I am ready, man. Ready to get it on. Check-it-out. I
> am the ultimate badass...state-of-the-badass-art. You
> do not want to fuck with me. Hey, Ripley, don't
> worry. Me and my squad of ultimate badasses will
> protect you. Check-it-out...

He slaps the servo-cannon controls in the gun bay above them.

> HUDSON
> Independently targeting particle-beam phalanx.
> VWAP! Fry half a city with this puppy. We got
> tactical smart-missiles, phased-plasma pulse-rifles,
> RPGs. We got sonic eeelectronic ballbreakers, we got
> nukes, we got knives...shark sticks –

ALIENS

Hicks grabs Hudson by his battle harness and pulls him into a seat. His voice is low, but it carries.

> HICKS
>
> Save it.

> HUDSON
>
> Sure, Hicks.

Ripley nods her thanks to Hicks. motors whine and the craft lurches. Burke, next to Ripley, grins eagerly like this is a sport fishing trip.

> BURKE
>
> Here we go.

She looks like she's in a gas chamber waiting for the pellet to drop.

EXT. *SULACO*   41

The Drop Ship lowers from the cargo lock on a massive launch rig. The night side of Acheron yawns below...

INT. COCKPIT   42

Ferro and Spunkmeyer run rapidly through the switches.

> FERRO
>
> Initiate release sequencer on my
> mark. Three. Two. One. Mark!

EXT. *SULACO* – DROP-SHIP   43

Hydraulics whine. Clamps slam back. The ship drops.

INT. DROP-SHIP – APC   44

Apone, stalking the aisle, snatches for a handhold. Bishop, Burke and Gorman groan at the sudden gees. Ripley closes her eyes...the point of no return.

EXT. DROP-SHIP   45

It screams down through the stratosphere, plunging into dark turbulence.

Scene 48: 'Terminal guidance locked in. Where's the damn beacon?'

INT. COCKPIT   46

Beyond the canopy is grey limbo. The craft shudders and lurches.

> FERRO
> Switching to DCS ranging.

> SPUNKMEYER
> Two-four-o. Nominal to profile. Picking up some hull ionisation.

> FERRO
> Got it. Rough air ahead. Stand by for some chop.

INT. HOLD – APC   47

Tight on Hicks: asleep in his seat harness.

ALIENS

Tight on Gorman: as the ship begins to buck, his eyes closed. Pale. Sweating. He rubs his hands on his knees repeatedly.

> RIPLEY
> How many drops is this for you, Lieutenant?

> GORMAN
> Thirty-eight-simulated.

> VASQUEZ
> How many combat drops?

> GORMAN
> Well...two. Including this one.

Vasquez and Drake exchange do-you-believe-this-shit expressions. Ripley looks accusingly at Burke.

INT. COCKPIT   48

> FERRO
> Turning on final. Coming around to a seven-zero-
> niner. Terminal guidance locked in. Where's the
> damn beacon?

EXT. DROP-SHIP   49

It emerges from the low cloud ceiling. From the twilight haze ahead the distant colony landing beacons become visible.

INT. HOLD – APC   50

Stumbling as the ship pitches, Ripley makes her way forward to the mobile tactical operations bay (MTOB), a control console lined with monitor screens. She joins Burke watching over Gorman's shoulder as the Lieutenant plays the board like a video director.

Tight on monitor console: revealing screens labelled with the names of the troopers. Two for each soldier. The upper screens show images from the image-intensified video cameras in their helmets. The lower screens are bio-monitors: EEG, EKG, and other graphic life-function readouts. Other screens show exterior views.

GORMAN
Let's see. Everybody on line. Drake, check your
camera. There seems to be a...

Close on Drake: as he whacks himself on the head with an ammo case. A familiar malfunction.

GORMAN
That's better. Pan it around a bit.

APONE
Awright. Fire-team A. Gear up. Let's move. Two
minutes. Somebody wake up Hicks.

A clatter of activity as they don backpacks and weapons. Vasquez and Drake buckle on their
smart-gun body harnesses. Ripley watches the AP station loom on the exterior screens.

RIPLEY
That the atmosphere processor?

BURKE
Yeah. Helluva piece of machinery. Completely
automated. We manufacture them, by the way.

EXT. SHIP – STATION   51

The tiny ship circles the roaring tower. A metal volcano thundering like the engines on God's
Lear jet.

INT. HOLD – APC   52

Gorman plays with the controls, zooming the image of the colony.

GORMAN
Hold at forty. Slow circle of the complex.

RIPLEY
The structure seems intact. They have power.

GORMAN
Okay, let's do it.

APONE
Awright! I want a nice clean dispersal this time.

Ripley turns as Vasquez squeezes past her.

                    VASQUEZ
          You staying in here?

                    RIPLEY
          You bet.

                    VASQUEZ
               (turning away)
          Figures.

                    GORMAN
          Okay, Ferro, set down on the landing grid.
          Immediate dust off on my 'clear', then stay on
          station.

                    APONE
          Ten seconds, people. Look sharp!

EXT. COLONY COMPLEX   53

The ship roars down, extending the loading ramp. The APC hits the ground a moment later,
pulling away from the ship as it leaps up in a cloud of spray and peels off, circling.

The APC pulls to the edge of the complex. The crew door opens. Troopers hit the ground
running. Spread out. They drop behind immediate cover. Apone scans with his image
intensifier visor lowered.

Apone's POV: through the starlight-scope visor. Bright as a sunny day, though contrasty and
lurid, we SEE the colony buildings. Trash blows in the street. No other movement.

                    GORMAN
               (voice-over; filtered)
          First squad up, on line. Hicks, get yours in a cordon.
          Watch the rear.

                    APONE
          Vasquez, take point. Let's move.

Sprinting in a skirmish line, Apone's team advances on the colony main entry lock. Parked
tightly across the doors are two heavy-duty tractors. Vasquez reaches one of the tractors, looks
inside. The controls are ripped out, as if by a crowbar or axe. She moves on.

EXT. COLONY BUILDING   54

Vasquez reaches the main doors, Drake flanking on the right. Apone tries the door controls. Nothing.

> APONE
> Sealed. Hudson, run a bypass.

Hudson, all business now, moves up and studies the door control panel. He prises off the facing and starts clipping on the bypass wires.

> APONE
> First squad, assemble on me at the main lock.

The wind roars around the bleak structures. A neon sign creaks overhead. Hudson makes a connection. The door shrieks in its tracks and rumbles aside. It jams partway open. Apone motions Vasquez inside. She eases over the wrecked tractor, through the doors. The others follow.

> GORMAN
> (voice-over; filtered)
> Second team, move up. Flanking positions.

NT. COLONY – MAIN CONCOURSE   55

Dollying slowly forward: following Vasquez and Apone as they move into the broad corridor. A few emergency lights are still on. Further down, rain drips through blast-holes in the ceiling. Evidence of a fire-fight with pulse-rifles.

On Vasquez: moving forward, her smart-gun cannon swinging slowly in an arc.

INT. APC   56

Ripley watches as the bobbing images reveal the empty colony buildings.

> GORMAN
> Quarter and search by twos. Second team move
> inside. Hicks, take the upper level. Use your motion
> trackers.

INT. MAIN CONCOURSE – SECOND LEVEL   57

ALIENS

Scene 54: 'The wind roars around the bleak structures. A neon sign creaks'

Hicks leads his squad up the stairwell to second level. They emerge cautiously. An empty corridor recedes into the dim distance. Hicks unslings a rugged piece of equipment. Aims it down the hall. He adjusts the 'gain'. It remains silent.

HICKS
Nothing. No movement.

They pass rooms and offices. Through doors they see increasing signs of struggle.

INT. APC   58

Ripley et al: watching.

BURKE
Looks like my room in college.

Nobody laughs.

INT. SECOND LEVEL   59

Hicks's group passes several burnt-out rooms. There are no bodies. In several offices the exterior windows are blown out, admitting wind and rain. Hicks picks up a half-eaten donut beside a coffee cup overflowing rainwater.

INT. LOWER LEVEL – QUARTERS   60

Apone's men are searching systematically in pairs. They pass through the colonists' modest apartments, little more than cubicles. Hudson, on tracker, flanks Vasquez as they move forward. Hudson touches a splash of colour on the wall. Dried blood. His tracker beeps.

Vasquez whirls, cannon aimed. The beeping grows more frequent as Hudson advances towards a half-open door. The door is splintered part-way out of its frame. Holes caused by pulse-rifle rounds pepper the walls. Vasquez eases up to the door. Kicks it in. Tenses to fire.

Inside, dangling from a piece of flex conduit, a junction-box swings like a pendulum in the wind from a broken window. It clacks against the rails of a child's bunk bed as it swings.

INT. DROP-SHIP – APC   61

Ripley watches Hicks' monitor.

> RIPLEY
> Wait! Tell him to...
> (plugs in headset jack)
> ...Hicks. Back up. Pan left. There!

The image shifts, revealing a section of wall corroded almost through in an irregular pattern.

> HICKS
> (voice-over; filtered)
> You seeing this okay? Looks melted.

Burke raises an eyebrow at Ripley.

> BURKE
> Hmm. Acid for blood.

> HICKS
> (voice-over; filtered)

Looks like somebody bagged them one of Ripley's
bad guys here.

INT. FIRST LEVEL   62

Hudson is looking up at something.

                              HUDSON
              Hey, if you like that, you're gonna love this...
Wider: showing the trooper standing beneath a gaping hole. Another hole, directly beneath, is
at his feet. The acid has melted right down through two levels into the maintenance level.

                              APONE
              Second squad? What's your status?

                              HICKS
                      (voice-over; filtered)
              Just finished our sweep. Nobody home.

                              APONE
                      (to Gorman)
              The place is dead, sir. Whatever happened, we
              missed it.

INT. APC   63

Gorman turns to the others.

                              GORMAN
              All right, the area's secured. Let's go in and see what
              their computer can tell us.
                      (into mike)
              First team head for operations. Hudson, see if you
              can get their CPU on line. Hicks, meet me at the
              south lock...

INT. FIRST LEVEL   62

                              GORMAN
                      (voice-over)
              ...We're coming in.

                              HUDSON
                      (cupping his mike)

He's coming in. I feel safer already.

> VASQUEZ
> (*sotto voce*)
> Pendejo jerk-off.

EXT. COLONY COMPLEX   65

Frost and Hicks emerge from the south lock just as the APC rolls up close to the entrance. The crew door slides back. Gorman emerges, followed by Burke and Bishop. Burke looks back to see Ripley stop in the APC doorway, eyeing the ominous colony structure. She meets his eyes. Shakes her head 'no'. Not ready.

> HUDSON
> (voice-over; filtered)
> Sir, the CPU is on-line.

> GORMAN
> Okay, stand by in operations.
> (to those present)
> Let's go.

INT. APC   66

The crew door cycles home with a clang. Ripley sits in the dark interior, lit by the tactical displays. The wind howls outside, an incredibly desolate sound. She hugs herself. Alone. Unarmed. She knows she's in a tank, but remembers the acid. Leaps up. Hits the door switch.

EXT. APC – SOUTH LOCK   67

The crew door opens and Ripley emerges. In time to see the lock doors rumbling closed.

> RIPLEY
> Burke!

The wind snatches her words away. The crew door whines shut behind her. She walks to the exterior lock door-controls and studies them. She punches some unfamiliar buttons. Nothing happens. She looks really nervous, alone in the howling wind. She hits another button. The door motors come to life and she relaxes a little. Glances behind her. And screams! There's a face right there! Right at her shoulder. She jumps back, gasping for breath.

> FROST
> Scare you?

RIPLEY

Jesus, Frost.

FROST

Sorry. Hicks said to keep an eye on you.

He gestures for her to precede him inside.

INT. CONTROL BLOCK CORRIDOR   68

Ripley catches up with the others as they move into the bowels of the complex.

GORMAN
(to Burke)
Looks like your company can write off its share of
this colony.

BURKE
(unconcerned)
It's insured.

On Ripley: as they move along the corridor...reacting to the fact that she is back in alien
country. She sees the ravaged administration complex. Fire-gutted offices. Hicks notices her
looking around nervously. He motions to Frost with his eyes and the trooper casually falls in
beside her on the other side, rifle at ready. A two-man protective cordon. She glances at Hicks.
He winks, but so fast maybe it's something in his eye. Trooper Drake emerges from a side
corridor ahead.

DRAKE
Sir, you should check this out...

INT. CORRIDOR   69

This wing is completely without power. The troopers switch on their pack lights and the beams
illuminate a scene of devastation worse than they have seen. Her expression reveals that Ripley
is about to turn and flee.

DRAKE
Right ahead here...

They approach a barricade blocking the corridor, a hastily welded wall of pipes, steel-plate,
outer-door panels. Acid holes have slashed through floor and walls in several places. The metal
is scratched and twisted by hideously powerful forces, peeled back like a soup can on one side.
They squeeze through the opening.

Scene 70: 'They seem to contain severed arthritic hands'

INT. MED LAB   70

The pack lights play over the devastation of the colonists' last-ditch battle. The equipment of the med labs has been uprooted to add to the barrier.

> FROST
> Last stand.

> GORMAN
> No bodies?

> DRAKE
> No, sir. Looks like it was a helluva fight.

ALIENS

Tight on Ripley: transfixed by something.

> RIPLEY
> (low)
> Over there.

The others turn and approach, seeing what she sees. She has entered a second room, part of the med-lab area. In a storage alcove at near eye level stand seven transparent cylinders. Stasis tubes.

They seem to contain severed arthritic hands, the palsied fingers curled in a death-rictus.

> BURKE
> Are these the same...?

Ripley nods, unable to speak. Burke leans closer in fascination, his face almost touching one cylinder...

> RIPLEY
> Watch it, Burke...

The creature inside lunges suddenly, slamming against the glass. Burke jumps back. From the 'palm' of the thing's body emerges a pearlescent tubule, which slithers tongue-like over the inside of the glass.

> HICKS
> (to Burke)
> It likes you.

Only two of the creatures seem to pulse with life. Burke taps the other stasis cylinders.

> BURKE
> These are dead. There's just the two alive.

Bishop takes a file folder from above one of the live specimens. Inside is a medical chart printout with handwritten entries.

> BISHOP
> (reading)
> Removed surgically before embryo implantation.
> Subject: Marachuk, John L. Died during procedure.
> (looking up)
> They killed him getting it off.

                              HICKS
            Poor bastard.

They are startled by a loud beep. They turn. Hicks is intent on his motion tracker, aimed back towards the shattered barricade. Beep. Beep.

                              HICKS
            Behind us.

He gestures at the corridor they just passed through.

                              RIPLEY
            One of us?

                              GORMAN
            Apone...where are your people?
            Anybody in D-Block?

                              APONE
            (voice-over; filtered)
            Negative. We're all in operations.

Vasquez swings the smart-gun to ready position. She and Hicks head towards the source of the signal, the others following.

[71 OUT]

INT. MED LAB   72

Hicks's tracker reads out more rapidly. Ripley reluctantly follows the group.

                              HICKS
            It's moving.

                              VASQUEZ
            Which way?

Hicks nods towards a complicated array of equipment. They move forward, weapons levelled. Frost trips over a metal cannister, sending it clanging. Ripley half climbs the wall.

Hicks's tracker beeps rapidly. Crash. Something moves in the dark, toppling a rack of equipment.

On Vasquez: pivoting smoothly to fire. In the same instant Hicks's rifle slashes into frame. Slams Vasquez's barrel upwards. A stream of tracer fire rips into the ceiling.

ALIENS

VASQUEZ

You fuck!

Hicks ignores her, moving past and aiming his light under a row of steel cabinets. He gestures to Ripley, who steps forward. Trusting his judgement. She crouches beside him.

Ripley's POV: lit by Hicks's pack light...a tiny cowering figure. A very dirty, very terrified Newt Jorden. She clutches a plastic food packet in one hand, its top gnawed part way through. In the other hand she grips the head of a large doll, holding it by the hair. Just the head.

RIPLEY

(soothingly)

Come on out. It's all right...

Ripley moves towards her, reaching slowly under the cabinet. The kid bolts like a shot, scuttling along beneath the cabinetry. Ripley scrambles to follow...to keep her in sight. Hicks makes a grab, catching one tiny ankle. He snaps his hand out a moment later.

HICKS

Ow! Shit. Watchit, she bites.

The girl reaches an air duct set in the baseboard, and scrambles inside.

DRAKE

Let her go, man. Who cares?

Ripley dives, squirms into the duct without thinking. Just ahead she sees Newt enter a dark space and slam a steel hatch. Ripley pushes the hatch open before the child can latch it, and crawls in after her.

Newt is backed into a cul-de-sac in the tiny steel chamber. Ripley shines her light around in amazement. It is a nest. A nest built by a child. Wadded up blankets and pillows line the space, mixed up with a haphazard array of toys, stuffed animals, dolls, cheap jewellery, comic books, empty food packets, even a battery-operated tape player. Newt edges along the far wall and dives for the hatch. Ripley grabs her, controlling her in a bear hug. The kid struggles wildly, like a cat at the vet's.

RIPLEY

It's okay, it's okay. It's over...you're going to be all
right now...it's okay...you're safe...

Newt goes limp, almost catatonic. Her stare vacant, traumatised. We read a dark nightmare world in her eyes.

Ripley's light falls on something amid the debris...a framed photograph of Newt, dressed up and smiling, a ribbon in her hair. In embossed gold letters underneath it says:
SECOND GRADE CITIZENSHIP AWARD
REBECCA JORDEN

INT. OPERATIONS – MANAGER'S OFFICE   73

Newt sits huddled in a chair, arms around her knees. Looking at a point in space.

> GORMAN
> What's her name again?

> DIETRICH
> Rebecca.

Gorman kneels in front of her while Dietrich watches the read-outs from a bio-monitoring cuff wrapped around Newt's tiny arm.

> GORMAN
> Now think, Rebecca. Concentrate.
> Just start at the beginning...

No response. Ripley enters, carrying a coffee mug.

> GORMAN
> Where are your parents? You have to try to...

> RIPLEY
> Gorman! Give it a rest, would you.

Gorman stands with a sigh of dismissal.

> GORMAN
> Total brainlock.

> DIETRICH
> Physically she's okay. Borderline malnutrition, but I
> don't think any permanent damage.

She unsnaps the bio-monitoring cuff.

> GORMAN
> Come on, we're wasting our time.

ALIENS

Gorman and the others exit, leaving only Ripley with Newt. Through the window of the office, out on the main floor of the operations room, we see Gorman join Burke and Bishop at a computer terminal.

Ripley kneels beside Newt, brushing the girl's unkempt hair out of her eyes in a gently, maternal fashion.

> RIPLEY
> Here, try this. A little instant hot chocolate.

She wraps the child's hands around the cup. Raises it to her lips for her. The girl drinks mechanically, spilling down her chin.

> RIPLEY
> Poor thing. You don't talk much, do you? That's okay
> with me. Most people do a lot of talking and they
> wind up not saying very much.

She sets the cup down and wipes the child's chin clean.

> RIPLEY
> Uh oh. I made a clean spot here. Now I've done it.
> Guess I'll just have to do the whole thing.

She pours water from a squeeze-bottle on to a small cloth and gently washes the little girl's face.

> RIPLEY
> Hard to believe...there's a little girl under all this.
> And a pretty one at that.

Newt doesn't seem to know she's there.

INT. OPERATIONS   74

The ground teams are gathered around a terminal in the computer centre...Hudson has the CPU main computer on-line and reading out.

Tight on monitor screen: as an abstract of the main-colony groundplan drifts across the screen. Searching.

Hudson bashes at the keyboard, his fingers dancing expertly.

> BURKE
> (to Gorman)

What's he scanning for?

                    GORMAN
        PDTs. Personal Data Transmitters. Every adult
        colonist has one surgically implanted.

                    HUDSON
        If they're within twenty clicks we'll read it out here,
        but so far...zip.

INT. OFFICE   75

Ripley is washing Newt's tiny hands with a cloth, pink skin emerging from black grime.

                    RIPLEY
        I don't know how you managed. You're one brave
        kid, Rebecca.

Newt's voice is all but inaudible.

                    NEWT
        N-newt.

Ripley leans closer. The single syllable was incomprehensible.

                    RIPLEY
        What did you say?

                    NEWT
        Newt. My n-name's Newt. Nobody calls me
        Rebecca, except my brother.

Ripley grins. She speaks quietly, not wanting to break the spell.

                    RIPLEY
        All right, Newt. I'm Ripley. Pleased to meet you. And
        who is this? Does she have a name?

Newt glances at the disembodied doll, still clutched in one filthy hand.

                    NEWT
        Casey.

ALIENS

                              RIPLEY
               Hello, Casey. And what about your brother, what's
               his name?

                              NEWT
               Timmy.

                              RIPLEY
               Is he around here too? Maybe hiding like you were?

Newt seems to close up, staring at her knees as if Ripley was not there.

                              RIPLEY
               Who else is there in your family, Newt? Sisters?

Newt shakes her head 'no', barely moving.

                              RIPLEY
               Mom and Dad?

The little girl nods, almost imperceptably.

                              RIPLEY
               Newt...look at me, Newt. Where are they?

                              NEWT
               Dead! They're dead. All right? Can I go now?

                              RIPLEY
               Don't you think you'd be safer here with us?

Newt shakes her head 'no' with chilling certainty.

                              RIPLEY
               Newt, these people are here to protect you. They're
               soldiers.

                              NEWT
                    (distantly)
               It won't make any difference.

INT. OPERATIONS   76

Everyone jumps as Hudson cries out triumphantly.

77

                    HUDSON
Hah! Stop your grinnin' and drop your linen!
Found 'em.

                    GORDON
Alive?

                    HUDSON
Unknown. But it looks like all of them. Over at the
processing station...sub-level four under the main
cooling towers.

Tight on screen: showing an amoeba-like cluster of flashing blue dots clumped tightly in one area.

                    HICKS
Looks like a goddamn town meeting.

                    GORMAN
Let's saddle up.

                    APONE
Awright, let's go, girls, they ain't payin' us by
the hour.

INT. OFFICE   76A

Hicks knocks and enters.

                    HICKS
We're moving out.

Newt uses the diversion, bolting like a rodent under the furniture, towards the door to a connecting office. Hicks leaps grabbing her arm, and the kid spins to bite him.

                    RIPLEY
Newt!

Hicks snaps his hand back as Ripley grabs the little girl by the shoulders. Newt stops struggling. Hicks rubs his hand where the child bit him earlier.

                    HICKS
Hope the kid don't have rabies.

ALIENS

                              RIPLEY
                        (to Newt)
                     Come on.

She leads the little girl out, following Hicks.

EXT. ACHERON – TWILIGHT   77

The APC roars across the Stygian landscape toward the atmosphere station two kilometres
away. Behind it the Drop Ship settles to the ground at the colony landing field.

INT. APC   78

The troopers sit, more subdued now, swaying and bouncing in the heavily sprung vehicle.
Ripley and Newt sit side by side just aft of the driver's cockpit, where Frost is in the saddle.

Ripley's gaze is rivetted to a monitor which the atmosphere station looms ahead.

EXT. APC STATION   79

The vast structure towers above the parked personnel carrier. Deploying in front of the APC,
backlit by its lights, the troopers cast long shadows. The base of the station is a depthless maze
of conduits and pressure vessels, like an oil refinery.

                              GORMAN
                     Forty metres in, bearing two-two-one there should
                     be a stairwell...

                              APONE
                     Check. Got it.

                              GORMAN
                     You want sub-level two. Next one down. Then
                     proceed on a one-two-five.

They descend the stairwell into the dark pit of machinery.

INT. APC   80

Huddled around the screens are Ripley, Burke and Gorman. Newt squeezes in from behind.

                              GORMAN
                     We're not making that out too well. What is it?

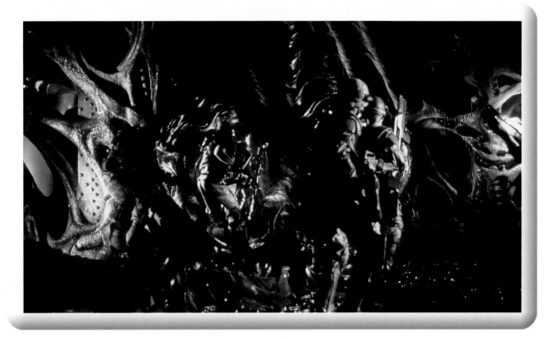

Scene 83: 'They enter the organic labyrinth, playing their lights over the walls'

HUDSON
(voice-over; static)
You tell me, man. I only work here.

INT. COMPLEX   81

The group stands before a bizarre tableau. Among the refinery-like lattice of pipes and conduits something new and not of human design has been added. It is a structure of some sort, extending from and crudely imitating the complex of plumbing, but made of some strange encrusted substance.

INT. APC   82

Ripley stares at the scene in dread fascination.

GORMAN
What is it?

                              RIPLEY
              I don't know.

                              GORMAN
                       (to team)
                    Proceed inside.

INT. ALIEN STRUCTURE   83

They enter the organic labyrinth, playing their lights over the walls, revealing a bio-mechanical lattice.

INT. APC   84

They watch the various helmet-camera POVs of the wall detail.

                              RIPLEY
                       (low)
                    Oh God...

Close on video: as it pans slowly...revealing a bas-relief of detritus from the colony: furniture, wiring, human bones, skulls...fused together with a translucent, epoxy-like substance.

                              DIETRICH
                    (voice-over; static)
              Looks like some sort of secreted resin.

                              RIPLEY
              Newt, go sit up front. Go on. Now!

                              BURKE
              They've been busy little creatures, haven't they?

INT. ALIEN STRUCTURE   85

Steam swirls around them as the troopers move deeper inside.

                              FROST
              Hotter'n hell in here.

                              HUDSON
              Yeah...but it's a dry heat.

Ripley leans forward suddenly, studying the graphic readout of the station ground plan.

> RIPLEY
> Lieutenant, what do those pulse-rifles fire?

> GORMAN
> Ten mm explosive-tip caseless, the standard light
> armour piercing round. Why?

> RIPLEY
> Well, look where your team is, they're right under
> the primary heat exchangers.

> GORMAN
> So?

> RIPLEY
> So, if they fire their weapons in there, they'll rupture
> the cooling system.

> BURKE
> Oh, oh. She's right.

> GORMAN
> So? So what?

> BURKE
> Look, this thing's a big fusion reactor, right? We're
> talking thermonuclear explosion. Adios muchachos.

> GORMAN
> Oh, great. Wonderful. Shit!
>   (into mike)
> Uh, Apone...look, we can't have any
> firing in there. I, uh, want you to
> collect magazines from everybody.

INT. ALIEN STRUCTURE   87

The troopers look at each other in dismay.

                              HUDSON
          Is he fucking crazy?

                              FROST
          What're we supposed to use, man?
          Harsh language?

                              GORMAN
                    (voice-over; static)
          Flame-units only. I want rifles
          slung. Just do it. And no grenades.

                              APONE
          Let's go. Pull 'em out.

He walks among the troopers, collecting the magazines from each one's weapons. He puts
them in a rucksack and hands it to Frost to carry.
Frost, Dietrich and Wierzbowski unsling their small flame-throwers. When Apone moves on,
Vasquez slips a spare magazine from concealment and inserts it in her weapon. Drake does the
same. Hicks hangs back in the shadows. He opens a leather quiver attached to his battle-harness.
Slides out an old-style pump twelve-gauge with a sawn-off butt stock. Chambers a round.

                              HICKS
                    (low, to Hudson)
          I always keep this handy. For
          close encounters.

                              APONE
                    (os)
          Let's move. Hicks, back us up.

INT. LARGE CHAMBER   88

The air is thick. Lights flare.

                              GORMAN
                    (voice-over; very faint)
          Any movement?

Hudson watches his tracker, scanning.

                              HUDSON
          Nothing. Zip.

Scene 88: 'The colonists have been brought here and entombed alive'

Apone stops, his expression changing. They face a wall of living horror. The colonists have been brought here and entombed alive...

Cocoons protrude from the niches and interstices of the structure. The cocoon material is the same translucent epoxy. The bodies are frozen in twisted positions. Ribcages burst outwards, exploded from within. Paralysed, then brought here as hosts for the embryos which grew within them.

Arrayed across the floor are a number of leathery ovoids, alien eggs, their tops open like flower petals. Apone shines his light into one. Empty and dry. His beam crosses the floor, finding one of the multilegged parasites, curled up and shrivelled like a dead spider. Others lie at the feet of the cocooned colonists, graphically illustrating the bizarre life cycle.

Dietrich moves close to examine one of the figures, perhaps the most 'recent'. A woman ghost-white and drained. The woman's eyes snap open. They seem to plead.

DIETRICH

Sir!

ALIENS

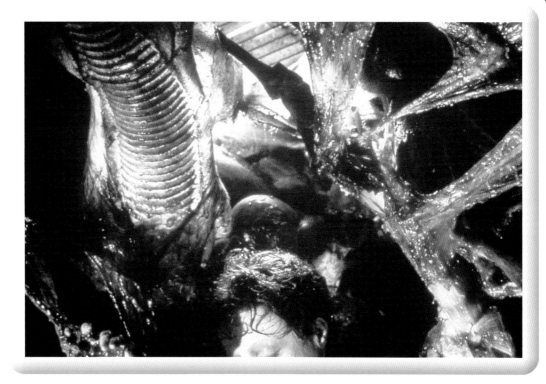

Scene 88: 'A woman ghost-white and drained'

The woman's lips move feebly.

>   WOMAN
>   Please... God... kill me.

INT. APC   89

Ripley watches the woman, white-knuckled.

INT. COCOON CHAMBER   90

The woman begins to convulse. She screams, a sawing shriek of mindless agony.

>   APONE
>   Flame-thrower! Move!

Frost hands it to him. Suddenly, the woman's chest explodes in a gout of blood. A small fanged head emerges, hissing viciously. Apone pulls the trigger. Then the other troopers carrying flame-throwers open fire. An orgy of purging fire. The cocoons vanish in the shimmering heat.

A shrill screeching begins, like a siren made from fingernails on blackboards. Unseen by the troopers, Shapes begin to emerge from the walls themselves...glistening bio-mechanoid forms. Visibility drops to zero as smoke fills the chamber.

> HUDSON
> Movement!

> APONE
> What's the position?

> HUDSON
> Can't lock up...

> APONE
> Talk to me, Hudson.

> HUDSON
> Uh, multiple signals...they're closing!

> APONE
> Go to infrared. Look sharp, people!

The squad members snap down their image-intensifier visors.

INT. APC   91

Gorman is playing with the gain controls on the monitors.

> GORMAN
> We can't see anything back here, Apone. What's going on?

Ripley senses it coming, like a wave at night. Dark, terrifying and inevitable.

> RIPLEY
> Pull your team out, Gorman.

INT. COCOON CHAMBER   92

In abstract glimpses we see the walls come alive...The troopers move in the smoky grotto, seeing without seeing.

>   HUDSON
>   I got readings in front and behind. Still closing.

>   FROST
>   Where, man? I don't see anything.

>   HUDSON
>   Look, I'm telling you, something's moving and it
>   ain't us.
>   DIETRICH
>   Maybe they don't show up on the infrared at all.

>   FROST
>   I say we back on outta here.

Dietrich, standing near a wall of the structure, grips her flame-thrower tightly. She doesn't see the nightmarish figure emerge from the wall behind her. It strikes, seizing her. She fires, reflexively, wild. The jet of flame engulfs Frost, nearby.

Crowe and Wierzbowski turn, horrified, to see the human torch drop his flaming satchel full of pulse-rifle magazines. They run. VOOM! They are catapulted forward by the blast, with Crowe striking a pillar head-on.

INT. APC   93

Ripley watches Crowe's monitor spin and go black. Frost's and Dietrich's have turned to static break-up. Their bio-readouts go flat-line.

>   GORMAN
>   Jesus Christ! Apone, what's going on?

INT. COCOON CHAMBER   94

Vasquez nods to Drake with grim satisfaction.

>   VASQUEZ
>   Let's rock.

They open up simultaneously. Vasquez moves ferret-quick in a pivoting dance. Thunder and lightning. Better than sex for her.

> GORMAN
> Who's firing, godammit? I ordered a hold fire!

> RIPLEY
> GET THEM OUT OF THERE! DO IT NOW!

> GORMAN
> Shut up! Just shut up! Uh...Apone, I want you to lay
> down a suppressing fire with the incinerators and
> fall back by squads to the APC, over.

> APONE
> (voice-over; heavy static)
> Say again? All after incinerators?

> GORMAN
> I said...

INT. COCOON CHAMBER   96

Apone adjusts his headset.

> GORMAN
> (voice-over; static)
> ...lay down (garbled)...squads to...(garbled)

Gorman's voice breaks up completely. A scream. Apone whirls uncertain.

> APONE
> Dietrich? Crowe? Sound off! Frost? Frost?

Nothing. Apone spins, isolated in the dense smoke. Can't see anything. Suddenly, his eyes snap
upwards and he raises his flame-thrower to fire.

INT. APC   97

Apone's monitor whites out as his flame-thrower fires, then spins crazily. Sounds of a vicious
struggle...then rolling static.

> GORMAN
> Apone? Apone?

The battle of phantoms unfolds on the video screens. Ripley flinches as another scream comes over the open frequency. Wierzbowski's monitor breaks up. His life-signs plummet. Voices blend and overlap.

                              HUDSON
                    (voice-over; freaked)
          The sarge's gone, man! Let's get the fuck out of here.

                              HICKS
                        (voice-over)
              Not that tunnel, the other one!

                              DRAKE
                        (voice-over)
              You sure? Watch it...behind you.
              Fucking move, will you!

Gorman is ashen. Confused. Gulping for air like a grouper. How could the situation have unravelled so fast?

                              GORMAN
                    I told them to fall back.

                              RIPLEY
                  They're cut off! Do something!

But he's gone. Total brain lock.

Tight on Ripley: as she struggles with a decision. She's terrified...of what she knows she's about to do. But more than that, she's furious. Shouldering past a paralysed Gorman, she runs up the aisle of the APC.

                              RIPLEY
                  Newt, put your seat belt on!

Ripley jumps into the driver's seat of the APC. Takes a deep breath. Starts slapping switches.

                              GORMAN
                    Ripley, what the hell...?

She slams the tractor into gear.

EXT. APC   98

89

As the drive wheels spin on the wet ground, the massive machine leaps forward.

INT. APC   99

Ripley sees smoke pouring out of the complex ahead as she slides sideways on to the descending rampway. She slams the left and right drive-wheel actuators viciously, spinning the machine in a roaring pivot. Gorman lunges forward along the aisle, abandoning his command console.

> GORMAN
> What are, you doing? Turn around!
> That's an order!

He claws at her, hysterical. Burke pulls him off.

INT. ALIEN STRUCTURE   100

The APC roars down into the smoky structure, tearing away outcropping of alien encrustation. Ripley hits the floodlights. Strobe-beacon. Siren. She homes on the flash of weapons-fire ahead.

INT. COCOON CHAMBER   101

The APC crashes inside, showering debris. Hicks, supporting a limping Hudson, appears out of the smoke. The APC pulls up broadside and Burke gets the crew door open.

Drake and Vasquez back out of the dense mist, firing as they fall back. Drake goes empty, slaps the buckles cutting loose his smart-gun harness and unslings a flame-thrower he has picked up.

Hicks pushes Hudson inside, leaps in after him and drags Vasquez inside, massive gear and all. She sees a dark shape lunge towards Drake. She fires one burst, prone. Clean body hit. The flash lights up the inhuman grin, blowing open the thing's thorax. A spray of bright yellow acid slashes across Drake's face and chest, eating into him like a hot knife through butter. He drops in boiling smoke, reflexively triggering his flame-thrower.

The jet of liquid fire arcs around as he falls, engulfing the back half of the APC.

INT. APC   102

Vasquez rolls aside as a gout of napalm shoots through the crew door, setting the interior on fire. Hicks is rolling the door closed when Vasquez lunges, clawing out the opening. He stops her, dragging her inside.

ALIENS

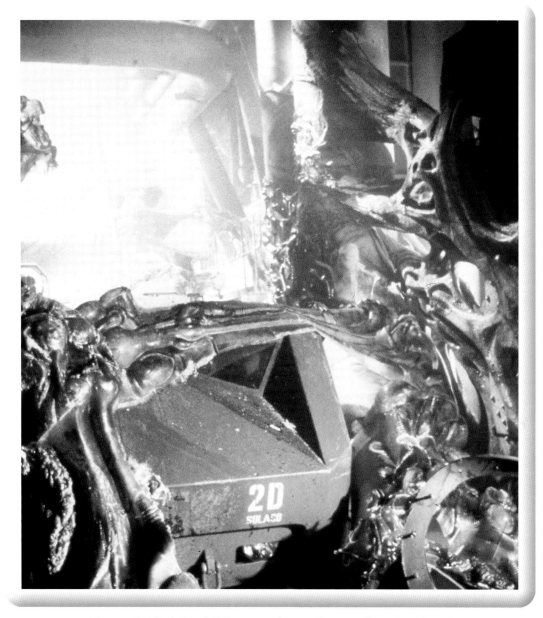

Scene 100: 'The APC roars down the smoky structure'

VASQUEZ
He's down! Drake's down!

Hicks screams right in her face.

HICKS
He's gone! Forget it, he's gone!

VASQUEZ
(irrational)
No. No, he's not. He's –

Burke and Hudson help him drag her from the door.

HICKS
(to Ripley)
Let's go!

Ripley jams reverse. Nails the throttle. The APC bellows backwards up the ramp. Hicks gets the door almost closed. Suddenly claws appear at the edge. The door is being slowly wrenched open from the outside. Hicks yells at a paralyzed Gorman.

HICKS
Get on the goddamn door!

Gorman backs away, eyes wide. Hicks jams his shoulder against the latching lever and frees one hand to raise his twelve-gauge. An alien head wedges through the opening, its hideous mouth opening. And Hicks jams his shotgun muzzle between its jaws and pulls the trigger! BLAM! The creature is flung backwards, its shattered head fountaining acid blood. The spray eats into the door, the deck, hits Hudson on the arm. He shrieks. They slide the door home and dog it tight.

EXT. APC   103

The armoured vehicle roars backwards up the ramp. Slams into a mass of conduit. Tears free.

INT./EXT. APC   104/105

The shock tears loose a storage rack and Gorman disappears under a pile of equipment. Ripley works the shifters, pivoting the massive machine. Everybody's shouting, trying to put out the fire. Pandemonium.

The APC rips away a section of catwalk and heads for clear air, its flank trailing fire like a comet. Ripley fights the controls as the big machine slews, broadsiding a control room out-building. Office furniture and splintered wall sections are strewn in the APC's wake.

Suddenly, an alien arm arcs down, right in front of Ripley's face. It smashes the windshield. Glistening, hideous jaws lunge inside.

Ripley recoils. Face-to-face once again with the same mind-numbing horror. She reacts instinctively. Slams both sets of brakes with all her strength. The huge wheels lock. The creature flips off, landing in the headlights. Ripley hits full throttle. The APC roars forward, smashing over the abomination. Its skeletal body is crushed under the massive wheels. The machine thunders out on to the open landscape and away from the station. A sound like bolts dropped in a meat grinder is coming from the APC's rear end. Hicks eases Ripley's hand back on the throttle lever. Her grip is white-knuckled.

> HICKS
> It's okay...we're clear. We're
> clear. Ease up.

The grinding clatter becomes deafening even as she slows the machine.

> HICKS
> Sounds like a blown transaxle.
> You're just grinding metal.

EXT. APC/LANDSCAPE   106

The personnel carrier limps to a halt, a smoking, acid-scarred mass...a half-kilometre from the station.

INT. APC   107

Ripley, still running on the adrenalin dynamo, spins out of her seat into the aisle, looking all around. She spots Newt, wedged into a tiny space between the driver's seat and a bulkhead. She is trembling, and looks terrified, but it's not the basket-case catatonia of before.

> RIPLEY
> You okay?

Newt gives her a thumbs-up, wan but stoic. Ripley goes back to the others. Hudson is holding his arm and staring in stunned dismay at nothing, playing it all back in his mind. Burke tries to have a look at his arm. He jerks away.

> HUDSON
> I'm all right, leave it!

Ripley joins Hicks who is bent over an unconscious Gorman, checking for a pulse. Gorman has a nasty forehead gash.

                    HICKS
        He's alive. Looks like concussion.

                   VASQUEZ
        He's dead!

She grabs Gorman by the collar, hauling him up roughly, ready to pulp him with her other fist.

                   VASQUEZ
        Wake up, pendejo! I'm gonna kill you, you useless
        fuck!

Hicks pushes her back. Right in her face.

                    HICKS
        Hold it. Hold it. Back off, right now.

Vasquez releases Gorman. His head smacks the deck.

                   HUDSON
        Hey...hey! Look, Wierzbowski and Dietrich aren't
        dead, man. Their signs are real low but they ain't
        dead.

They turn to see Hudson at the MTOB monitors, pointing at the bio-function screens.

                   VASQUEZ
        Well, I guess we better just go back in and get them.

                   HUDSON
        I ain't going back. Fuck that.

Hudson is pale, his voice panicky.

                   RIPLEY
        You can't help them. Right now they're being
        cocooned just like those colonists.

                   HUDSON
        Oh, God. Jesus. This ain't happening.

Ripley and Vasquez lock eyes. Ripley doesn't want it to be 'I told you so' but Vasquez reads it
that way. She turns away with a snap.

ALIENS

Scene 108: 'A dissection of one of the dead parasites'

INT. MED LAB   108

Bishop is hunched over an ocular probe doing a dissection of one of the dead parasites. Spunkmeyer enters with some electronics gear on a hand truck and parks it near Bishop's work table.

                              SPUNKMEYER
                    Need anything else?

Bishop waves 'no' without looking up.

EXT. COLONY – DROP-SHIP   109

Spunkmeyer emerges, crossing the tarmac to the loading ramp of the ship. As he nears the top of the ramp, his boot slips...skidding on something wet. Kneeling, he touches a small puddle of thick slime. He shrugs, and hits the controls to retract the ramp and close the doors.

INT. APC   110

On Vasquez: wired and intense.

VASQUEZ

All right, we got seven canisters of CN-20...we roll them down there and nerve-gas the whole nest.

RIPLEY

No good. We don't know if it'll affect them.

HUDSON

Look, let's just bug out and call it even, okay?

RIPLEY

I say we take off and nuke the entire site from orbit. It's the only way to be sure.

BURKE

Whoah! Hold on a second. This installation has a substantial dollar value attached to it –

RIPLEY

They can bill me. I got a tab running.

BURKE

I know this is an emotional moment, but let's not make snap judgements. This is clearly an important species we're dealing with here. We can't just arbitrarily exterminate them –

RIPLEY

Wrong.

VASQUEZ

Yeah. Watch us.

HUDSON

Hey, maybe you haven't been keeping up on current events, but we just got our asses kicked, pal!

BURKE

I'm sorry, I just can't authorise this action.

RIPLEY

I believe Corporal Hicks has authority here.

> BURKE

Corporal Hicks!?

> RIPLEY

This operation is under military jurisdiction and
Hicks is next in chain of command. Right?

> HICKS

Looks that way.

Burke starts to lose it and it's not a pretty sight.

> BURKE

Look, this is a multimillion-dollar installation. He
can't make that kind of decision. He's just a grunt!
> (glances at Hicks)
No offence.

> HICKS

None taken. Ferro, you copying?

> FERRO

> (voice-over; static)
Standing by.

> HICKS

Prep for dust-off. We're gonna need an immediate
evac.
> (to Burke)
I think we'll take off and nuke the site from orbit. It's
the only way to be sure.

He winks. Burke looks like a kid whose toy has been snatched.

EXT. DROP-SHIP   111

The ship rises through the spray thrown up by the down blast of the VTOL jets, hovering above
the complex like a huge insect, its searchlights blazing.

EXT. APC   112

The group is filing out of the personnel carrier, which is clearly a write-off. Hicks and Hudson
have Gorman between them, and the others emerge into the wind. They watch the ship roar in
on its final approach.

Scene 113: 'An impression of leering jaws which blur forward,
then a whirl of motion and a truncated scream'

INT. DROP-SHIP COCKPIT   113

Ferro flicks the intercom switch several times. Thumps her headset mike.

> FERRO
> Spunkmeyer? Goddammit.

The compartment door behind her slides slowly back.

> FERRO
> (turning)
> Where the fu–

Her eyes widen. It's not Spunkmeyer.

An impression of leering jaws which blur forward, then a whirl of motion and a truncated
scream. The throttle levers are slammed forward in the mêlée.

They watch in dismay as the approaching ship dips and veers wildly. Its main engines roar full on and the craft accelerates towards them even as it loses altitude. It skims the ground. Clips a rock formation. The ship slews, side-slipping. It hits a ridge. Tumbles, bursting into flame, breaking up. It arcs into the air, end over end, a Catherine wheel juggernaut.

                    RIPLEY
          Run!

She grabs Newt and sprints for cover as a tumbling section of the ship's massive engine module slams into the APC and it explodes into twisted wreckage. A Drop Ship skips again, like a stone, engulfed in flames...and crashes into the station. A tremendous fireball.

The remainder of the ground team watches their hopes of getting off the planet, and most of their superior fire power, reduced to flaming debris. There is a moment of stunned silence, then...

                    HUDSON
               (hysterical)
          Well that's great! That's just fucking great, man.
          Now what the fuck are we supposed to do, man?
          We're in some real pretty shit now!

                    HICKS
          Are you finished?
               (to Ripley)
          You okay?

She nods. She can't disguise her stricken expression when she looks at Newt, but the little girl seems relatively calm. She shrugs with fatalistic acceptance.

                    NEWT
          I guess we're not leaving, right?

                    RIPLEY
          I'm sorry, Newt.

                    NEWT
          You don't have to be sorry. It wasn't your fault.

                    HUDSON
               (kicking rocks)

Just tell me what the fuck we're supposed to do
now. What're we gonna do now?

                    BURKE
Maybe we could build a fire and sing songs.

                    NEWT
We should get back, 'cause it'll be dark soon. They
come mostly at night. Mostly.

Ripley follows Newt's look to the AP station looming in the twilight, the burning Drop Ship
wreckage jammed into its basal structure.

EXT. CONTROL BLOCK – NIGHT   115

The wind howls mournfully around the metal buildings, dry and cold.

INT. OPERATIONS   116

The weary and demoralised group is gathered to take stock of their grim options. Vasquez and
Hudson are just setting down a scorched and dented packing case, one of several culled from
the APC wreckage. Hicks indicates their remaining inventory of weapons, lying on a table.

                    HICKS
This is all we could salvage. We've got four pulse-
rifles, with about fifty rounds each. That ain't so
good. About fifteen M-40 grenades and one flame
thrower less than half full...one damaged. And we've
got four of these robot sentry units with scanners
and display intact.

He opens one of the scorched cases, revealing a high-tech servo-actuated machine gun with
optical sensing equipment, packed in foam.

                    RIPLEY
How long after we're declared overdue can we
expect a rescue?

                    HICKS
About seventeen days.

ALIENS

HUDSON

We're not going to make it seventeen hours! Those
things are going to come in here, just like they did
before, man...they're going to come in here and get
us, man, long before...

RIPLEY

She survived longer than that with no weapons and
no training.

Ripley indicates Newt, who salutes Hudson smartly.

RIPLEY

So you better just start dealing with it. Just deal with
it, Hudson...because we need you and I'm tired of
your bullshit. Now get on a terminal and call up some
kind of floorplan file. Construction blueprints, I don't
care, anything that shows the layout of this place. I
want to see air ducts, electrical access tunnels, sub-
basements. Every possible way into this complex.

Hudson gathers himself, thankful for the direction. Hicks nods approval of her handling of it.

HUDSON

Aye-firmative. I'm on it.

BISHOP

I'll be in medical. I'd like to continue my analysis.

RIPLEY

Fine. You do that.

INT. OPERATIONS   117

Burke, Ripley, Hudson and Hicks are bent over a large horizontal video screen, like an
illumination chart table. Newt hops from one foot to the other to see.

RIPLEY

This service tunnel is how they're
moving back and forth.

HUDSON

Yeah, right, it runs from the processing station right
into the sub-level here.

He traces a finger.

> RIPLEY
> All right. There's a pressure door at this end. The
> first thing we do is put a remote sentry in the tunnel
> and seal that door.

> HICKS
> We gotta figure on them getting into the complex.

> RIPLEY
> That's right. So we repair the barricades at these
> intersections...
> > (pointing)
> ...and weld plate-steel over these ducts here and
> here. Then they can only come at us from these two
> corridors, so we put the other two sentry units here.

Hicks contemplates her game plan and raises his head, satisfied.

> HICKS
> Outstanding. Then all we need's a deck of cards. All
> right, let's move like we got a purpose.

> HUDSON
> Aye-firmative.

> NEWT
> > (imitating Hudson)
> Aye-firmative.

INT. SERVICE TUNNEL – SUB-LEVEL   118

A long straight service tunnel, lined with conduit, seems to go on for ever. Vasquez and
Hudson have finished setting up two of the robot sentry guns on tripods in the tunnel.

> VASQUEZ
> > (shouting)
> Testing!

She hurls a wastebasket down the tunnel, into the automatic field of fire. The sentry guns
swivel smoothly, the wastebasket bounces once ...and is riddled by two quick bursts. They
retreat behind a heavy steel fire door which they roll closed on its track. Vasquez, using a
portable welding torch, begins sealing the door to its frame, as Hudson paces nervously.

ALIENS

                              HUDSON
                    Hudson here. A and B sentries are in place and
                    keyed. We're sealing the tunnel.

INT. SECOND LEVEL CORRIDOR   119

Hicks pauses in his work.

                              HICKS
                         (into mike)
                    Roger.

He and Ripley are covering an air-duct opening with a metal plate, welding it in place,
showering sparks in the dark corridor. Behind them Burke and Newt are moving back and forth
with cartons of food on a hand truck, stacking it inside the operations centre. Hicks sets down
his welder and removes what looks like a wristwatch from his arm. It is a standard issue
locating beeper.

                              HICKS
                    Here, put this on. Then I can find you anywhere in
                    the complex on this –

He indicates a tiny locator hooked to his battle harness. He shrugs, a little self-consciously.

                              HICKS
                    Just a...precaution. You know.

Ripley pauses for a moment, regarding him quizzically.

                              RIPLEY
                    Thanks.

                              HICKS
                    Uh, what's next?

She consults a printout of the floor plan.

EXT. CONTROL BLOCK   120

The wind has died utterly and in the eerie stillness a diffuse mist has rolled in to shroud the
complex. Everything looks underwater. There is no movement.

INT. CORRIDOR   121

In the barricaded corridor sentry guns C and D sit waiting, their 'ARMED' lights flashing green. Through a hole torn in the ceiling at the far end of the corridor the fog swirls in. Water drips. An expectant hush.

INT. MED LAB ANNEX/SURGERY   122

Ripley carries an exhausted Newt through the inner connecting rooms of the medical wing. She reaches an operating room which is small but very high tech...vaultlike metal walls, strange equipment. Several metal cots have been set up, displacing OR equipment which is pushed into one corner.

Newt is resting her head on Ripley's shoulder, barely awake...out of steam. Ripley sets her on one of the cots and Newt lies down.

> RIPLEY
> Now you just lie here and have a nap. You're
> exhausted.

> NEWT
> I don't want to...I have scary dreams.

This obviously strikes a chord with Ripley, but she feigns cheerfulness.

> RIPLEY
> I'll bet Casey doesn't have bad dreams.

Ripley lifts the doll's head from Newt's tiny fingers and looks inside. It is, of course, empty.

> RIPLEY
> Nothing bad in here. Maybe you could just try to be
> like her.

Ripley closes the doll's eyes and hands her back. Newt rolls her eyes as if to say 'don't pull that six-year-old shit on me, lady, I'm seven'.

> NEWT
> Ripley...she doesn't have bad dreams because she's
> just a piece of plastic.

> RIPLEY
> Oh. Sorry, Newt.

She turns, reaching for a portable space heater sitting nearby, and slides it closer to the bed. She switches it on. It hums and emits a cosy orange glow.

ALIENS

NEWT

My mommy always said there were no monsters. No
real ones. But there are.

Ripley's expression becomes sober. She brushes damp hair back from the child's pale forehead.

RIPLEY

Yes, there are, aren't there.

NEWT

Why do they tell little kids that?

Newt's voice reveals her deep sense of betrayal.

RIPLEY

Well, some kids can't handle it like you can.

NEWT

Did one of those things grow inside her?

Ripley begins pulling blankets up and tucking them in around her tiny body.

RIPLEY

I don't know, Newt. That's the truth.

NEWT

Isn't that how babies come? I mean, people babies
...they grow inside you?

RIPLEY

No, it's different, honey.

NEWT

Did you ever have a baby?

RIPLEY

Yes. A little girl.

NEWT

Where is she?

RIPLEY

Gone.

                         NEWT
          You mean dead.

It's more statement than question. Ripley nods slowly.

Ripley unsnaps the tracer bracelet given to her by Hicks and puts it on Newt's tiny wrist,
cinching it down.

                         RIPLEY
          Here, this is for luck.

She switches off the light and starts to rise. Newt grabs her arm. A plaintive voice in the dark.

                         NEWT
          Don't go! Please.

                         RIPLEY
          I'll be right in the other room. And look...I can see
          you on that camera right up there.

Newt looks at the video security camera above the door.

                         RIPLEY
          Newt...I won't leave you, honey.
          I mean it. That's a promise.

                         NEWT
          You promise?

                         RIPLEY
          Cross my heart.

                         NEWT
          And hope to die?

Ripley flinches at the innocently grim expression.

                         RIPLEY
          And hope to die.

Newt grabs her in a desperate hug and Ripley returns it slowly, a bit overwhelmed at first, then
with fierce emotion. The child's need is so vast, Ripley prays she has made a promise she can
keep.

ALIENS

                            RIPLEY
                Now go to sleep...and don't dream.

Ripley exits and Newt turns on her side, gazing at the bracelet.

INT. MED LAB   123

Ripley stands over Lieutenant Gorman, lying motionless on a gurney, his head bandaged.
Bishop, crouched over his instruments, is still analysing the facehugger specimens. Hudson
and Vasquez are nearby, their weapons cradled.

                            RIPLEY
                Okay, now let me get this straight.
                They grabbed the colonists, took them
                over there, and immobilised them to
                be hosts for more of those...

Ripley points at the stasis cylinders containing the facehugger specimens.

                            RIPLEY
                Which would mean lots of those parasites, right?
                One for each person...over a hundred at least.

                            BISHOP
                Yes. That follows.

                            RIPLEY
                But each one of these things comes from an egg,
                right? So who lays the eggs?

                            BISHOP
                I don't know yet. It must be something we haven't
                seen.

                            HUDSON
                Hey, maybe it's like an ant hive.

                            VASQUEZ
                Bees. Bees have hives.

                            HUDSON
                You know what I mean. There's like one female that
                runs the show.

> BISHOP
> That's right. The queen.

> HUDSON
> Yeah, the momma. And she's badass, man. Big.

Hudson gestures, about an inch long.

> VASQUEZ
> These things ain't ants.

> RIPLEY
> I want those specimens destroyed as soon as you're
> done with them. You understand?

Bishop glances at the creatures, pulsing malevolently in their cylinders.

> BISHOP
> Mr Burke gave instructions that they were to be kept
> alive in stasis for return to the Company labs. He
> was very specific.

Ripley feels the fabric of her self-restraint tearing. She slaps the intercom switch.

> RIPLEY
> Burke!

INT. MED LAB ANNEXE   124

In a small observation chamber separated from the med lab by a glass partition, Ripley and
Burke have squared off.

> RIPLEY
> Look, Burke, we had an agreement!

> BURKE
> I know, I know, but we're dealing with changing
> scenarios here. This thing is major, Ripley. You gotta
> go with its energy. Look, you're the representative of
> the Company who discovered this species, your
> percentage is going to be some serious money. I
> mean serious.

Ripley stares at him like he's a particularly disagreeable fungus.

ALIENS

RIPLEY

You son of a bitch.

BURKE

Look, those specimens are worth millions to the bio-
weapons division. Now, if you're smart we can both
come out of this heroes. Set up for life.

RIPLEY

You'll never get a dangerous organism past ICC
quarantine.

BURKE

They can't impound it if they don't know about it.

RIPLEY

But they will know about it, Burke. From me.
Just like they'll know how you were responsible
for the deaths of one hundred and fifty-seven
colonists here –

BURKE

Now, wait a second –

RIPLEY

You sent them to that ship. I just checked the
coronary log...directive dated six-twelve-seventy-
nine. Signed Burke, Carter J.

Ripley's fury is peaking, now that the frustration and rage finally have a target to focus on.

RIPLEY

You sent them out there and you didn't
even warn them, Burke. Why didn't you
warn them?

BURKE

Look, maybe that ship didn't even exist, right? And if
I'd made it a major security situation, the
administration would've stepped in. Then no
exclusive rights, nothing.
        (shrugs)
It was a bad call, that's all.

Ripley snaps. She slams him against the wall, surprising herself and him.

> RIPLEY
> Bad call? These people are dead, Burke! Do you have
> any idea what you've done here?
> (she releases him)
> Well, I'm going to see they nail your hide to the
> wall...kiddo.

She steps back, shaking, and looks at him with utter loathing, as if the depths of human greed are a far more horrific revelation than any alien.

> BURKE
> I expected more of you, Ripley, I thought you would
> be smarter than this.

> RIPLEY
> Happy to disappoint you.

She turns away and strides out. The doors close. Burke stares after her, his mind a whirl of options.

INT. CORRIDOR   125

Ripley is walking toward operations when a strident alarm begins to sound. She breaks into a run.

INT. OPERATIONS   126

Ripley double-times it to Hicks's tactical console where Hudson and Vasquez have already gathered. Hicks slaps a switch, killing the alarm.

> HICKS
> They're coming. They're in the tunnel.

The trilling of the motion sensor remains, speeding up. Two red lights on the tactical display light up simultaneously with an echoing crash of gunfire which vibrates the floor.

> HICKS
> Guns A and B. Tracking and firing on multiple
> targets.

The RSS guns pound away, echoing through the complex. Their separate bursts overlap in an irregular rhythm. A counter on the display counts down the number of rounds fired.

> HUDSON
> They must be wall-to-wall in there. Look at those
> ammo counters go. It's a shooting gallery down
> there.

INT. SERVICE TUNNEL   127

Tight on the RSS gun blasting stroboscopically in the tunnels. Their barrels are over-heating, glowing cherry red. One clicks empty and sits smoking, still swivelling to track targets it can't fire upon.

INT. OPERATIONS   128

The digital counter on B-gun reads zero.

> HICKS
> B-gun's dry. Twenty on A. Ten. Five. That's it.

Silence. Then a gong-like booming echoes eerily up from sub-level.

> RIPLEY
> They're at the pressure door.

The booming increases in volume and ferocity.

> HUDSON
> Man, listen to that.

Mixed with the echoing crash-clang is a nerve-racking screech of claws on steel. The intercom buzzes, startling them.

> BISHOP
> (voice-over)
> Bishop here. I'm afraid I have some bad news.

> HUDSON
> Well, that's a switch.

INT. OPERATIONS – MINUTES LATER   129

Everyone, including Bishop, is crowded at the window, intently watching the AP station which is a dim silhouette in the mist. Suddenly a column of flame, like an acetylene torch, jets upwards from the complex at the base of the cone.

BISHOP

That's it. Emergency venting.

HICKS

How long until it blows?

BISHOP

Four hours. The blast radius will be about thirty
kilometres. About equal to twenty megatons.

HICKS

We got problems.

HUDSON

I don't fucking believe this. Do you believe this?

RIPLEY

Why can't we shut it down from here?

BISHOP

I'm sorry. The crash did too much damage. The
overload is inevitable, at this point.

HUDSON

Oh, man. And I was gettin' short, too! Four more
weeks and out. Now I'm gonna buy it on this fuckin'
rock. It ain't half fair, man!

VASQUEZ

Hudson, give us a break.

They watch as another gas jet lights up the fog-shrouded landscape. Ripley turns to Hicks.

RIPLEY

We need the other Drop Ship from the *Sulaco*. Can
we bring it down on remote, somehow?

HUDSON

How? The transmitter was on the APC. It's wasted.

RIPLEY

I don't care how! Think of a way. Think of
something.

ALIENS

HUDSON
Think of what? We're fucked.

RIPLEY
What about the colony transmitter? That up-link
tower down at the other end. Why can't we use that?

BISHOP
No, I checked. The hardwiring between here and
there was damaged. We can't align the dish.

Ripley is wound up like a dynamo, her mind spinning out options, grim solutions.

RIPLEY
Well then somebody's just going to have to go out
there. Take a portable terminal and go out there and
patch in manually.

HUDSON
Oh, right! Right! With those things running around.
No way.

BISHOP
(quietly)
I'll go.

RIPLEY
What?

BISHOP
Well, I'm really the only one qualified to remote-pilot
the ship anyway.

HUDSON
Yeah, right. Bishop should go. Good idea.

BISHOP
Believe me, I'd prefer not to. I may be synthetic but
I'm not stupid.

RIPLEY
All right. Let's get on it. What'll you need?

VASQUEZ
Listen. It's stopped.

They listen. Nothing. An instant later comes the high-pitched trilling of a motion-sensor alarm.
Hicks looks at the tactical board.

HICKS
Well, they're into the complex.

INT. MED LAB   130

One of the acid holes from the colonists' seige has yielded access to sub-floor conduits. Bishop,
lying in the opening, reaches up to grasp the portable terminal as Ripley hands it down to him.
He pushes it into the constricted shaft ahead of him. She then hands him a small satchel
containing tools and assorted patch cables, a service pistol and a small cutting torch.

RIPLEY
How long?

BISHOP
Let's see, this duct runs almost to the up-link
assembly. One hundred eighty metres. Say, forty
minutes to crawl down there. One hour to patch in
and align the antenna. Thirty minutes to prep the
ship, then about fifty minutes flight time.

Ripley looks at her watch.

RIPLEY
It's going to be close. Okay, get going.

BISHOP
(cheerfully)
See you soon.

He squirms into the shaft, pushing the equipment along ahead of him with a scraping rhythm.
Vasquez slides a metal plate over the hole and begins spot-welding it in place.

INT. CONDUIT   131

Bishop looks back as the welder seals him in. He sighs fatalistically and squirms forward.
Ahead of him the conduit dwindles straight to seeming infinity.

INT. MED LAB   132

Ripley jumps as an alarm suddenly blares through the complex.

> HICKS
> (voice-over)
> They're in the approach corridors.

> RIPLEY
> On my way.

Ripley jumps up, unslinging a flame-thrower from her shoulder in one motion, and sprints for operations with Vasquez. The sound of sentry guns opening up in staccato bursts echoes from close by.

INT. OPERATIONS   133

Ripley runs to the tactical console where Hicks is mesmerised by the images from the surveillance cameras. The flashes of the sentry guns flare-out the sensitive video, but impressions of figures moving in the smoky corridor are occasionally visible. The robot sentries hammer away, driving streamers of tracer fire into the swirling mist.

> HICKS
> Twenty metres and closing. Fifteen.
> C and D guns down about fifty per cent.

The digital readouts whirl through descending numbers. An inhuman shrill screeching is audible between bursts of fire.

> RIPLEY
> How many?

> HICKS
> Can't tell. Lots. D gun's down to twenty. Ten. It's
> out.

Then the firing from the remaining gun stops abruptly. The video image is a swirling wall of smoke. There are black and twisted shapes scattered at the edge of visibility. However, nothing emerges from the wall of smoke. The motion-sensor tone shuts off.

> RIPLEY
> They retreated. The guns stopped them.

The moment stretches. Everyone exhales slowly.

                    HICKS
        Yeah. But look...

The digital counters for the two sentry guns read '0' and '10' respectively. Less than a second's worth of firing.

                    HICKS
        Next time they can walk right up and
        knock.

                    RIPLEY
        But they don't know that. They're probably looking
        for other ways to get in. That'll take them a while.

                    HUDSON
        Maybe we got 'em demoralised.

                    HICKS
            (to Vasquez and Hudson)
        I want you two walking the perimeter. I know we're
        all in strung-out shape but stay frosty and alert.
        We've got to stop any entries before they get out of
        hand.

The two troopers nod and head for the corridor. Ripley sighs and picks up a cup of cold coffee, draining it in one gulp.

                    HICKS
        How long since you slept? Twenty-four hours?

Ripley shrugs. She seems soul-weary, drained by the nerve-racking tension. When she answers, her voice seems distant, detached.

                    RIPLEY
            (grimly)
        They'll get us.

                    HICKS
        Maybe. Maybe not.

                    RIPLEY
        Hicks, I'm not going to wind up like those others.
        You'll take care of it, won't you, if it comes to that?

ALIENS

                              HICKS
                    If it comes to that, I'll do us both. Let's see that it
                    doesn't. Here, I'd like to introduce you to a close
                    personal friend of mine.

He picks up his pulse-rifle, snaps open the bolt, drops out the magazine and hands it to her.

                              HICKS
                    M-41A 10mm pulse-rifle, over and under with a
                    30mm pump-action grenade launcher.

Ripley hefts the weapon. It is heavy and awkward.

                              RIPLEY
                    Okay. What do I do?

INT. CONDUIT   134

Bishop is in claustrophobic limbo between two echoing infinities. He approaches an irregular
hole which admits a tiny shaft of light. He puts his eyes up to the acid-etched opening.

HIS POV: as drooling jaws flash towards us, slamming against the steel with a vicious scraping
snap.

Bishop flattens himself away from the opening and inches along, looking pale and strained. He
glances at his watch.

INT. OPERATIONS   135

Ripley has the stock of the M-41A snugged up to her cheek and is awkwardly trying to keep up
with Hicks's instructions.

                              HICKS
                    Just pull it in real tight. It will kick some. When the
                    counter here reads zero, hit this...Just let it drop
                    right out. Get the other one in quick. Just slap it in
                    hard, it likes abuse. Now, pull the bolt. You're ready
                    again.

Ripley repeats the action, not very smoothly. Her hands are trembling. She indicates a stout
tube underneath the slender pulse-rifle barrel.

                              RIPLEY
                    What's this?

HICKS

Well, that's the grenade launcher...you probably
don't want to mess with that.

RIPLEY

Look, you started this. Now show me everything. I
can handle myself.

HICKS

Yeah. I've noticed.

INT. CORRIDOR   136

Dollying with Ripley walking down the corridor, now carrying her new-found friend, the
M-41A. Gorman steps out of the door to the med lab, looking weak but sound. Burke is right
behind him.

RIPLEY

How do you feel?

GORMAN

All right, I guess. One hell of a hangover. Look,
Ripley...I...

RIPLEY

Forget it.

She shoulders by him into the med lab. Gorman turns to see Vasquez staring at him with cold,
slitted eyes.

INT. MED LAB – ANNEX   137

Ripley crosses the deserted lab, passing through the annexe to the small OR where she left
Newt.

INT. SURGERY   138

Entering the darkened chamber, Ripley looks around. Newt is nowhere to be seen. On a hunch
she kneels down and peers under the bed. Newt is curled up there, jammed as far back as she
can get, fast asleep. Still clutching 'Casey'.

Ripley stares at Newt's tiny face, so angelic despite the demons that have chased her through
her dreams and the reality between dreams. Ripley lays the rifle on top of the cot and crawls
carefully underneath. Without waking the little girl, she slips her arms around her. Newt cries
out, a vague inarticulate plea. Ripley rocks her gently.

ALIENS

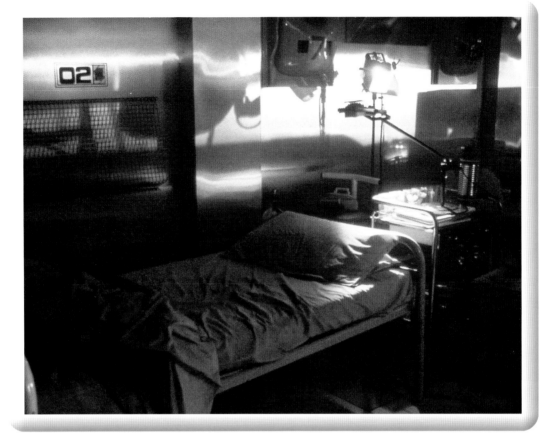

Scene 138: 'Ripley looks around. Newt is nowhere to be seen'

RIPLEY
There, there. Ssshh. It's all right.

EXT. UPLINK TOWER – VIEW OF AP STATION   139

A view of the processing station from the colony landing field.

Pan on to Bishop, foreground, hunched against the wind at the base of the telemetry tower. He has a test-bay panel open and the portable terminal patched in. His jacket is draped over the keyboard and monitor unit to protect it from the elements and he is typing frenetically.

Scene 141 : 'Two stasis cylinders. They are both empty'

                              BISHOP
                    Now, if I did it right…

He punches a key marked 'ENABLE'.

INT. *SULACO* CARGO LOCK – IN ORBIT   140

The drop-bay is empty and silent, with the remaning ship brooding in the shadows. A klaxon sounds and rotating clearance lights come on. Hydraulics whine to life. Drop Ship Two moves out on its overhead track and is lowered into the drop-bay for launch-prep. Service booms and fuelling couplers move in automatically around the hull.

INT. SURGERY   141

Tight on Ripley as she awakens with a start. She checks her watch...an hour has passed. She sees something and freezes. Across the room, just inside the door to the med lab, are two stasis cylinders. Their tops are hinged open, and the suspension fields are switched off. They are both empty. Ripley realises the inescapable certainty of a lethal presence.

                            RIPLEY
                    (whispers)
                Newt. Newt, wake up.

                            NEWT
            Wha...? Where are...?

                            RIPLEY
            Sssh. Don't move. We're in trouble.

Newt nods, now wide awake. They listen in the darkness for the slightest betrayal of movement. Ripley reaches up and, clutching the springs of the underside of the cot, begins to inch it away from the wall.

When the space is wide enough she cautiously slides herself up between the wall and the edge of the cot, reaching for the rifle she left lying on top of the mattress. Her eyes clear the edge of the bed. The rifle is gone.
She snaps her head around. A scuttling shape leaps towards her. She ducks. The obscene thing hits the wall above her. Reflexively she slams the bed against the wall, pinning the creature inches above her face. Its legs and tail writhe with incredible ferocity.

Ripley heaves Newt across the polished floor and in a frenzied scramble rolls from beneath the cot. She flips it over, trapping the creature underneath.

They back away, gasping. The creature scuttles from beneath the bed and disappears under a bank of cabinets in a blur. Ripley hugs Newt close and heads towards the door, moving as if every object in the room had a million volts running through it. She reaches the door. Hits the wall switch. Nothing happens. Disabled from outside. She tries the lights. Nothing. She pounds on the door. The acoustically dampened door panel thunks dully. She moves to the observation window.

                            RIPLEY
                    (shouting)

Hey...hey!

She pounds the window. Through the double thickness window we can see that the lab is dark and empty. Ripley whirls, hearing a loathsome scrabbling behind her. Newt starts to whimper, feeding off her fear. She steps in front of the surveillance camera and waves her arms in a circle.

>   RIPLEY
>   Hicks! Hicks!

INT. OPERATIONS   142

Tight on the video monitor showing Ripley waving her arms. There is no sound, a surreal pantomime. A hand enters frame and switches off the monitor. Ripley's image vanishes.

Wider: as Burke straightens casually from the console. Hicks is talking via headset with Bishop and hasn't noticed Ripley's plight or Burke's action.

>   HICKS
>   (into mike)
>   Roger. Check back when you've
>   activated the launch cycle.
>   (turning)
>   He's at the up-link tower.

>   BURKE
>   (calmly)
>   Excellent.

INT. SURGERY   143

Ripley picks up a steel chair and slams it against the observation window. It bounces back from the high-impact material.

Ripley turns, studying the room. Newt starts a thin, high wailing.

Ripley steadies herself, realising Newt's terror and the child's dependence on her. She gets an idea. Removes her lighter from a jacket pocket and picks up some papers from the counter. Moving cautiously she boosts Newt up on to the surgical table in the centre of the room and clambers up after her.

>   NEWT
>   Ripley...I'm scared.

>   RIPLEY
>   I know, honey. Me too.

ALIENS

Ripley lights the papers and holds the flaming mass under the temperature-sensor of a fire-control system SPRINKLER HEAD. It triggers, spraying the room from several sources with water. An ALARM sounds throughout the complex.

INT. OPERATIONS   144

Hicks jumps at the sound of the alarm, finally identifying its source among the lights flashing on his board. He bolts for the door, yelling into his headset as he moves.

> HICKS
> Vasquez, Hudson, meet me in
> Medical! We got a fire!

Ripley and Newt are drenched as the sprinklers continue to drizzle in the darkness. She is eye level with a complex surgical multilight. She looks into its tangle of arms and cables, inches away. Looks away. Her eyes snap back. Something leaps at her face. She screams and topples off the table, splashing to the floor. Newt shrieks and scrambles away as Ripley hurls the chittering creature off of her. It slams against a wall of cabinets, clings for a moment, then leaps back as if driven by a steel spring. Ripley scrambles desperately, pulling equipment over on top of herself, clawing across the floor in a frenzy of motion.

The creature scuttles up her body. She tears at it, but it is incredibly powerful for its size. It moves like lightning towards her head, avoiding her fumbling hands. Newt screams abjectly, backing away, until she is pressed up against a desk in one corner. Ripley has both hands up, forcing the pulsing body back from her face. The thing's tail whips around her throat and begins to tighten, forcing the underside of its body close to her. Ripley thrashes about, knocking over equipment, sending instruments clattering.

INT. OPERATIONS   145

Angle on Newt: as crablike legs appear from behind the desk right behind her. She sees it and, thinking fast, jams the desk against the wall, pinning the writhing thing. The desk jumps and shudders against all the pressure her tiny body can bring to bear on it. She wails between gritted teeth as the second creature gets one leg free, then another and another.

The legs of the chittering thing claw at Ripley's head, getting a surer grip even as she whips her head from side to side. The obscene tubule extrudes wetly from the sheath on the creature's underside, forcing itself between the arms she has crossed tightly over her face.

A figure appears at the observation window, a silhouette behind the misted-over glass. A hand wipes a clear spot. Hicks's eyes appear. He steps back. WHAM! A burst of pulse-fire shatters the tempered glass. Hicks dives into the crazed spiderweb pattern and explodes into the room. He hits rolling, and slides across to Ripley. He gets his fingers around the thrashing legs of the vicious beast and pulls. Between the two of them they force it away from her face, though Ripley is losing strength as the tail tightens sickeningly around her throat. Hudson leaps into the room, flings Newt away from the desk to go skidding across the wet floor, and blasts the second creature against the wall. Point-blank. Acid and smoke.

Gorman appears at Ripley's side and grabs the tail, unwinding its writhing length like a boa constrictor coil from her throat. All of them grip the struggling, shrieking creature.

                          HICKS
               The corner! Ready?

                          HUDSON
               Do it!

Hicks hurls the thing into the corner. It scrabbles upright in an instant and leaps back towards them. WHAM! Hudson gets it clean. Ripley collapses, gagging. The alarm and sprinklers shut off automatically. Hicks sees the stasis cylinders.

                          RIPLEY
                    (coughing)
               Burke...it was Burke.

INT. OPERATIONS   146

Angle on Hudson: looking decidedly stressed-out. He grips his rifle tightly, aimed right at camera.

                          HUDSON
               I say we grease this ratfuck son of a bitch right now!

The group is gathered around Burke who sits in a chair, maintaining an icy calm although beads of sweat betray intense concealed tension.

                          HICKS
                    (pacing)
               I don't get it. It doesn't make any goddamn sense.

ALIENS

RIPLEY

He figured he could get an alien back through
quarantine if one of us was impregnated...whatever
you call it – then frozen for the trip back. Nobody
would know about the embryos we were carrying.
Me and Newt.

HICKS

Wait a minute. We'd know about it.

RIPLEY

The only way it would work is if he sabotaged
certain freezers on the ship. Then he could jettison
the bodies and make up any story he liked.

HUDSON

Fuuuck! He's dead.
        (to Burke)
You're dog meat, pal.

BURKE

This is total paranoid delusion. It's pitiful.

RIPLEY

You know, Burke, I don't know which species is
worse. You don't see them screwing each other over
for a fucking percentage.

HICKS

Let's waste him.
        (to Burke)
No offence.

Ripley shakes her head. The rage giving way to a sickened emptiness.

RIPLEY

Just find someplace to lock him up until it's time to –

The lights go out. Everyone stops in the sudden darkness, realising instinctively it is a new
escalation in the struggle. Hicks looks at the board. Everything is out. Doors. Video screens.

RIPLEY

They cut the power.

HUDSON
What do you mean, they cut the power? How could
they cut the power, man? They're animals.

Ripley picks up her rifle and thumbs off the safety.

RIPLEY
Newt! Stay close.
(to the others)
Let's get some trackers going. Come on, get moving.
Gorman, watch Burke.

Hudson and Vasquez pick up their scanners and move to the door. Vasquez has to slide it open
manually on its track.

INT. CORRIDOR   147

The two troopers separate and move rapidly to the barriers at opposite ends of the control block.

RIPLEY
(voice-over)
Anything?

Beep. Hudson's tracker lights up, a faint signal.

HUDSON
There's something.

He pans it around. Back down the corridor. It beeps again, louder.

HUDSON
It's inside the complex.

VASQUEZ
(voice-over)
You're just reading me.

HUDSON
No. No! It ain't you. They're inside. Inside the
perimeter. They're in here.

RIPLEY
Hudson, stay cool. Vasquez?

Angle on Vasquez: swinging her tracker and rifle together. She aims it behind her. Beep.

> VASQUEZ
> (cool)
> Hudson may be right.

INT. OPERATIONS 148

Ripley and Hicks share a look...'here we go'.

> HICKS
> (low)
> It's game time.

> RIPLEY
> Get back here, both of you. Fall back to operations.

INT. CORRIDOR 149

Hudson backtracks nervously, peering all around. He looks stretched to the limit.

> HUDSON
> This signal's weird...must be some interference or
> something. There's movement all over the place...

> RIPLEY
> (voice-over)
> Just get back here!

Hudson reaches the door to operations at a run, a moment before Vasquez. They pull the door shut and lock it.

INT. OPERATIONS 150

Hudson joins Ripley and Hicks, who are laying out their armament. Flame-thrower. Grenades. M-41A magazines.
Hudson's tracker beeps. Then again. The tone continues through the scene, its rhythm increasing.

> HUDSON
> Movement! Signal's clean. Range twenty meters.

> RIPLEY
> (to Vasquez)
> Seal the door. Move fast.

Vasquez picks up a hand-welder and moves to comply.

> HUDSON
> Seventeen metres.

> HICKS
> Definitely inside the barricade.

Sparks shower around Vasquez as she begins welding the door.

> RIPLEY
> They found a way in, something we missed.

> HICKS
> We didn't miss anything.

> HUDSON
> Fifteen metres.

> RIPLEY
> Something under the floors, not on the plans. I don't know!

She picks up Vasquez's scanner and aims it the same direction as Hudson's.

> HUDSON
> Twelve metres. Man, this is a big fucking signal. Ten metres.

> HICKS
> They're right on us.

> RIPLEY
> Vasquez, how you doing?

Vasquez is heedlessly showering herself with molten metal as she welds the door shut. Working like a demon.

> HUDSON
> Nine metres. Eight.

> RIPLEY
> Can't be. That's inside the room!

HUDSON
It's readin' right. Look!

Ripley fiddles with her tracker, adjusting the tuning.

HICKS
Well, you're not reading it right!

HUDSON
Six metres. Five. What the fu–

He looks at Ripley. It dawns on both of them at the same time. She feels a cold premonitory dread as she angles her tracker upward to the ceiling, almost overhead. The tone gets louder. Hicks climbs on to a file cabinet and raises a panel of the acoustic drop-ceiling. He shines his light inside.

INT. OPERATIONS   151

Hicks's POV

A soul-wrenching nightmare image. Moving in the beam of his light are alien warriors. They are crawling like bats, upside down, clinging to the pipes and beams of the structural ceiling. The inner sanctum is utterly violated. Hicks' POV spins, revealing a lunging shape, coming straight at him from behind.

INT. OPERATIONS   152

Hicks falls into the room, firing, just as the creatures detach en masse from the handholds. The ceiling explodes, raining debris. Nightmare shapes drop into the room. Newt screams. Hudson opens fire. Vasquez grabs Hicks, pulls him up, firing one-handed with her flame-thrower. Ripley scoops up Newt and staggers back. Gorman turns to fire and Burke bolts for the only remaining exit, the corridor connecting to the med lab. In the strobe-like glare of the pulse-rifles we see flashes of aliens, moving forward in the smoke from the flame-thrower fires.

RIPLEY
Medical! Get to medical!

INT. MED LAB CORRIDOR   153

Dollying behind her as she sprints. Ahead of her Burke clears the door to the med lab. He slides it closed. Ripley slams into the door. Hears it lock from the far side.

RIPLEY
Burke! Open the door!

NEWT

Look!

Behind her a warrior is moving down the corridor like a locomotive. Shaking, Ripley raises her rifle. She squeezes the trigger. Nothing happens. Ripley checks the safety. The safety is off. The digital counter. The magazine is full. Newt begins to wail. The thing is almost on Ripley, filling the corridor, when she remembers. She snaps the bolt back, chambering a round. Whips the stock to her shoulder. Fires. Flash-crack! A flashbulb glimpse of shrieking jaws as the silhouette is hurled back, screeching insanely.

INT. OPERATIONS   154

The fire-control system has tripped, with sprinklers spraying the room and a mindless siren wailing. Total pandemonium.

HUDSON

Let's go! Let's go!

HICKS

Fuckin' A!

Hudson screams as floor panels lift under him, and clawed arms seize him lightning fast, dragging him down. Another skeletal shape leaps on him from above. He disappears into the sub-floor crawlway. Hicks, Vasquez and Gorman make it to the med lab access corridor.

INT. CORRIDOR   155

The troopers seem to materialise out of the smoke.

HICKS

Hold your fire!

RIPLEY
(indicating door)

It's locked.

HICKS

Stand back.

Hicks snaps the torch off his belt and cuts into the lock. Inhuman shapes enter the far end of the corridor. Vasquez hands her flame-thrower to Gorman and unslings her rifle. She starts loading thirty mm grenades into the launcher, like oversize twelve-gauge shells. Hicks kicks the door in, molten droplets flying.

INT. MED LAB ANNEX   156

They enter a small cubicle, Vasquez trailing. She slides the door almost closed, then fires three grenades rapid-fire through the gap. She slams the door home as the grenades detonate, the explosion sounding gong-like through the metal.

Ripley sprints across the room, trying the far door. Burke has locked it as well. Hicks switches his hand-torch from cut to weld and starts sealing the door they just passed through.

INT. MED LAB   157

Burke, hyperventilating with terror, backs across the dark chamber. Gasping, almost paralysed with fear, he crosses to the door leading to the main concourse. His fingers reach for the latch. It moves by itself. The door opens slowly.

On Burke: his eyes wide, transfixed by his fate.

                                                                    CUT TO:

INT. MED LAB ANNEXE   158

The door dimples with a clanging impact, separating slightly from its frame. Another crash, the squeal of tortured steel. Newt grabs Ripley by the hand and tugs her across the room.

                              NEWT
                    Come on! This way.

She leads Ripley to an air vent set low in the wall and expertly unlatches the grille, swinging it open. Newt starts inside but Ripley pulls her back.

                              RIPLEY
                    Stay behind me.

Ripley trades her rifle for Gorman's flame-thrower before he can protest and enters the air shaft, which is a tight fit. Newt scrambles in behind, followed by Hicks, Gorman and Vasquez on rearguard. Glancing back fearfully Newt pushes on Ripley's butt as they crawl rapidly through the shaft.

                              NEWT
                    Come on. Crawl faster.

                              RIPLEY
                    Do you know how to get to the landing field from
                    here?

                              NEWT
                Sure. Go left.

Ripley turns into a larger main duct where there is enough room to crab-walk in a low crouch.
She runs, scraping her back on the ceiling. The troopers' armour clatters in the confined space.
They approach an intersection. She fires the flame-thrower around the corner, then looks. Clear.

                              NEWT
                Go right.

They sprint into the narrow connecting duct, the maze becoming a blur. Ripley fires the flame-
thrower periodically, as they pass side ducts covered by louvred grilles or vertical shafts going
to higher or lower levels.

                              HICKS
                     (into headset)
                Bishop, you read me? Come in, over.

There is a long pause then Bishop's voice, almost unintelligible with interference, comes over
the radio.

                             BISHOP
                     (voice-over; static)
                Yes, I read you. Not very well...

EXT. UP-LINK RELAY – LANDING FIELD   159

Bishop is huddled against the base of the telemetry mast, out of the wind which is now gusting
viciously.

                             BISHOP
                     (yelling; overenunciating)
                The ship is on its way. ETA about sixteen minutes. I've
                got my hands full flying...the weather's come up a bit.

Bishop's fingers are blurring over the terminal keys. In the b.g. the station has become a raging
demon, wreathed in boiling steam and electrical discharges.

INT. AIR DUCT   160

                              HICKS
                All right, stand by there. We're on our way. Over.

ALIENS

The beam of Ripley's light wavers hypnotically in the tunnel ahead. She blinks, seeing something...not sure. A glinting obscene form moving towards them, filling the tunnel at the absolute limit of the light's power.

RIPLEY
Back. Go back!

They try to crawl back, jamming together. Behind them, the way they have come, a grating is battered in with a ferocious clang and the deadly silhouette of a warrior flows into the duct. They are trapped. Vasquez opens fire with her pulse-rifle. Hicks snaps out his hand-welder and cuts into the wall of the duct. Vasquez goes empty and reloads with icy precision. Bracing his back, Hicks kicks hard at the cherry-hot metal. It bends aside.

Beyond is a narrow service way, lined with pipes and conduit. Hicks slides through the searing hole, lifting Newt safely through as Ripley hands her out. Ripley follows and turns to help Gorman. Vasquez's pulse-gun runs empty. She draws her service pistol. Suddenly she looks up as a warrior screeches down from a vertical shaft, right above her.

She fires with incredible rapidity...Bam! Bam! Bam! Rolls aside. It lands on her legs and she snaps her head to one side just its tail-stinger buries into the metal wall beside her cheek. She fires again, emptying the pistol, kicking the thrashing shape away.

Acid cuts through her armour, searing into her thigh. She grits her teeth against the white-hot pain. Gorman sees Vasquez hit, unable to move. Sees the creatures coming the other way...and turns away from the escape hole. He crawls back to her, grabs her battle harness and starts dragging her towards safety. Too late. They are cut off. Vasquez sees him, barely conscious.

VASQUEZ
You always were an asshole, Gorman.

She seizes his hand in a deathly grip, but we recognise it as the 'power greeting' she shared with Drake...something for the chosen few. Gorman returns the grip. He hands her two grenades and arms two himself.

INT. SERVICE WAY   161

Rushing with Ripley, Newt and Hicks at a full tilt run. The service way lights up with a powerful blast behind them and they stumble with the shockwave. Newt breaks out ahead and it's all Ripley and Hicks can do to keep up.

NEWT
This way. Come on, we're almost there!

RIPLEY

Newt, wait!

The kid moves like lightning, diving and dodging around obstacles. They reach a large metal housing and Newt crawls inside.

NEWT

Here! Go up. There's a shortcut across the roof.

It is a junction of several shafts, including a vertical duct with ladder rungs leading up to an exterior vent hood. The 'floor' is actually the top of a large blower drum, a vaned cylinder.

Ripley crosses to the ladder, seizes a rung to steady herself, and reaches back for Newt. The blower rotates suddenly as their weight shifts and Newt falls, slipping nightmarishly through a narrow gap into another duct, a chute angling into the depths at forty-five degrees. She catches the lip of the chute and holds on.

NEWT

Riiiipppleee –

Ripley dives, getting one arm through the opening as Hicks steadies the drum, but she can't squeeze through the gap. She strains, her hand groping for Newt's. Their fingers miss, inches apart.
In a desperate lunge Hicks seizes the sleeve of Newt's oversize jacket just as she loses her grip and she slips out of it. With an echoing scream Newt plummets, sliding down the chute into darkness, disappearing around a bend. Ripley screams after the child.

RIPLEY

Newt!

The shaft recedes into darkness. No answer. Ripley yells again. Nothing. Then...a plaintive call from the darkness. Echoey, distorted, terrified.

NEWT
(os)
Mooommeee...

Hicks grabs Ripley's arm.

HICKS

Come on, we can find her with this.

He jerks the locator off his belt and switches it on. Ripley nods, then yells down the chute into blackness.

ALIENS

RIPLEY
Newt! Stay right where you are.
Don't move!

INT. CORRIDOR/STAIRWELL   162

Kicking out a ventilator grille, Hicks emerges on to a stairwell landing, followed by Ripley. He studies the locator's signal.

HICKS
This way.

INT. SUB-BASEMENT   163

Newt is in a low grotto-like chamber, filled with pipes and machines. It is flooded, almost up to Newt's waist. She looks up, seeing light streaming through a grating.

Newt climbs some pipes towards the overhead grille, hearing voices above.

INT. CORRIDOR   164

Ripley follows Hicks, sprinting along the corridor, intent on the locator's signal.

HICKS
We're close.

RIPLEY
(shouting)
Newt.

NEWT
(os)
Here! I'm here. I'm here!

Halfway along the corridor, Ripley stops. Looking down through the floor grating she sees Newt's tear-streaked face. Newt reaches up. Her tiny fingers wriggle up through the bars of the grate. Ripley squeezes the child's precious fingertips.

RIPLEY
Climb down, honey. We have to
cut through.

Newt backs away, climbing down the pipe as Hicks cuts into the bars with his hand-torch.

Newt, standing waist-deep in water, watches sparks shower blindingly as Hicks cuts. Silently a glistening shape rises in one graceful motion from the water behind her. It stands, dripping, dwarfing her tiny form. She screams as the shadow engulfs her.

INT. CORRIDOR   166

Ripley panics, hearing the screaming below, then splashing. She and Hicks kick desperately at the grating, smashing it down. Ripley lunges into the hole with her light. The surface of the water reflects the beam placidly. Newt is gone. Bobbing in the water, eyes staring, is 'Casey' the doll head. It sinks slowly, distorting, vanishing in darkness.

Hicks pulls Ripley away from the hole. She struggles furiously, trying to tear out of his grip.

> RIPLEY
>> No! Nooooo!

He drags her back. It takes all his strength.

> HICKS
>> (intense)
>> She's gone. Let's go!

He sees something moving towards them through a lattice of pipes. Ripley is irrational. Hysterical.

> RIPLEY
>> No! No! She's alive! She's alive!
>> They don't kill you! They –

> HICKS
>> All right! She's alive. I believe it. But we gotta get
>> moving! Now!

He drags her towards an elevator not far away at the end of the tunnel. Gets her inside, slamming her against the back wall. Hits the button to go to surface level. An alien warrior leaps into the tunnel, starts toward them. The doors are closing. Not fast enough. The creature gets one arm through, the doors closing on it. They open again, an automatic safety feature.

ALIENS

The warrior hisses, lunging. Hicks fires, point-blank. It spins away, screeching. Acid sluices between the closing doors, across Hicks's armoured chest plate. The lift starts upwards. Hick's fingers race with the clasps. Galvanised out of her hysteria, Ripley claws at his armour, helping him as much as she can. He screams as the acid contacts his chest and arm. He shucks out of the combat armour like a madman as acrid fumes fill the air. The elevator stops. The doors part and they stumble out.

EXT. COLONY/NORTH LOCK   166A

Ripley supports Hicks who is doubled over in agony as they emerge into the storm-blasted night.

                         RIPLEY
          Come on, you can make it. Almost there! Come on,
          Hicks.

EXT LANDING FIELD/UP-LINK TOWER BASE   167

Drop-ship two descends towards the landing grid, side-slipping in hurricane gusts. Bishop stands, guiding it with the portable terminal. The ship sets down hard. Slides sideways. Stops. Bishop turns as Ripley and Hicks stumble towards him. He goes to them, helping to support Hicks and they run towards the ship, buffeted by the gale. Ripley shouts, her words barely audible over the wind.

                         RIPLEY
          HOW MUCH TIME?

                         BISHOP
          WE'RE OKAY. TWENTY-SIX MINUTES!

                         RIPLEY
          WE'RE NOT LEAVING!

The loading ramp deploys and they run into the ship.

EXT. PROCESSING STATION   168

An infernal engine, roaring out of control. Steam blasts and swirls, lightning zaps around the superstructure and columns of incandescent gas thunder hundreds of feet into the air.

We approach, hypnotically. The Drop Ship enters frame, moving towards the station. It pivots, hovering in the blasting turbulence, and settles on to a narrow landing platform twenty levels above the ground.

Scene 170: 'This is the most terrifying thing she has ever done'

ALIENS

Ripley finishes winding tape around a bulky object and drops the roll. She has crudely fastened an M-41A assault rifle together, side by side, with a flame-thrower. She works rapidly, snatching magazines, grenades, belts and other gear from the fully stocked ordnance racks of the Drop Ship.

Hicks is sprawled in a flight seat, the contents of a field medical kit strewn around him. He's out of the game...contorted with pain. Bishop comes aft from the pilot's compartment.

                              BISHOP
                    Ripley...

                              RIPLEY
                    She's alive. They brought her here
                    and you know it. It's not too late.

                              BISHOP
                    In nineteen minutes this place will be a cloud of
                    vapour the size of Nebraska.

Ripley is stuffing gear rapidly into a satchel, her hands flying.

                              RIPLEY
                    Hicks, don't let him leave.

                              HICKS
                    (grimacing with pain)
                    We ain't going anywhere.

She hefts the hybrid weapon, grabs the satchel and spins to the door controls. The door opens. Wind and machine thunder blast in.

                              RIPLEY
                    See you, Hicks.

Hicks is holding a wad of gauze plastered over his face.

                              HICKS
                    Dwayne. It's Dwayne.

Ripley grabs his hand. They share a moment, albeit brief. Mutual respect in the valley of death.

                              RIPLEY
                    Ellen.

139

Scene 173: 'Ripley pumps the slide on her grenade launcher'

                          HICKS
                  (nods with satisfaction)
                  Don't be long, Ellen.

Ripley runs down the ramp, crossing the platform to the open doors of a large freight elevator. The doors close.

INT. FREIGHT ELEVATOR   170

ALIENS

The elevator descends. Ripley removes her jacket and dons a battle harness directly over her T-shirt. Her eyes burn with a determination that holds the gut-panic in check. She checks her weapons. Attaches a bandolier of grenades to her harness. Primes the flame-thrower. She checks the marking flares jammed in the thigh pockets of her jump pants.

This is the most terrifying thing she has ever done. She begins to hyperventilate, soaking with sweat. The elevator descends. The lift motors whine, slowing. It hits bottom with a bump. The safety cage retracts. Slowly, expectantly, the doors open...

Her POV: through the parting doors...an empty corridor. Dark, swirling with steam, a ruddy glow visible here and there. It seems to have been a descent into Dantean hell. Like the beating of a vast heart the pounding of massive pumps echoes through the station.

INT. CORRIDOR   171

Ripley moves out of the lift, knuckles white on the rifle. Behind her we see a second elevator next to hers, its lift cage somewhere on a higher floor. Not far ahead the bio-mechanoid catacomb begins. She enters the maze, darting glances at Hicks's locator, taped to the top of her weapon. A voice echoes down the tunnels, calm and mechanical.

> VOICE
> Attention. Emergency. All personnel must evacuate
> immediately. You now have fifteen minutes to reach
> minimum safe distance.

INT. CATACOMB   172

Range and direction read out in rapid-fire alpha-numics on the locator display.

Ripley blinks sweat out of her eyes, moving through the swirling steam of the alien maze. She approaches an intersecting tunnel. Flashing emergency lights illuminate the insane fresco of the walls. She spins, firing the flame-thrower. Nothing there. She moves forward. The locator signal strengthens as she turns, crouches through a low passage, turns again. At each intersection she quickly lights a fifteen minute marking flare and drops it. For the way back. She has to turn sideways, inching through a fissure between two walls of death...cocoon niches, a human bas-relief sealed in resin.

Suddenly something shoots out, grabbing her! A hand. She recovers, then recognises the face sealed in the wall. Carter Burke.

> BURKE
> Ripley...help me. I can feel it...inside. Oh, God...it's
> moving! Oh Gooood...

Scene 175: 'The Alien Queen glowers over her eggs'

She looks at him. No one deserves this.

She hands him a grenade, popping the safety cap, placing his thumb over the priming button.

> VOICE
> You now have thirteen minutes to reach minimum
> safe distance.

ALIENS

Ripley moves ahead. The locator signal shows she is almost there. A concussion rocks the place, like an earthquake, jarring her almost off her feet. The whole station seems to shudder. Following the tracker she turns a corner and stops. The range indicator reads zero. She looks down, horrified to see Newt's tracer bracelet lying on the floor of the tunnel. All hope recedes, disintegrating into mindless chaos.

INT. EGG CHAMBER   173

Newt is cocooned in a pillar-like structure at the edge of a cluster of alien eggs. Her eyelids flutter open and she becomes aware of her surroundings. The egg nearest her begins to move ...opening like an obscene flower. Newt stares, transfixed by terror, as jointed legs appear over the lip of the ovoid one by one. She screams.

INT. CATACOMB   174

Ripley hears the scream and breaks into a run.

INT. EGG CHAMBER   175

Newt watches the facehugger emerge and turn towards her. Ripley runs in just as it is tensing to leap, and fires, blasting it with a burst from the assault rifle. The flash illuminates the figure of an adult warrior, nearby. It spins, moving straight for Ripley. Firing from the hip she drills it with two controlled bursts which catapult it back. She steps towards it, firing again. Her expression is murderous. And again.

It spins on to its back. She unleashes the flame-thrower and it vanishes in a fireball. Ripley runs to Newt and begins tearing at the fresh resinous cocoon material, freeing the child. She swings her up on to her back.

NEWT
(weakly)
I knew you'd come.

RIPLEY
Newt, I want you to hang on, now.
Hang on real tight. Okay?

Newt nods groggily and hooks her arms and legs through Ripley's battle harness. Ripley turns to retrace her steps only to have an explosion on a lower level engulf the passageway in an enormous fireball. She retreats, moving into a large chamber, its floor an expanse of eggs. A piercing shriek fills the chamber. She turns. And there it is...A massive silhouette in the mist, the ALIEN QUEEN glowers over her eggs like a great, glistening black insect-Buddha. What's bigger and meaner than the Alien? His momma. Her fanged head is an unimaginable horror.

Her six limbs, the four arms and two powerful legs, are folded grotesquely over her distended abdomen. The egg-filled abdomen swells and swells into a great pulsing tubular sac, suspended from a lattice of pipes and conduits by a web-like membrane as if some vast coil of intestine was draped carelessly among the machinery.

As Ripley backs away from the Queen, deeper into the egg chamber she becomes aware of a number of warriors moving towards her from the dim recesses. She fires the flame-thrower above the rows of eggs and then lowers her aim towards the eggs, while staring fixedly at the Queen. The warriors freeze. A nightmare tableau. Ripley fires another warning jet of flame. The warriors move back into the shadows, clearly at the Queen's direction. A Mexican stand-off between two females fighting for their young. Ripley backs slowly across the chamber until she reaches an exit tunnel. Then she unleashes the flame-thrower, igniting the field of eggs with an insane fury. The Queen goes berserk, screeching like some psychotic steam whistle.
Ripley pumps the slide on her grenade launcher. She fires. Pumps and fires again. Four times. The grenades punch deep into the egg sac and explode, ripping it open from within. Eggs and tons of gelatinous matter pour across the chamber floor.

Everything disappears behind a wall of fire. Ripley drops a magazine and grabs another from her belt, ramming it home just as a warrior leaps from the inferno like a living fireball. She blasts it back to hell with a long burst. She unslings the bandolier of grenades, primes one, and throws the whole thing as far as she can into the egg chamber. Dashing into the catacombs, she is hurled forward by the shock wave of multiple explosions.

INT. CATACOMB   176

Ripley runs, blindly, with panting intensity verging on hysteria. She sees one of the flares she dropped and turns. Sees another, sprinting towards it as the foundations of the world shake.

INT. EGG CHAMBER   177

Lashing in a frenzy, the Queen detaches from the egg sac, ripping away and dragging torn cartilage and tissue behind it.

INT. CATACOMBS – CORRIDOR   179

Ripley uses the flame-thrower ahead of her, firing bursts of pulse-rifle fire down side corridors at indistinct shapes and shadows. The weapon is empty when she reaches the freight elevators. A mass of debris, falling down the shaft from a high level, has demolished the lift cage she descended in. She slams the control for the other cage and hears the sound of the lift motor's whine as it begins its slow descent from several levels up. An enraged screech echoes in the corridor. Ripley sees a silhouette moving in the smoke...the Queen. Her last cartridge is reading zeros. The grenades are gone. Ripley drops the weapon and looks up the shaft to the descending lift...then at the approaching figure. The elevator won't be in time. She runs to a ladder set in the wall as a horrendous screech beats in her ears. She scrambles up the rungs.

ALIENS

INT. SECOND LEVEL   180

Ripley struggles up through a narrow hatch, Newt clinging to her. She dives aside as a powerful black arm shoots up through the opening, its razor claws slamming into the grille floor inches from her.
Looking down through the grille she sees the great horrifying jaws directly below her, wet and leering. She scrambles up, running, as the grille floor lifts and buckles behind her with the titanic force of the creature below. It hurls itself with insane ferocity against the metal, pacing her from below as she runs.

INT. STAIRWELL   181

Ripley reaches an open grid emergency stairwell and sprints upwards. It rocks and shudders with the station's death throes.

INT. CORRIDOR – ELEVATORS   182/183

The lift reaches bottom, the doors rolling open. The Queen turns and freezes, as if contemplating the open lift cage.

INT. STAIRWELL   184

Ripley stumbles, smashing her knees against the metal stairs. As she rises she hears the lift motors start up. Looking down through the latticework of the station she sees the lift cage start ominously upwards.

EXT. LANDING PLATFORM   185

Ripley, with Newt still clinging to her, slams through the door opening on to the platform. Through wind-whipped streamers of smoke she sees...the ship is gone.

                          RIPLEY
            BISHOP!

Her shouts become inarticulate screams of hatred, outrage at the final betrayal. She scans the sky. Nothing.

The lift rises ponderously into view. Ripley turns, backing away from the doors toward the railing. There is no place to run to on the platform. Explosions detonate in the complex far below and huge fireballs well upward through the machinery. The platform bucks wildly. Nearby a cooling tower collapses with a thunderous roar and the shriek of rending steel. Ripley stares transfixed as the lift stops. The safety cage parts.

RIPLEY
(to Newt, low)
Close your eyes, baby.

The lift doors begin to open. A glimpse of the apparition within.
Angle on Ripley and Newt: as the Drop Ship rises right behind them, its hovering jets roaring.

VOICE
You now have thirty seconds to reach...

Ripley leaps for the loading boom projecting down from the cargo bay and it raises them into the ship. A tremendous explosion rips through the complex nearby, slamming the ship sideways. Its extended landing legs foul in a tangle of conduit, grinding with a hideous squeal of metal on metal.

INT./EXT. DROP-SHIP STATION   186/187

Ripley leaps into a seat with Newt, cradling her. Begins strapping in. Bishop wrestles with the controls. The landing legs retract, ripping free. Ripley slams her seat harness latches home.

RIPLEY
Punch it, Bishop.

The entire lower level of the station disappears in a fireball. The air vibrates with intense heat waves and concussion. The Drop Ship engines fire. Ripley is slammed back in her seat. The ship vaults out and up, Bishop standing it on its tail, pouring on the gees. Ripley and Newt see everything shake into a blur.

EXT. STRATOSPHERE   188

The Drop Ship lunges up out of the cloud layer into the clear high night. Below, the clouds light up from beneath from horizon to horizon.

A sun-hot dome of energy bursts up through the cloud layer, whiting out the frame. The tiny ship is slammed by the shockwave, tossed forwards...and climbs, scorched but functioning, towards the stars.

INT. DROP-SHIP   189

Ripley and Newt watch the blinding glare fade away and they sit, wide-eyed, trembling, realising they are finally and truly safe. Newt starts to cry quietly and Ripley strokes her hair.

RIPLEY
It's okay, baby. We made it. It's over.

ALIENS

INT. *SULACO* CARGO LOCK – IN ORBIT – LATER   190

The scorched and battered ship once again sits in its drop bay, steam blasting from cooling vents beside the engine. Rotating clearance lights sweep the dark chamber hypnotically.

INT. DROP-SHIP   191

Bishop stands behind Ripley as she kneels beside a comatose Hicks.

> BISHOP
> I gave him a shot, for the pain, but I think he's going to be okay. We'll need to get a stretcher to carry him up to medical.

Ripley nods and, picking up Newt, precedes Bishop down the aisle to the loading ramp.

> BISHOP
> I'm sorry if I gave you a scare but that platform was just becoming too unstable...

INT. CARGO LOCK – DROP SHIP   192

Bishop continues as they move down the ramp.

> BISHOP
> I had to circle and hope things didn't get too rough to take you off.

Ripley turns to him, stopping partway down the ramp. She puts her hand on his shoulder.

> RIPLEY
> You did okay, Bishop.

> BISHOP
> Well, thanks, I –

He notices a tiny, innocuous drop of liquid splash onto the ramp next to his shoe. SSSSSS. Acid. Something bursts from his chest, spraying Ripley with milk-like android blood. It is the razor-sharp scorpion tail of the Alien Queen. Driven right through him from behind. Bishop thrashes, seizing the protruding section of tail in his hands, as it slowly lifts him off the deck. Above them the Queen glowers from its place of concealment among the hydraulic mechanisms inside one landing-leg bay. It blends perfectly with the machinery until it begins to emerge. Seizing Bishop in two great hands it rips him apart and flings him aside, shredded, like a doll. It descends slowly to the deck, the rotating lights glistening across its shiny black limbs, dripping acid and rage. Still smoking where Ripley half fried it. The Queen is huge, powerful...and very pissed off. It descends slowly, its six limbs unfolding in inhuman geometries.

Ripley moves with nightmarish slowness herself, staring hypnotised...terrified to break and run. She lowers Newt to the deck, never taking her eyes off the creature.

> RIPLEY
>
> Go!

Newt runs for cover. The alien drops to the deck, pivoting towards the motion. Ripley waves her arms, decoying.

> RIPLEY
>
> Here!

Without warning it moves like lightning, straight at her. Ripley spins, sprinting, as the creature leaps for her. Its feet slam, echoing, on the deck behind her. She clears a door. Hits the switch. It whirrs closed. Boom. The alien hits a moment later.

INT. DARK CHAMBER   193

Ripley moves ferret-quick among dark, unrecognisable machines.

Various angles: very tight on what she is doing...her feet going into stirrup-like mechanisms. Velcro straps fastened over them. Fingers stabbing buttons in a sequence. Her hand closing on a complex grip-control. The hum of powerful motors. The whine of hydraulics.

INT. CARGO LOCK   194

The Queen turns its attention from the doors to Newt as the little girl crawls into a system of trench-like service channels which cross the deck.

INT. CHANNEL   195

Newt scurries like a rabbit as the looming figure of the alien appears above, seen through the bars. A section of grille is ripped away behind her.

INT. CARGO LOCK   196

The Queen spins at the sound of door motors behind her. The parting doors REVEAL an inhuman silhouette standing there.

Ripley steps out, wearing two tons of hardened steel. The power loader. Like medieval armour with the power of a bulldozer. She takes a step...the massive foot crash-clangs to the deck. She takes another, advancing.

ALIENS

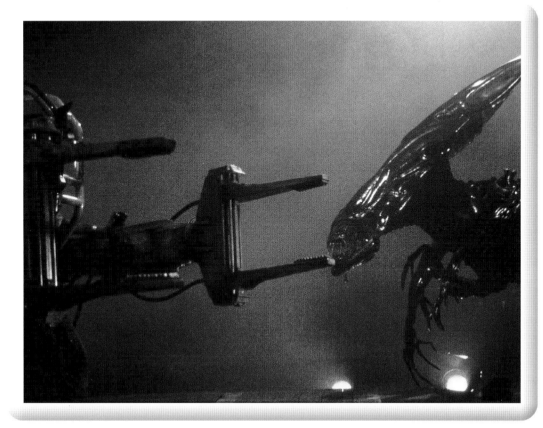

Scene 196: 'Ripley steps out, wearing two tons of hardened steel'

RIPLEY
Get away from her, you bitch.

The Queen screeches pure lethality and leaps. Wallop! A roundhouse from one great hydraulic arm catches it on its hideous skull and slams it into a wall. It rebounds into a massive backhand. Crash! It goes backwards into heavy loading equipment.

RIPLEY
(screaming)
Come on!

Scene 196: 'The Queen emerges as a blur of rage, lashing with fury'

The Queen emerges as a blur of rage, lashing with unbelievable fury. The battle is joined. Claws swipe, tail lashes. Ripley parries with radical swipes of the steel forks. They circle in a whirling blur, demolishing everything in their path. The cavernous chamber echoes with nightmarish sounds...WHINE, CRASH, CLANG, SCREECH. They lock in a death embrace. Ripley closes the forks, crushing two of the creature's limbs. It lashes and writhes with incredible fury, coming within inches of her exposed body. She lifts it off the ground. The hind legs rip at her, slamming against the safety cage, denting it in. The striking teeth extend almost a metre from inside its fanged maw, shooting between the crash-bars.

ALIENS

She ducks and the teeth slam into the seat cushion behind her head in a spray of drool. Yellow acid foams down the hydraulic arms towards her.

The creature rips at high-pressure hoses. Purple hydraulic fluid sprays...machine blood mixing with alien blood. They topple, off balance. The Queen pins her. Ripley hits a switch. The power-loader's cutting torch flares on, directly in the thing's face. They roll together, over the lip of a rectangular pit, a vertical loading airlock.

INT. LOADING LOCK   197

They crash together five metres below, twisted in the loader's wreckage. The alien shrieks, pinned.

Ripley pulls her arm out of the controls of the loader and claws towards the panel of airlock actuating buttons. She slaps the red 'inner door override' and latches the 'HOLD' locking-key down. A klaxon begins to sound. She hits 'outer door open' and there is a hurricane shriek of air as the doors on which they are lying separate, revealing the infinite pit of stars below.

All this time the alien has been lashing at her in a frenzy and she has been parrying desperately in the confined space. The airlock becomes a wind tunnel, blasting and buffeting her as she struggles to unstrap from the loader. The air of the vast ship howls past her into space as she claws her way up a service ladder.

INT. CARGO BAY   198

Newt screams as the hurricane airstream sucks her across the floor towards the airlock. Bishop, torn virtually in two, grips a stanchion and reaches desperately for Newt as she slides past him. He catches her arm and hangs on as she dangles doll-like in the airblast.

INT. LOADING DOCK   199

The alien seizes Ripley's ankle. She locks her arms around a ladder rung, feels them almost torn out of their shoulder sockets.

The door opens further, all of space yawning below. The loader tumbles clear, falling away. It drags the alien, still clutching one of Ripley's lucky hi-tops, into the depths of space. Its shriek fades, is gone.

With all her strength Ripley fights the blasting air, crawling over the lip of the inner doorway. She releases the override from a second panel. The inner doors close. The turbulent air eddies and settles.

She lies on her back, drained of all strength. Gasping for breath. Weakly she turns her head, seeing Bishop still holding Newt by the arm. Encrusted with his own vanilla milkshake blood, Bishop gives her a small, grim smile.

                          BISHOP
            Not bad for a human.

He winks. Ripley crosses to Newt.

                          NEWT
                   (weakly)
            Mommy...Mommy ?

                          RIPLEY
            Right here, baby. Right here.

Ripley hugs her desperately.

INT. HYPERSLEEP   200

Ripley sits at the edge of an open hypersleep capsule in which Newt is lying. Behind them, already going under, is Hicks and in a further capsule, Bishop, wrapped in a plastic membrane.

                          NEWT
            Are we going to sleep all the way back?

                          RIPLEY
            That's right.

                          NEWT
            Can we dream?

                          RIPLEY
            Yes, honey. I think we both can.

Ripley brushes a strand of hair from Newt's forehead.

Dissolve to Ripley in capsule...where we started. Except now it's a two-shot, with Newt behind, perfect in sleep.

FREEZE FRAME

                                                           FADE OUT.

                    THE END

ALIENS

THE ALIENS SCRIPT CUTS
BY PAUL M. SAMMON

Shortly before *Aliens*' original 18 July 1986 release, writer/director James Cameron edited approximately twenty minutes out of his SF/action classic. This left the running time of *Aliens*' initial '*Theatrical Cut*' at 137 minutes. Five years later, Cameron was able to reinstate seventeen minutes of that deleted footage. The occasion? A 1991, non-theatrical American release, entitled '*Aliens Special Wide Screen Collector's Edition*' (hereafter shortened to the '*Special Edition*').

The *Aliens Special Edition* was an expanded, boxed-set laserdisc version of *Aliens*' *Theatrical Cut*. Interested reviewers soon trumpeted the fact that the *Special Edition* restored one of *Aliens*' most important sub-plots – Ripley's daughter. Not so well known was the fact that while supervising the *Special Edition*, Cameron had also completed a handful of *Aliens* special-effects shots. Why? Because those same, originally uncompleted effects had initially been earmarked for the twenty minutes of footage ultimately dropped from the *Theatrical Cut*.

Therefore, the occasion of the 1991 *Aliens Special Edition* provided Cameron with an opportunity to finish those previously uncompleted F/X, a chore he and his effects technicians attacked with characteristic passion and creativity. *Aliens*' writer/director then incorporated the finished F/X into *Aliens*' newly restored footage. Among other previously unseen sequences was a scene of Newt's family discovering the ruins of the first *Alien*'s derelict spacecraft, on the still foreboding but recently colonised LV-426.

The release of the *Aliens Special Edition* now meant that there were two versions of *Aliens* available to American home viewers: the original, 137-minute *Theatrical Cut* (on video), and an expanded, 154-minute version (on laserdisc). Although 20th Century Fox went on to release a videocassette version of *Aliens Special Edition* to British, Japanese and German markets in 1992, Americans would have to wait until 1999 for a video release of *Aliens Special Edition* in their own country. This meant that, at least until 1999, the original 1986 *Theatrical Cut* was the version of *Aliens* with which most Americans were familiar.

Today, despite the ever-widening availability of the *Special Edition*, the *Aliens Theatrical Cut* remains the most well-known version of *Aliens* globally. So why make such distinctions in a book concerning the *Aliens* screenplay? Because, again, of the additional scenes that were filmed and then edited out of *Aliens,* footage based on over seventeen pages of Cameron's highly praised script. Those deleted pages are presented and examined here (at least in book form) for the very first time.

'The *Aliens* Script Cuts' primarily concerns itself with collating the differences between the two versions of *Aliens*. It achieves this by, first, cataloging the scripted scenes edited out of the *Theatrical Cut* but reinstated for the *Special Edition*. Second, it includes certain *Aliens* screenplay segments that were never filmed, or were shot but *not* reinstated into the *Aliens Special Edition* (such as Ripley's discovery of the cocooned Burke). These are labelled NOT IN THE *ALIENS THEATRICAL CUT* OR *SPECIAL EDITION*. Third, sequences where Cameron heavily rewrote an *Aliens* scene before shooting it are also included; for such sequences, both action and dialogue have been faithfully transcribed, and any text that originally appeared in the *Theatrical Cut* for said scenes has likewise been precisely reproduced. In short, three types of out-take appear here:

i   scripted but cut from the *Theatrical Cut* and included in the *Special Edition*
ii   scripted and/or shot but omitted from both versions
iii   unscripted but appearing in either film (or both) as a change or an addition

Each *Aliens* screenplay cut is preceded by a title I have created to describe that sequence, as well as by the scene number originally assigned that sequence in the script.

It is critical to note that 'The *Aliens* Script Cuts' does not claim to be the definitive examination of its subject. Not *every* difference between the *Aliens* screenplay, the *Theatrical Cut*, the *Special Edition*, or what James Cameron originally shot for *Aliens* is included here (such as Scene 5). Such an undertaking would consume far too many extra pages in a project that's already reached its textual limit, particularly given the minor but extensive dialogue variations which took place between Cameron's writing of the *Aliens* script and his shooting it.

Those looking for additional information on the *Aliens* script edits (as well as further insights into the *Aliens Special Edition*) would be well served by first picking up either a DVD or videocassette copy of 20th Century Fox Home Entertainment's superb *Aliens: Special Edition*. Both formats feature excellent widescreen transfers of the expanded *Theatrical Cut*; the DVD version, in particular, includes many supplemental chapters detailing *Aliens'* entire history. Hard-core Xenomorph fanatics can also find additional *Aliens* info on one the Internet's many *Aliens*-related websites (*ALIEN MOVIES RESOURCE PAGES* is one good starting point; their URL is http://www.acs.ucalgary.ca/~naflande/).

Finally, to close in a spirit of naked self-promotion, some readers may be interested to know that my upcoming book *The Complete Aliens* features an extensive section spotlighting *all* the differences between the *Aliens Theatrical Cut* and *Special Edition*. It also includes an in-depth examination of the creation, shooting and editing of James Cameron's tense, exciting and still-fascinating *Aliens* script.

Ripley aims a remote control device at a park-like 'Hi-Resolution Video Loop'

THE CUTS

1) A VIRTUAL PARK

A) SCENE 4

B) After: Scene 3 / (Ripley) hugs Jones to her and rocks with him like a child, still shattered by the nightmare.

NOTE: *This, the first instance of restored material in the* Aliens Special Edition, *was also* Aliens' *most significant edit. Taking place within the Earth-orbiting 'Gateway Station' after Ellen Ripley has been rescued from the long-lost shuttlecraft* Narcissus, *Scene 4 begins with Ripley seated before a 'High Resolution Environmental Wall Screen', on which is displayed the closed-loop image of a verdant landscape (sort of a computer-less 'Virtual Park'). During a subsequent conversation with Company man Carter Burke, viewers learn that Ripley is a working mother, one who'd left a young daughter (Amanda) back on Earth while Ripley completed her duties aboard the* Nostromo. *Scene 4 then concluded by showing a sobbing Ripley suffering tremendous guilt over literally sleeping through her daughter's subsequent life and death (which occurred during Ripley's 57-year-long hypersleep).*

James Cameron has told this author that he originally dropped the 'Virtual Park' sequence because Cameron felt it both interfered with Aliens' *pacing, and because the film-maker 'was worried that my idea of Ripley losing one daughter before finding another might be dramatically obvious, too "on the nose" or corny'. Yet the painful sense of loss exhibited by Sigourney Weaver during this sequence actually adds a subtle, melancholy undertone to the* Special Edition, *while likewise adding extra urgency to Ripley's battle against the aliens and their Queen for Newt's life (after all, Ripley has already lost one child!).*

Contrast these Special Edition *shadings to the Newt/Ripley relationship displayed in the* Aliens Theatrical Cut. *That version of* Aliens *contains absolutely no mention of Ripley's daughter – a deletion that dilutes the strength of (and removes the primary motivation for)* Aliens' *Newt/Ripley dynamic.*

EXT. PARK

Sunlight streams in shafts through a stand of poplars, beyond which a verdant meadow is visible. Jones stalks towards a bird hopping among fallen leaves. He leaps. And smacks into a wall.

> RIPLEY
> (voice-over)
> That's brilliant, Jones.

Wider: As Jones steps back confused from the high-resolution environmental wall screen, a sort of cinerama video-loop. Ripley sits on a bench in what we now see is an atrium off the medical center. Burke enters in his usual mode, casual haste.

> BURKE
> Sorry...I've been running behind all morning.

> RIPLEY
> Have they located my daughter yet?

> BURKE
> Well, I was going to wait until after the inquest...

He opens his briefcase, removing a sheet of printer hard copy, including a telestat photo.

> RIPLEY
> Is she...?

> BURKE
> (scanning)
> Amanda Ripley-McClaren. Married name, I guess. Age: sixty-six...at time of death. Two years ago.
> (looks at her)
> I'm sorry.

Ripley studies the photograph, stunned. The face of a woman in her mid-sixties. It could be anybody. She tries to reconcile the face with the little girl she once knew.

> RIPLEY
> Amy.

> BURKE
> (reading)
> Cancer. Hmmmm. They still haven't licked that one. Cremated. Interred Westlake Repository, Little Chute, Wisconsin. No children.

Ripley gazes off, into the pseudo-landscape, into the past.

> RIPLEY
> No children.
> (a beat, then)
> I promised her I'd be home for her birthday. Her eleventh birthday.

> BURKE
> Some promises you just can't keep.

Let's get one thing straight...Ripley can be one tough lady. But the terror, the loss, the emptiness are, in this moment, overwhelming. She cries silently. Burke puts a reassuring hand on her arm.

> BURKE
> The hearing convenes at 09.30. You don't want to be late.

2) COURT OF INQUIRY FINDING

SCENE 7 (NOT IN THE *ALIENS THEATRICAL CUT* OR *SPECIAL EDITION*) & SCENE 8
After: Scene 6 / Ripley: 'Then you can just kiss all this goodbye, just kiss it goodbye.'
NOTE: *Following Ripley's outburst during the Weyland-Yutani Board of Inquiry, a scene in the* Aliens *script (but not in the* Special Edition*) showed Ripley and Burke getting coffee and donuts while awaiting the Board's decision. A subsequent moment (which* does *appear on the* Special Edition*) then gave Weyland-Yutani rep Van Leuwen some additional dialogue, lines that reflected the Board's scepticism re. the disappearance of the* Nostromo *and her crew.*

INT. CORRIDOR

Ripley kicks the wall next to Burke who is getting coffee and donuts at a vending machine.

> BURKE
> You had them eating out of your hand, kiddo.

> RIPLEY
> They had their minds made up before I even went in there. They think I'm some kind of headcase.

> BURKE
> (cheerfully)
> You are a headcase. Have a donut.

INT. CONFERENCE ROOM – TIGHT ON RIPLEY – LATER

Van Leuwen clears his throat.

> VAN LEUWEN
> It is the finding of this board of inquiry that Warrant Officer Ellen Ripley, NOC-14472, has acted with questionable judgment and is unfit to hold an ICC licence as a commercial flight officer.

Burke watches Ripley taking it on the chin, white-lipped but subdued.

> VAN LEUWEN
> Said licence is hereby suspended indefinitely. No criminal charges will be filed at this time and you are released on own recognisance for a six month period of psychometric probation, to include monthly review by an ICC psychiatric tech...

Ripley's video-dossier fills the screen behind her. At the bottom a new entry prints out: FILE CLOSED.

3) HADLEY'S HOPE

SCENES 10–13
After: Scene 9 / It closes in her face.
NOTE: *These* Special Edition *scenes all took place on the home of A1's crashed derelict ship, the mysterious 'planetoid' which, in his* Aliens *script, Cameron called both 'LV-426' and 'Acheron' (in Greek mythology, Acheron is one of four rivers flowing through Hades; in this case, the river of pain and woe). Said scenes were originally meant to occur immediately after Ripley's grilling by the Company's Board of Inquiry.*
    Interestingly, the deletion of this early Acheron footage from the Aliens Theatrical Cut *prevented 1986 audiences from witnessing the only scenes in* Aliens *concerned with the normal, day-to-day activities of LV-426's human outpost (note how the* Special Edition

Artist Ron Cobb's pre-production painting of the Atmosphere Processor and human colony on Acheron, also known as 'LV-426'

further humanised this off-world colony by *including a group of children riding their tricycles – ! – through the Main Concourse in Scene 12).*

EXT. ALIEN LANDSCAPE – DAY

Panning slowly across a storm-blasted vista of tortured rock and bleak twilight on to a metal sign which reads:
HADLEY'S HOPE – POP. 159

Some local has added 'have a nice day' with a spray can. Gale-force wind screeches around the corroded sign. In the background is the colony, a squat complex surrounded by an angled storm-barrier wall.

EXT. COLONY COMPLEX

Several angles establishing the town, a cluster of bunkerlike buildings huddling in the wind. Visible across two kilometres of

ALIENS

barren heath, background, is the massive atmosphere processor, looking like an oil refinery bred with an active volcano.

INT. COLONY MAIN CONCOURSE

A wide corridor bustling with routine activity. We see a cross-section of the hardy frontier stock who have come to live in this godforsaken wilderness. Some children race in the corridor on wheeled plastic toys.

INT. OPERATIONS ROOM/CONTROL BLOCK

The nerve-centre of the colony, jammed with computer terminals, displays, technicians.

Dollying ahead of Simpson, the harried operations manager, as he is approached by his assistant, LYDECKER.

> SIMPSON
> What?

> LYDECKER
> You remember you sent some wildcatters out to the middle of nowhere last week? Out past the Ilium range.

> SIMPSON
> Yeah. What?

> LYDECKER
> One of them's on the horn, mom-and-pop survey team. Says he's on to something and wants to know will his claim be honoured.

> SIMPSON
> Why wouldn't his claim be honoured?

> LYDECKER
> Well, because you sent them to that particular middle of nowhere on

company orders, maybe. I don't know.

> SIMPSON
> Christ. Some honch in a cushy office on Earth says go look at a grid reference, we look. They don't say why, and I don't ask. I don't ask because it takes two weeks to get an answer out here and the answer's always 'don't ask'.

> LYDECKER
> So what do I tell this guy?

> SIMPSON
> Tell him, as far as I'm concerned, he finds something it's his.

4) NEWT'S FAMILY / THE DERELICT REVISITED

A) SCENES 14–19
B) After: Scene 13 / Simpson: 'Tell him, as far as I'm concerned, he finds something, it's his.'
NOTE: *Now we are introduced to Newt and the rest of her family (the Jordens, freelance prospectors): Newt's brother Tim, her mother Anne, and father Russ, all of whom are rolling along the forbidding landscape of LV-426 inside a futuristic all-terrain vehicle.*

This particular deletion was the second most important bit of footage to be reinstated in the Special Edition. *Its significance hinges on the introduction of Newt's family, their discovery of the derelict ship, and the revelation that it is Newt's own parents who brought the alien scourge back to Acheron's human colony. Running nearly five minutes long, Scenes 14–19 also represented the longest single sequence to be excised from the Aliens Theatrical Cut.*

EXT. ACHERON – THE MIDDLE OF NOWHERE – DAY

An eight-wheeled tractor roars across corrugated rock, blasting through soggy drifts of volcanic ash.

INT. TRACTOR

At the controls, intent on a pinging scope, is RUSS JORDEN, independent prospector. Beside him is his wife/partner Anne and in the back their two kids are playing among the heavy sampling equipment.

> JORDEN
> (a gloating cackle)
> Look at this fat, juicy magnetic profile. And it's mine, mine, mine.

> ANNE
> Half mine, dear.

NEWT, their six-year-old daughter, yells from the back.

> NEWT
> And half mine!

> JORDEN
> I got too many partners.

> NEWT
> Daddy, when are we going back to town?

> JORDEN
> When we get rich, Newt.

> NEWT
> You always say that. I wanna go back, Dad, can we?

Her older brother TIM sticks his jeering face close to hers.

> TIM
> Yeah, so you can play 'Monster Maze'.

Well, we're not gonna let you play any more. You cheat!

> NEWT
> Do not!

> TIM
> Do too! You go in places we can't fit.

> NEWT
> So! That's why I'm the best.

> ANNE
> Knock it off! I catch either of you playing in the air ducts again I'll tan your hides.

> NEWT
> Mom. All the kids play it...

> JORDEN
> (reverently)
> Holy shiiit!

Angle through front canopy: on a bizarre shape looming ahead. An enormous bone-like mass projecting upwards from the bed of ash. Canted on its side and buckled against a rock outcropping by the lava flow, it is still recognisable as an extraterrestrial ship. Bio-mechanoid. Non-human design.

> JORDEN
> Folks, we have scored big this time!

The tractor moves around the base of the vast enigma, approaching a gash in the hull.

> ANNE
> Shouldn't we call in?

> JORDEN
> Let's wait 'til we know what to call it in as.

ALIENS

ANNE
(nervous)
How about 'big weird thing'?

EXT. TRACTOR

Jorden and Anne step down, wearing environment suits. Carrying lights, packs, cameras, test gear. Their breath clouds in the chill air.

ANNE
You kids stay inside. I mean it! We'll be right back.

They trudge towards the alien derelict.

They pause at the enormous gash in the hull. Blackness inside.

INT./EXT. TRACTOR

Newt has her face pressed to the glass, steaming it. Watching her parents enter the strange ship. Tim grabs her from behind. She shrieks.

TIM
Cheater!

EXT. LANDSCAPE – NIGHT

The tractor and the derelict are dark and motionless. The wind howls around them.

INT. TRACTOR

Tim is curled up in the driver's seat. Newt shakes him awake, trying hard not to cry.

NEWT
Timmy – they've been gone a long time.

Tim considers the night. The wind. The vast landscape. He bites his lip.

TIM
It'll be okay, Newt. Dad knows what he's doing.

Crash! Newt screams as the door beside her is ripped open. A dark shape lunges inside! Anne, panting and terrified, grabs the dash mike.

ANNE
Mayday! Mayday! This is Alpha Kilo Two-Four-Niner calling Hadley Control. Repeat. This is...

As Anne shouts the Mayday, Newt looks past her, to the ground. Russ Jorden lies there inert, dragged somehow by Anne from inside the ship. There is something on his face. An appalling multilegged creature, pulsing with obscene life. Newt begins to scream hysterically, competing with the shrieking wind which rises to a crescendo as we:

CUT TO:

INT. RIPLEY'S APARTMENT – GATEWAY – DAY

Silence. Ripley, looking haggard, sits at a table in the dining alcove contemplating the smoke rising from her cigarette.

5) BUILDING BETTER WORLDS

SCENE 22
After: Scene 22/Burke: 'But if it's not, I want you there...as an adviser. That's all.'
NOTE: *During Burke and Gorman's visit to Ripley's Gateway apartment, Burke has extra dialogue regarding the Company's interest in the LV-426 colony. These lines appear only in the* Special Edition, *beginning immediately*

after Burke tells Ripley '...I want you there...as an adviser. That's all.'

INT. RIPLEY'S APARTMENT – A LITTLE LATER

BURKE
Look, we don't know what's going on out there. It may just be a down transmitter. But if it's not, I want you there...as an adviser. That's all.

GORMAN
You wouldn't be going in with the troops. I can guarantee your safety.

BURKE
These Colonial Marines are some tough hombres, and they're packing state-of-the-art firepower. Nothing they can't handle...right, Lieutenant?

GORMAN
We're trained to deal with these kinds of situations.

RIPLEY
(to Burke)
What about you? Why are you going?

BURKE
Well, the corporation co-financed that colony with the Colonial Administration, against mineral rights. We're getting into a lot of terraforming...'Building Better Worlds'.

RIPLEY
Yeah, yeah. I saw the commercial.

6) PROWLING THE SULACO
A) SCENE 28
B) After: Scene 27 / DROP-SHIPS
NOTE: *In Cameron's original* Aliens *cut, footage of a long tracking shot showed the*

camera prowling through the Sulaco *spacecraft (during 'Scene 28') shortly before Ripley and the Colonial Marines awoke from hypersleep. This* Aliens *'ship tour' is very similar to* Alien's *own opening prowl through the corridors of the* Nostromo, *which occurred just before the* Nostromo's *hypersleep capsules open; Cameron obviously was tipping his hat to the first* Alien *by using a similar 'ship introduction' here. The* Special Edition *'Sulaco prowl' then underlined Cameron's homage to* Alien *by cutting to a close-up of an unattended toy gyroscope spinning merrily away on a* Sulaco *tabletop – echoing similar shots of* Alien's *'Dippy Bird' toys, which are seen bobbing for water on the* Nostromo's *galley table.*

EXT. DEEP SPACE – THREE WEEKS LATER

An empty starfield. Metal spires slice across frame, followed by a mountain of steel. A massive military transport ship, the *Sulaco*. Ugly, battered-functional.

INT. CARGO LOCK

An enormous chamber, cavernous and dark. Squatting in the shadows are two orbit-to-surface shuttles. Drop-ships.

(The following is a description by Paul M. Sammon of the missing 'Scene 28' as seen in Aliens Special Edition).

INT. *SULACO*

The camera prowls through the quiet, seemingly empty ship.

We see a swinging, unlatched locker door (on which hangs a pin-up). Watch as the camera tracks down a dark, equipment-littered corridor. Enter the *Sulaco*'s

ALIENS

Some of the custom-made Colonial Marine props created for Aliens

enormous 'Cargo Lock', which holds an empty power loader and Drop Ship.

Now we witness a close-up of a toy gyroscope spinning on a tabletop. Track past the Colonial Marines' clothing lockers, before finally stopping at their sealed hypersleep capsules.

7) BISHOP'S KNIFE TRICK

A) SCENE 32
B) After: Scene 32 / Frost tosses Bishop a K-Bar combat knife and Bishop slaps his palm on the table.

NOTE: *During Scene 32 in Cameron's script (and in all filmed versions of* Aliens), *the 'synthetic' Bishop demonstrates his paranormal reflexes by, first, laying his hand on a table. The android then rams the point of a knife between his outstretched fingers with superhuman speed.*

However, one minor variation in this scene does exist between its scripted and filmed counterparts. In the screenplay, Bishop performs the 'knife trick' on his own hand; in the film (all versions), Hudson's hand is trapped beneath Bishop's, and the android plunges the knife tip between both men's fingers.

8) STATE OF THE BADASS ART

A) SCENE 40
B) After: Scene 40/ Ripley watches him [Hudson] working his way towards her.

NOTE: *Hudson playfully boasted to Ripley about the Colonial Marines awesome firepower during a moment found only in the* Special Edition. *This scene took place within the Drop Ship/APC, shortly before those vehicles reached LV-426.*

INT./EXT. APC

Ripley double times into the APC with the line of hulking troopers. They take seats and begin strapping in. A klaxon sounds and the APC drives up a ramp into the Drop Ship.

Hudson prowls the aisle, his movements predatory and exaggerated. Ripley watches him working his way toward her.

> HUDSON
> I am ready, man. Ready to get it on. Check-it-out. I am the ultimate badass… state-of-the-badass-art. You do not want to fuck with me. Hey, Ripley, don't worry. Me and my squad of ultimate badasses will protect you. Check-it-out…

He slaps the servo-cannon controls in the gun bay above them.

> HUDSON
> Independently targeting particle-beam phalanx. VWAP! Fry half a city with this puppy. We got tactical smart-missiles, phased-plasma pulse-rifles, RPGs. We got sonic eeelectronic ballbreakers, we got nukes, we got knives…sharp sticks –

Hicks grabs Hudson by his battle harness and pulls him into a seat. His voice is low, but it carries.

> HICKS
> Save it.

> HUDSON
> Sure, Hicks.

9) FALSE ALARM

A) SCENE 60
B) After: Scene 59 / Hicks picks up a half-eaten donut beside a coffee cup overflowing with rainwater.

ALIENS

James Cameron's pre-production sketch of the
Marines' self-targeting 'Smart Gun'

NOTE: Aliens Special Edition *included an
extra scene between Vasquez and Hudson:
right after the Marines first entered the
deserted LV-426 colony. In the* Theatrical Cut,
*this sequence would have followed a short
shot of Vasquez and Hudson walking down a
Colony corridor as Hudson looks at his
motion tracker – it would have ended just
before the shot of Hicks walking past a
deserted office desk, on which rests a soggy
croissant and glass coffee cup. However, this
extra scene has no corresponding entry in
Cameron's script, other than the general*

*information outlined in Scene 60; apparently,
Cameron rewrote this sequence before filming
it, resulting in a substantially different scene
than the one in the* Aliens *screenplay.*

*In order to differentiate the two versions, I
will first reprint Scene 60 as it appears in the
23 September 1985* Aliens *script:*

INT. LOWER LEVEL – QUARTERS

Apone's men are searching systematically in
pairs. They pass through the colonists' modest
apartments, little more than cubicles. Hudson,

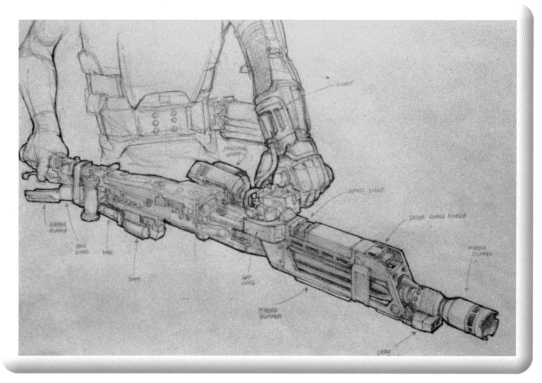

Another of James Cameron's pre-production sketches of the 'Smart Gun'

on tracker, flanks Vasquez as they move forward. Hudson touches a splash of colour on the wall. Dried blood. His tracker beeps.

Vasquez whirls, cannon aimed. The beeping grows more frequent as Hudson advances towards a half-open door. The door is splintered part-way out of its frame. Holes caused by pulse-rifle rounds pepper the walls. Vasquez eases up to the door. Kicks it in. Tenses to fire.

Inside, dangling from a piece of flex conduit, a junction-box swings like a pendulum in the wind from a broken window. It clacks against the rails of a child's bunk bed as it swings. *Now, here is the same sequence of Vasquez/Hudson investigating the movement caught by their beeping tracker as it plays in the* Special Edition. *Scene descriptions here are by Paul M. Sammon; dialogue is that heard in the* Special Edition.

INT. LOWER LEVEL – QUARTERS

Vasquez and Hudson walk uneasily down a deserted corridor. They stop as a pinging sound comes from Hudson's motion tracker.

ALIENS

CUT TO:

A close-up of the tracker's readout screen, on which can be seen a glowing dot.

CUT TO:

Hudson, looking up.

CUT TO:

Gorman inside the APC, seated before the Marines readout control centre. The Lieutenant glides his chair over to Hudson's screen.

CUT TO:

Hudson, back in the corridor. He silently signals Vasquez to wait, then directs her attention towards a half-opened door.

CUT TO:

Another close-up of Hudson's tracker. The DOT moves closer on the device's readout screen.

CUT TO:

Hudson pointing at the room behind the half-opened door.

> HUDSON
> (whispering to Vasquez)
> It's right in here!

Hudson suddenly kicks the door fully open. Vasquez enters the room beyond, Smart Gun at the ready. Hudson follows her.
They come to another door. This one is closed. Hudson gently touches it with his hand. He looks at Vasquez. She nods.

> HUDSON
> Now!

Hudson KICKS the door open.

> VASQUEZ
> NOW!

> HUDSON
> (yelling)
> Hyaaaaaaaaa!

Both Marines race into the next room, Hudson first this time. Hearts racing, they discover – a yellow plastic hamster habitat.

The habitat sits harmlessly on a table. One hamster (the source of the moving dot on Hudson's motion tracker) races through a translucent tube.

> VASQUEZ
> (sarcastic)
> Good one, Hudson.

> HUDSON
> (radioing to Gorman)
> Uhhh Sir, uhh we have a negative situation here..uh..Movin' on, sir.

CUT TO:

A sweating Gorman, looking peeved.

10) ENTERING THE COMPLEX
SCENES 65–67
After: Scene 64 / Vasquez: 'Pendejo jerk-off.'
NOTE: *The* Special Edition Aliens *features a sequence of the Marines' Armoured Personnel Carrier stopping before an outer entrance to the colony called 'the South Lock'. Ripley, Burke, Gorman and Bishop then disembark from the APC, are met by Hicks and Frost, and enter the colony through the Lock. This*

*deleted moment would have occurred in the
Theatrical Cut after Gorman announced that
he was 'coming in' to the colony, whereupon
Vasquez calls him a 'jerk-off'; it would have
ended just before a shot of Gorman (who is
now inside the colony) ducking beneath a
mass of twisted metal and stepping into a
main corridor.*

   *What follows is the extra sequence as
described in Cameron's script:*

INT. FIRST LEVEL

GORMAN
(voice-over)
...We're coming in.

HUDSON
(cupping his mike)
He's coming in. I feel safer already.

VASQUEZ
(*sotto voce*)
Pendejo jerk-off.

EXT. COLONY COMPLEX

Frost and Hicks emerge from the south lock
just as the APC rolls up close to the entrance.
The crew door slides back. Gorman emerges,
followed by Burke and Bishop. Burke looks
back to see Ripley stop in the APC doorway,
eyeing the ominous colony structure. She
meets his eyes. Shakes her head 'no'. Not
ready.

HUDSON
(voice-over; filtered)
Sir, the CPU is on-line.

GORMAN
Okay, stand by in operations.
(to those present)
Let's go.

INT. APC

The crew door cycles home with a clang.
Ripley sits in the dark interior, lit by the
tactical displays. The wind howls outside, an
incredibly desolate sound. She hugs herself.
Alone. Unarmed. She knows she's in a tank,
but remembers the acid. Leaps up. Hits the
door switch.

EXT. APC – SOUTH LOCK

The crew door opens and Ripley emerges. In
time to see the lock doors rumbling closed.

RIPLEY
Burke!

The wind snatches her words away. The crew
door whines shut behind her. She walks to the
exterior lock door controls and studies them.
She punches some unfamiliar buttons.
Nothing happens. She looks really nervous,
alone in the howling wind. She hits another
button. The door motors come to life and she
relaxes a little. Glances behind her. And
screams! There's a face right there! Right at her
shoulder. She jumps back, gasping for breath.

FROST
Scare you?

RIPLEY
Jesus, Frost.

FROST
Sorry. Hicks said to keep an eye on you.

He gestures for her to precede him inside.

*Interestingly, this sequence, like the one of
Vasquez/Hudson discovering the hamster
habitat, was changed before shooting. Said
tweaking resulted in a different version of*

ALIENS

Scenes 65–67, especially of the moment in which Ripley demonstrates her fearful unwillingness to enter the colony. Footage of the altered Scenes 65–67 were then edited into the Special Edition.

The following transcription describes Scenes 65–67 as they appears in the Special Edition; *action descriptions by Paul M. Sammon, dialogue as heard in the* Special Edition *itself.*

EXT. COLONY

The APC drives through the rain towards the colony's 'South Lock'. As it stops before this entrance, the lock's doors open, and Hicks and Frost step out.

                                    CUT TO:

The APC door sliding open. Gorman, Burke and Ripley leave the vehicle. As they do, Gorman receives a message from Hudson on his headset.

                    HUDSON
            (os, on radio to Gorman)
    Sir, we got the CPU online. No problem.

                    GORMAN
                (into his headset)
    Good. Stand by in operations.
                (Gorman slides shut
                the APC's door)
    Okay, let's go.

                                    CUT TO:

A close-up of Ripley, looking anxious.

                                    CUT TO:

A wide shot of Gorman, Burke and Ripley hurrying through the rain and around the front of the APC. They walk up the South Lock's outer ramp, where Hicks and Frost wait for them. At the same time, Bishop exits the APC from the driver's side and races to join the group.

Gorman, Burke and Bishop enter through the South Lock. Ripley pauses for a moment. Her expression subtly conveys fear and hesitation. Hicks catches sight of this – he and Frost also stop.

                    HICKS
                (to Ripley)
            Are you allright?

                    RIPLEY
                (nodding)
    Yes.

The three pass through the South Lock. Its doors slide shut behind them. They are now in the colony.

I I) SEARCHING THE COMPLEX
A) SCENES 68–69, 70 (partial)
B) After: Scene 67 / He [Frost] gestures for her [Ripley] to precede him inside.
Scenes of Gorman receiving information on the Colony as he first enters the complex, as well as the moments when Ripley/the Marines first enter the Colony's Med Lab, also differ from the manner in which they appeared in the Special Edition *as opposed to the* Aliens *script.*

First, Scenes 68, 69 and the beginning of Scene 70 as they read in the screenplay:

INT. CONTROL BLOCK CORRIDOR

Ripley catches up with the others as they move into the bowels of the complex.

GORMAN
(to Burke)
Looks like your company can write off its
share of this colony.

BURKE
(unconcerned)
It's insured.

On Ripley: as they move along the
corridor...reacting to the fact that she is back
in alien country. She sees the ravaged
administration complex. Fire-gutted offices.
Hicks notices her looking around nervously.
He motions to Frost with his eyes and the
trooper casually falls in beside her on the
other side, rifle at ready. A two-man
protective cordon. She glances at Hicks. He
winks, but so fast maybe it's something in
his eye. Trooper Drake emerges from a side
corridor ahead.

DRAKE
Sir, you should check this out...

INT. CORRIDOR

This wing is completely without power. The
troopers switch on their pack lights and the
beams illuminate a scene of devastation
worse than they have seen. Her expression
reveals that Ripley is about to turn and flee.

DRAKE
Right ahead here...

They approach a barricade blocking the
corridor, a hastily welded wall of pipes, steel-
plate, outer-door panels. Acid holes have
slashed through floor and walls in several
places. The metal is scratched and twisted by
hideously powerful forces, peeled back like a
soup can on one side. They squeeze through
the opening.

INT. MED LAB

The pack lights play over the devastation of
the colonists' last-ditch battle. The
equipment of the med labs has been
uprooted to add to the barrier.

FROST
Last stand.

GORMAN
No bodies?

DRAKE
No, sir. Looks like it was a helluva fight.

Tight on Ripley: transfixed by something.

RIPLEY
(low)
Over there.

The others turn and approach, seeing what
she sees. She has entered a second room,
part of the med-lab area. In a storage alcove
at near eye level stand seven transparent
cylinders. Stasis tubes.

They seem to contain severed arthritic hands,
the palsied fingers curled in a death-rictus.

BURKE
Are these the same...?

Ripley nods, unable to speak. Burke leans
closer in fascination, his face almost
touching one cylinder...

RIPLEY
Watch it, Burke...

The creature inside lunges suddenly,
slamming against the glass. Burke jumps
back. From the 'palm' of the thing's body

ALIENS

emerges a pearlescent tubule, which slithers tongue-like over the inside of the glass.

> HICKS
> (to Burke)
> It likes you.

Here is the same sequence as it plays out in Special Edition *(note the dialogue changes between Frost, Drake and Hicks). Actions described by Paul M. Sammon, dialogue transcribed from the* Special Edition.

INT. CONTROL BLOCK CORRIDOR

Ripley, Burke, Frost, Bishop, Hicks and Gorman step into the shattered control block corridor. They silently regard the ominous wreckage as Drake appears and approaches Gorman.

> DRAKE
> Sir. They sealed off this wing at both ends. Welded the doors, blocked off the stairs with heavy equipment.

> GORMAN
> Mm-huh.

> DRAKE
> But it looks like the barricade didn't hold.

> GORMAN
> Any bodies?

> DRAKE
> No sir.

> FROST
> (to Hicks)
> Last stand. Must've been a helluva fight.

> HICKS
> Yeah. Looks that way.

INT. CORRIDOR

The small group begins cautiously advancing down the corridor.

> GORMAN
> (off)
> Allright, Drake. This way. We should be able to cut through the med lab to operations.

Cautiously led by Drake (with his extended Smart Gun), the group passes through an arch into –

INT. MED LAB

Drake silently pads down a med lab aisle, both sides flanked by machinery.

> CUT TO:

Bishop, Burke and Gorman walk down another Med Lab aisle. At the far end of the lab Ripley, Hicks and Frost parallel their progress.

> CUT TO:

Ripley, stopping in her tracks. She's seen something.
REVERSE ANGLE

Ripley has spotted three liquid-filled stasis tubes, holding three apparently dead facehuggers. She and Hicks cautiously approach them.

> HICKS
> (low)
> Lieutenant? Gorman!

Gorman appears behind the rest of the group as Hicks cautiously approaches a tube. He stops. Stares at the inert facehugger within. Burke joins him.

> BURKE
> (to Ripley, indicating facehuggers)
> Are those the same ones?

Ripley nods. Burke leans very closely towards the stasis tube.

> RIPLEY
> Careful, Burke!

Burke looks around at Ripley. Turns back towards the tube. As he does, the previously motionless facehugger lunges at him! Burke steps back, startled.

> HICKS
> (to Burke)
> Looks like love at first sight to me.

Scene 70 in the Special Edition *now proceeds the same way as written in the* Aliens' *screenplay.*

12) 'MAGNIFICENT, ISN'T IT?'

A) SCENE 108
B) After: Scene 75 / Newt: 'It won't make any difference.'
NOTE: *A short* Aliens *moment between Bishop and a Marine named Spunkmeyer was enhanced during its transition from screenplay to screen.*

In the script, this sequence (Scene 108) had Spunkmeyer delivering equipment to an oblivious Bishop, who's examining a dead Facehugger with intense interest. The filmed version of the same scene in Aliens, *however, makes the unspoken fascination Bishop feels towards this creature more explicit. This, in turn, helps make viewers more suspicious of Bishop's loyalties – especially when one recalls the dangerous admiration another android (Ash) felt towards A1's title creature.*

Incidentally, the appearance of the originally numbered Scene 108 right after Scene 75 in the filmed Aliens *suggests that Cameron decided to slightly reshuffle* Aliens' *narrative during the film's post-production editing process; in this case, by placing Scene 108 at an earlier point in* Aliens' *plot than was originally intended.*

First, Scene 108 as written:

INT. MED LAB

Bishop is hunched over an ocular probe doing a dissection of one of the dead parasites. Spunkmeyer enters with some electronics gear on a hand truck and parks it near Bishop's work table.

> SPUNKMEYER
> Need anything else?

Bishop waves no without looking up.
Now, the same sequence as seen/heard in the film:

INT. MED LAB

Bishop is hunched over the ocular probe. He is dissecting one of the dead facehuggers, which is splayed on its back. He pokes at it with a long, tweezer-like probe, totally absorbed in his work.

Behind him, Spunkmeyer enters the room. He's pushing a cart heaped with equipment. Spunkmeyer parks the cart behind the android. Bishop ignores him. Remains staring through the high-tech microscope.

ALIENS

SPUNKMEYER
Need anything else?

Bishop quickly turns, obviously startled by
the sound of Spunkmeyer's voice. The
synthetic human stares blankly at the
marine.

SPUNKMEYER
Hello, Bishop. Do you need anything else?

Bishop now notes the cart beside him. He
looks back at Spunkmeyer blankly.

BISHOP
No.

Bishop turns back, dips his eyes to the ocular
probe. Spunkmeyer has been dismissed. But
he doesn't leave.

SPUNKMEYER
That's a nice pet you got there, Bishop.

BISHOP
(enthused)
Magnificent, isn't it?

13) NEWT & HICKS
(NOT IN THE *THEATRICAL CUT* OR
***SPECIAL EDITION*)**
A)SCENE 76A
**B) After: Scene 76 / Apone: 'Awright, let's
go girls, they ain't payin' us by the hour.'**
NOTE: *The following scene from James
Cameron's* Aliens *script does not appear in
either the* Theatrical Cut *or the* Special
Edition*: it was originally intended to appear
immediately after the scene of Hudson
locating the missing colonists through their
implanted 'Personal-Data Transmitters':*

INT. OFFICE

Hicks knocks and enters.

HICKS
We're moving out.

Newt uses the diversion, bolting like a rodent
under the furniture, towards the door to a
connecting office. Hicks leaps grabbing her
arm, and the kid spins to bite him.

RIPLEY
Newt!

Hicks snaps his hand back as Ripley grabs
the little girl by the shoulders. Newt stops
struggling. Hicks rubs his hand where the
child bit him earlier.

HICKS
Hope the kid don't have rabies.

RIPLEY
(to Newt)
Come on.

She leads the little girl out, following Hicks.

14) RADIO CHATTER
A)SCENES 81–84
**B) After: Scene 80 / Hudson: 'You tell me,
man. I only work here.'**
Note: *Although the action and dialogue heard
throughout Scenes 81–84 in the filmed*
Aliens*(all versions) essentially mimics the
same relevant passages in Cameron's script,*
Aliens *the motion picture adds many
unscripted background conversations between
the Colonial Marines and Sergeant Apone
during these sequences (which take place
between the time the marines first enter the
LV-426 Atmosphere Processor and the
moment they later discover the 'secreted resin'
laid down by the Xenomorphs hiding*

underneath this facility). *These conversations are, for the most part, inconsequential. Sergeant Apone can be heard snapping out an unscripted order or two; we further hear a lot of idle chatter and tech-filled jargon between the other marines, who stay in touch via their communication headsets. Most of this extra dialogue has also been sonically treated ('filtered') to sound like static-y radio transmissions.*

15) THE SENTRY GUNS: 'THIS IS ALL WE COULD SALVAGE.'

SCENE 116
After: Scene 115 / The wind howls mournfully around the metal buildings, dry and cold.
NOTE: *The* Aliens Special Edition *included a number of extra scenes featuring 'Robot Sentry Units', advanced Colonial Marine weapons that were essentially high-tech machine guns. These 'remote sentries' engaged their targets automatically, and appeared in at least a half-dozen different* Special Edition *sequences. However, all scenes and references to the sentry guns were deleted from* Aliens Theatrical Cut.

The first Robot Sentry Units reference debuted in the Special Edition *during a scene of Hicks (in the colony's operations room) discussing what equipment had been salvaged from the wrecked APC / Drop Ship:*

INT. OPERATION

The weary and demoralised group is gathered to take stock of their grim options. Vasquez and Hudson are just setting down a scorched and dented packing case, one of several culled from the APC wreckage. Hicks indicates their remaining inventory of weapons, lying on a table.

> HICKS
> This is all we could salvage. We've got four pulse-rifles, with about fifty rounds each. That ain't so good. About fifteen M-40 grenades and one flame-thrower less than half full...one damaged. And we've got four of these robot-sentry units with scanners and display intact.

He opens one of the scorched cases, revealing a high-tech servo-actuated machine gun with optical sensing equipment, packed in foam.

> RIPLEY
> How long after we're declared overdue can we expect a rescue?

16) THE SENTRY GUNS: STRATEGIC PLACEMENT

SCENE 117
After: Scene 116 / Ripley: 'Fine. You do that.'
NOTE: *The second* Special Edition *Sentry Gun scene took place as Ripley and the marines examined the colony's blueprints for information as to how best barricade themselves against the marauding aliens. Interestingly,* Aliens Theatrical Cut *(as opposed to its* Special Edition*) used different dialogue during Ripley and Hicks's exchange in this sequence. Said changes were created by looping new dialogue over the actors original lines during post-production. This substitution was then concealed by laying in these newly looped sentences over various visual cutaways, ones that showed the* Aliens *characters standing around the blueprint display table.*

For the record, the way this dialogue runs in the theatrical version of Aliens *is:*

> RIPLEY
> Well, there's a pressure door at this end. We could close that, weld it shut. That

ALIENS

should hold them for awhile.

HICKS
But we gotta figure on them getting into
the complex.

RIPLEY
That's right. So, we repair the barricades
at these two intersections. And weld
plate steel over these ducts here, and
here, and here. That should seal off med
lab and operations.

HICKS
Outstanding. Now all we need is a deck
of cards.

Contrast the preceding with the manner in
which the dialogue in the same scene plays
out in Cameron's script, which the Special
Edition *closely follows:*

INT. OPERATIONS

Burke, Ripley, Hudson and Hicks are bent
over a large horizontal video screen, like an
illumination chart table. Newt hops from one
foot to the other to see.

RIPLEY
This service tunnel is how they're
moving back and forth.

HUDSON
Yeah, right, it runs from the processing
station right into the sub-level here.

He traces a finger.

RIPLEY
All right. There's a pressure door at this
end. The first thing we do is put a remote
sentry in the tunnel and seal that door.

HICKS
We gotta figure on them getting into the
complex.

RIPLEY
That's right. So we repair the barricades
at these intersections...
(pointing)
...and weld plate steel over these ducts
here and here. Then they can only come
at us from these two corridors, so we put
the other two sentry units here.

Hicks contemplates her game plan and raises
his head, satisfied.

HICKS
Outstanding. Then all we need's a deck
of cards. All right, let's move
like we got a purpose.

HUDSON
Aye-firmative.

NEWT
(imitating Hudson)
Aye-firmative.

17) THE SENTRY GUNS: THE TEST

SCENE 118
After: Scene 117 / Newt: 'Aye-firmative.'
NOTE: *Also included in the* Special Edition
was a sequence of Hicks using remote TV
cameras and a laptop computer to arm the
sentry guns; the same deleted scene revealed
Vasquez and Hudson in a colony corridor
testing the now-activated weapons.
   Cameron must have rethought this
sequence between the time he wrote and
filmed it, as Scene 118 plays out differently in
its scripted and Special Edition *forms. In*
addition, while the Theatrical Cut *did retain a*

James Cameron's early design sketch of the Alien Queen

portion of Scene 118, only its final moments (which had Hudson saying, 'We're sealing the tunnel. Baby, hurry up! Come on!' before the corridor's doors slammed shut), remained in the Aliens *distributed to theatres in 1986.*

Here is Scene 118 from the Aliens *script:*

INT. SERVICE TUNNEL – SUB-LEVEL

A long straight service tunnel, lined with conduit, seems to go on for ever. Vasquez and Hudson have finished setting up two of the robot sentry guns on tripods in the tunnel.

VASQUEZ
(shouting)
Testing!

She hurls a wastebasket down the tunnel, into the automatic field of fire. The sentry guns swivel smoothly, the wastebasket bounces once...and is riddled by two quick bursts. They retreat behind a heavy steel fire door which they roll closed on its track. Vasquez, using a portable welding torch, begins sealing the door to its frame, as Hudson paces nervously.

ALIENS

HUDSON
Hudson here. A and B sentries are in place and keyed. We're sealing the tunnel.

Now, here is the same (greatly expanded) sequence as seen in the Special Edition. *Action descriptions by Paul M. Sammon, dialogue transcribed from the* Special Edition:

CLOSE-UP – TV MONITOR

We see a closed-circuit image of Vasquez and Hudson in a service tunnel.

CUT TO:

INT. COLONY – TACTICAL CONSOLE

Hicks sits at a tactical console with six monitors, watching Hudson and Vasquez's progress. He swivels in his chair and bends over. Near him are two closed laptop computers. Hicks opens both. Reveals two screens displaying greenish-yellow characters. He begins typing on one of the laptop keyboards.

CUT TO:

CLOSE-UP – LAPTOP SCREEN
A close-up of a laptop screen reveals the words 'REMOTE SENTRY WEAPON SYSTEM'. A sub-menu on this screen flashes 'AUTO'.

INT. COLONY – SERVICE TUNNEL

A close-up of a hand plugging a power cord into a sentry gun. A light blinks on the weapon. We hear Hudson's voice.

HUDSON
(os)
Do your thing, baby.

CUT TO:

A wide shot, showing that two sentry guns have been placed side-by-side in a service tunnel. Hudson is hurriedly moving away from one gun past Vasquez, who is activating her own gun.

HUDSON
(to Vasquez)
Come on, come on, Vasquez, let's get the hell out of here.
(Hudson speaks on his headset radio, to Hicks)
Hudson here. A and B sentries are in place and keyed.

HICKS
(os, through headset)
Roger.

CUT TO:

A close-up of Hicks's hands typing out commands on a laptop.

HICKS
(os)
Stand by. Arming now.

CUT TO:

A close-up of one of Hicks's laptop screens displaying the word 'ARMED'.

HICKS
(os)
Test it, Hudson.

CUT TO:

Hudson and Vasquez back in the service tunnel.

HUDSON
(to Vasquez)
Do it!

VASQUEZ
Fire in the hole!

Vasquez tosses a small metal canister over the sentry guns. As soon as it falls into their field of fire, both guns open up, blasting the canister to atoms.

HUDSON
Okay, great! Lets get the hell out of here!

Vasquez and Hudson slip through an open door at their backs. Camera favours Hudson as he keys the door closed.

HUDSON
(radioing to Hicks)
We're sealing the tunnels.
(Looks at door closing)
Baby, hurry up! Come on...

The bottom of the door slams shut.

18) THE SENTRY GUNS: READY FOR ACTION

A) SCENE 121
B) After: Scene 120 / There is no movement
NOTE: *Before the beginning of the scene in the med lab, where Ripley tucks Newt into bed, the* Special Edition *included a tracking shot of two sentry guns (located at the intersection of two brightly lit corridors) rotating on their tripods and automatically scanning the area. This shot begins on the* Special Edition *just after Hicks gives Ripley a wristwatch-like 'locator' and we see an exterior shot of the operations centre with its metal shutters closed; it ends just before Ripley carries Newt through an opening door into the med lab. As Cameron's screenplay describes:*

INT. CORRIDOR

In the barricaded corridor sentry guns C and D sit waiting, their 'armed' lights flashing green. Through a hole torn in the ceiling at the far end of the corridor the fog swirls in. Water drips. An expectant hush.

19) NEWT & RIPLEY'S BABY

A) SCENE 122
B) After: Scene 122 / Newt: 'Why do they tell little kids that?'
NOTE: *Some additional* Special Edition *dialogue between Newt and Ripley (concerning Newt's mother, Ripley's daughter, and the origin of babies) took place in the med lab during the* Special Edition *scene of Ripley putting Newt to bed. This exchange, obviously cut from theatrical prints since it referenced the likewise excised Scene 4 ('A Virtual Park') begins in the* Special Edition *immediately after Newt questions Ripley as to why adults tell children that monsters don't exist. The dialogue heard in the* Theatrical Cut *version of this scene then picks up just before Ripley gives Newt Ripley's locator device and tells the child, 'Here, take this.'*

INT. MED LAB ANNEXE/SURGERY

… (Ripley) turns, reaching for a portable space heater sitting nearby, and slides it closer to the bed. She switches it on. It hums and emits a cosy orange glow.

NEWT
My mommy always said there were no monsters. No real ones. But there are.

Ripley's expression becomes sober. She brushes damp hair back from the child's pale forehead.

ALIENS

RIPLEY
Yes, there are, aren't there.

NEWT
Why do they tell little kids that?

Newt's voice reveals her deep sense of betrayal.

RIPLEY
Well, some kids can't handle it like you can.

NEWT
Did one of those things grow inside her?

Ripley begins pulling blankets up and tucking them in around her tiny body.

RIPLEY
I don't know, Newt. That's the truth.

NEWT
Isn't that how babies come? I mean, people babies...they grow inside you?

RIPLEY
No, it's different, honey.

NEWT
Did you ever have a baby?

RIPLEY
Yes. A little girl.

NEWT
Where is she?

RIPLEY
Gone.

NEWT
You mean dead.

It's more statement than question. Ripley nods slowly.

Ripley unsnaps the tracer bracelet given to her by Hicks and puts it on Newt's tiny wrist, cinching it down.

20) ANTS & BEES

SCENE 123
After: Scene 123/ Bishop: 'It must be something we haven't seen.'
NOTE: *When Ripley, Bishop, Hudson and Vasquez are in the med lab discussing who – or what – might be laying alien eggs on LV-426, the* Special Edition *includes some additional dialogue speculating on the creatures' life cycles.*

The following script excerpt describes the beginning of this scene, which can be found in Aliens Theatrical Cut:

INT. MED LAB

Ripley stands over Lieutenant Gorman, lying motionless on a gurney, his head bandaged. Bishop, crouched over his instruments, is still analysing the facehugger specimens. Hudson and Vasquez are nearby, their weapons cradled.

RIPLEY
Okay, now let me get this straight. They grabbed the colonists, took them over there, and immobilised them to be hosts for more of those...

Ripley points at the stasis cylinders containing the facehugger specimens.

RIPLEY
Which would mean lots of those parasites, right? One for each person... over a hundred at least.

BISHOP
Yes. That follows.

RIPLEY
But each one of these things comes from an egg, right? So who lays the eggs?

BISHOP
I don't know yet. It must be something we haven't seen.

Now, the same scene as it continues in the Special Edition:

HUDSON
Hey, maybe it's like an ant hive.

VASQUEZ
Bees. Bees have hives.

HUDSON
You know what I mean. There's like one female that runs the show.

BISHOP
That's right. The Queen.

HUDSON
Yeah, the momma. And she's badass, man. Big.

Hudson gestures, about an inch long.

VASQUEZ
These things ain't ants.

Both the Theatrical Cut *and* Special Edition *then conclude this scene with:*

RIPLEY
(to Bishop)
I want those specimens destroyed as soon as you're done with them. You understand?

Bishop glances at the creatures, pulsing malevolently in their cylinders.

BISHOP
Mr Burke gave instructions that they were to be kept alive in stasis for return to the Company labs. He was very specific.

Ripley feels the fabric of her self-restraint tearing. She slaps the intercom switch.

RIPLEY
Burke!

21) BURKE'S PRIORITIES
(NOT IN THE *ALIENS THEATRICAL CUT* OR *SPECIAL EDITION*)
A) SCENE 124
B) After: Scene 123 / Ripley: 'Burke!'
NOTE: *Neither* Aliens Theatrical Cut or Special Edition *included this short, scripted, opening scene confrontation between Ripley and Burke, after Ripley discovers Burke's new plans for the facehuggers:*

INT. MED LAB ANNEXE

In a small observation chamber separated from the med lab by a glass partition, Ripley and Burke have squared off.

RIPLEY
Look, Burke, we had an agreement!

BURKE
I know, I know, but we're dealing with changing scenarios here. This thing is major, Ripley. You gotta go with its energy. Look, you're the representative of the Company who discovered this species, your percentage is going to be some serious money. I mean serious.

Ripley stares at him like he's a particularly disagreeable fungus.

RIPLEY
You son of a bitch.

22) SENTRY GUNS A & B
SCENES 125–128
After: Scene 124/ Ripley: 'Happy to disappoint you.'
NOTE: *Following Ripley's confrontation with Burke in the Med Lab over the latter's plan to smuggle aliens back to earth, the* Special Edition *included a sequence showing the Xenomorphs attempting to make their way past sentry guns A and B in a service tunnel.*

This deleted footage started just after Burke, in the med lab, tells Ripley, 'I thought you'd be smarter than this,' and Ripley replies, 'Happy to disappoint you'. It ended just before Ripley and the others are then seen watching excess gas being vented from the atmosphere processor, whereupon Ripley says, 'It's very pretty Bishop, but what are we looking for?'

INT. CORRIDOR

Ripley is walking towards operations when a strident alarm begins to sound. She breaks into a run.

INT. OPERATIONS

Ripley double-times it to Hicks's tactical console where Hudson and Vasquez have already gathered. Hicks slaps a switch, killing the alarm.

HICKS
They're coming. They're in the tunnel.

The trilling of the motion sensor remains, speeding up. Two red lights on the tactical display light up simultaneously with an echoing crash of gunfire which vibrates the floor.

HICKS
Guns A and B. Tracking and firing on multiple targets.

The RSS (robot sentry) guns pound away, echoing through the complex. Their separate bursts overlap in an irregular rhythm. A counter on the display counts down the number of rounds fired.

HUDSON
They must be wall-to-wall in there. Look at those ammo counters go. It's a shooting gallery down there.

INT. SERVICE TUNNEL – TIGHT ON THE RSS GUN

Blasting stroboscopically in the tunnels. Their barrels are overheating, glowing cherry red. One clicks empty and sits smoking, still swivelling to track targets it can't fire upon.

INT. OPERATIONS

The digital counter on B-gun reads zero.

HICKS
B-gun's dry. Twenty on A. Ten. Five. That's it.

Silence. Then a gong-like booming echoes eerily up from the sub-level.

RIPLEY
They're at the pressure door.

The booming increases in volume and ferocity.

HUDSON
Man, listen to that.

Mixed with the echoing crash-clang is a nerve-racking screech of claws on steel. The intercom buzzes, startling them.

BISHOP
(voice-over)
Bishop here. I'm afraid I have some bad news.

HUDSON
Well, that's a switch.

23) AN ALARMED MOTION-SENSOR
(NOT IN THE *ALIENS THEATRICAL CUT* OR *SPECIAL EDITION*)
A)SCENE 129
B)After: Scene 129 / Bishop: 'I may be synthetic but I'm not stupid.'
The tag-end of the (scripted and mostly filmed) scene of Bishop volunteering to repair the colony's 'uplink antennae' in order to summon the second Drop Ship does not appear in either the Theatrical or Special Edition *versions of* Aliens. *Both of these variants conclude this sequence with Bishop saying he'll take on the job, then adding that 'I may be synthetic, but I'm not stupid'.* Aliens' *screenplay, however, then continues with Ripley asking Bishop:*

INT. OPERATIONS – MINUTES LATER

RIPLEY
All right. Let's get on it. What'll you need?

VASQUEZ
Listen. It's stopped.

(Vasquez is referring to the sound of distant aliens trying to break through the colony's pressure doors – PMS.)

They listen. Nothing. An instant later comes the high-pitched trilling of a motion-sensor alarm. Hicks looks at the tactical board.

HICKS
Well, they're into the complex.

24) SENTRY GUNS C & D
SCENES 132–133
After: Scene 131 / Ahead of him the conduit dwindles straight to seeming infinity.
NOTE: *The final excised sentry gun sequence takes place in the* Special Edition *after Vasquez and Ripley have sealed Bishop in a claustrophobic, pipe-like conduit, which the android will wiggles through towards the uplink antenna. The* Special Edition *then shows the remaining sentry guns (C and D) ripping through a large group of aliens trying to advance down a Colony corridor.*

INT. MED LAB

Ripley jumps as an alarm suddenly blares through the complex.

HICKS
(voice-over)
They're in the approach corridors.

RIPLEY
On my way.

Ripley jumps up, unslinging a flame-thrower from her shoulder in one motion, and sprints for operations with Vasquez. The sound of sentry guns opening up in staccato bursts echoes from close by.

ALIENS

INT. OPERATIONS

Ripley runs to the tactical console where Hicks is mesmerised by the images from the surveillance cameras. The flashes of the sentry guns flare out the sensitive video, but impressions of figures moving in the smoky corridor are occasionally visible. The robot sentries hammer away, driving streamers of tracer fire into the swirling mist.

> HICKS
> Twenty metres and closing. Fifteen. C and D guns down about fifty per cent.

The digital readouts whirl through descending numbers. An inhuman shrill screeching is audible between bursts of fire.

> RIPLEY
> How many?

> HICKS
> Can't tell. Lots. D gun's down to twenty. Ten. It's out.

Then the firing from the remaining gun stops abruptly. The video image is a swirling wall of smoke. There are black and twisted shapes scattered at the edge of visibility. However, nothing emerges from the wall of smoke. The motion-sensor tone shuts off.

> RIPLEY
> They retreated. The guns stopped them.

The moment stretches. Everyone exhales slowly.

> HICKS
> Yeah. But look...

The digital counters for the two sentry guns read 0 and 10 respectively. Less than a second's worth of firing.

> HICKS
> Next time they can walk right up and knock.

> RIPLEY
> But they don't know that. They're probably looking for other ways to get in. That'll take them a while.

> HUDSON
> Maybe we got 'em demoralised.

> HICKS
> (to Vasquez and Hudson)
> I want you two walking the perimeter. Move!
> (Vasquez and Hudson begin to leave)
> I know we're all in strung-out shape but stay frosty and alert. We've got to stop any entries before they get out of hand.

The two troopers nod and head for the corridor. Ripley sighs and picks up a cup of cold coffee, draining it in one gulp.

Interestingly, the closing part of Scene 133 (*Special Edition* version) was slightly re-edited by Cameron, and then inserted into *Aliens Theatrical Cut*.
The major difference between the Special Edition *and* Theatrical *renditions of Scene 133 is one of length, as the* Theatrical Cut *drops almost the entire first half of the Scene 133 that's displayed in the* Special Edition. *Additionally, the* Theatrical Cut *begins its version of Scene 133 with Ripley drinking from her coffee cup; then, in the next shot, we see Hicks telling Vasquez/Hudson, 'I want you two walkin' perimeter'. During the same moment in the* Special Edition *Scene 133, however, it is Hicks we first see telling*

*Vasquez/Hudson 'I want you two walkin'
perimeter. Move!' – then we see Ripley
drinking from her coffee cup. At which point
both versions of Scene 133 continue in an
identical fashion, with Hicks showing Ripley
how to handle a Colonial Marine pulse rifle.
Also note that in the Special Edition, Hicks
closes his order to Vasquez and Hudson about
walking perimeter with the command 'Move!'
But the word 'Move!' does not appear in the
Theatrical Cut's version of Hicks dialogue.*

25) DWAYNE & ELLEN
SCENE 169
**After: Scene 169 / Hicks: 'We ain't going
anywhere.'**
NOTE: *Just before Ripley leaves the Drop Ship
in order to rescue Newt from the sub-levels of
the atmosphere processor, the* Special Edition
Aliens *included an unexpected moment
where Ripley and Hicks finally learned each
other's first names. This deleted exchange
began inside the Drop Ship right after Ripley
says, 'Hicks, don't let him (Bishop) leave,'
and Hicks replies, 'He ain't goin' anywhere'.
The additional footage then ended just before
we saw Ripley running down the Drop Ship's
open ramp into the processor.*

INT. DROP-SHIP

Ripley hefts the hybrid weapon, grabs the
satchel and spins to the door controls. The
door opens. Wind and machine thunder
blast in.

RIPLEY
See you, Hicks.

Hicks is holding a wad of gauze plastered
over his face.

HICKS
Dwayne. It's Dwayne.

Ripley grabs his hand. They share a moment,
albeit brief. Mutual respect in the valley of
death.

RIPLEY
Ellen.

HICKS
(nods with satisfaction)
Don't be long, Ellen.

Ripley stares at the smiling Hicks for a
moment. Then she turns, and leaves. Runs
down the ramp, crossing the platform to the
open doors of a large freight elevator. The
doors close.

26) BURKE COCOONED
**(NOT IN THE *THEATRICAL CUT* OR
SPECIAL EDITION)**
SCENE 172
**After: Scene 172 / A human bas-relief
sealed in resin.**
NOTE: Aliens *most famous 'lost' scene – that
is, footage that was shot but not subsequently
included in either the* Special Edition *or*
Aliens Theatrical Cut *– is probably the
'Cocooned Burke' sequence. Here, Ripley
discovers an agonised but still-living Carter
Burke trapped within a hardened mass of
alien resin during her search for the
kidnapped Newt in the atmosphere
processor's Xenomorph-infested sub-level 3.
This moment was not intended as a simple
shock effect; instead, the Cocooned Burke
scene was meant to reveal the ultimate (and
ironic) fate of the man who had come to LV-
426 to exploit the aliens.*

As it now stands in both the Theatrical
Cut *and* Special Edition, *Burke's ultimate
destiny is left to the viewer's imagination,
since all versions of* Aliens *portray Burke's
final moment as the one in which the
duplicitous Company man encounters an*

ALIENS

Ron Cobb's design sketch for a LV-426 colony 'Tow Lorry',
a futuristic work vehicle

alien while trying to escape from the Xenomorphs' final assault on the Colonial Marines – whereupon Burke is summarily dropped from Aliens' narrative. Yet James Cameron actually filmed the 'Cocooned Burke' scene. However, Aliens' writer/director later decided he was not happy with its overall effectiveness; Cameron also felt the sequence interfered with Aliens' pacing at a critical moment. Whereupon Cameron simply cut out the 'Cocooned Burke' sequence out of the film.

Since then, the 'Cocooned Burke' scene has not resurfaced on any DVD, video or film incarnation of Aliens. One still photograph of this sequence, however, does exist, and has appeared in a handful of magazines since Aliens' original release. The photo takes the form of a medium close-up, and shows Ripley standing next to the cocooned Burke in the darkened bowels of sub-level 3 (that same photograph, incidentally, is reproduced in this book).

Today it is still possible to reconstruct where the scene revealing Burke's ultimate fate would have occurred in the cinematic

This shot of Ripley disovering the traitorous Burke cocooned did not appear in either the Theatrical Cut or Special Edition

Aliens *by referring to* Aliens' *script. For Cameron's screenplay clearly indicates that the 'Cocooned Burke' scene was originally to have begun right after Ripley drops a marker flare during her search for Newt – it then would have ended just before Ripley discovers Newt's discarded locator bracelet (please note that the Catacomb heading in the following extract refers to sub-level 3 of the Hadley's Hope Atmosphere Processor):*

INT. CATACOMB

Range and direction read out in rapid-fire alpha-numerics on Ripley's locator display.

Ripley blinks sweat out of her eyes, moving through the swirling steam of the alien maze. She approaches an intersecting tunnel. Flashing emergency lights illuminate the insane fresco of the walls. She spins, firing the flame-thrower. Nothing there. She moves forward. The locator signal strengthens as she turns, crouches through a low passage, turns again.At each intersection she quickly lights a fifteen-minute marking flare and

Syd Mead's pre-production sketch of the Sulaco's hanger bay

drops it. For the way back. She has to turn sideways, inching through a fissure between two walls of death...cocoon niches, human bas-relief sealed in resin.

Suddenly something shoots out, grabbing her! A hand. She recovers, then recognizes the face sealed in the wall. Carter Burke.

> BURKE
> Ripley...help me.I can feel it...inside. Oh, God...it's moving! Oh Gooood...

She looks at him. No one deserves this.

She hands him a grenade, popping the safety cap, placing his thumb over the priming button.

> VOICE
> You now have thirteen minutes to reach minimum safe distance.

Ripley moves ahead.The locator signals shows she is almost there. A concussion rocks the place, like an earthquake, jarring her almost off her feet.The whole station seems to shudder. A siren begins to wail a demented rhythm. Following the tracker she

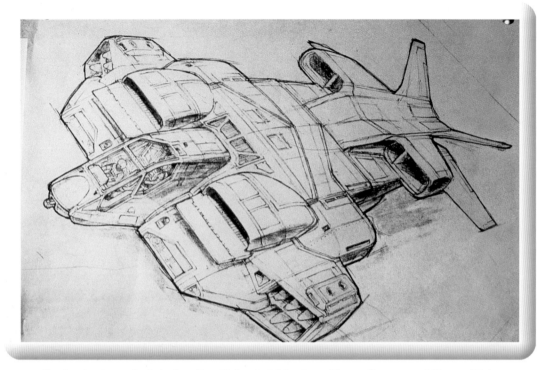

Early design sketch for the Colonial Marines' heavily armed Drop Ship

turns a corner and stops. The range indicator reads zero. She looks down, horrified to see Newt's tracer bracelet lying on the floor of the tunnel. All hope recedes, disintegrating into mindless chaos.

27) UP THE SUB-LEVEL STAIRCASE

(NOT IN THE *THEATRICAL CUT* OR *SPECIAL EDITION*)
A) SCENES 178–185
B) After: Scene 177 / Lashing in a frenzy, the Queen detaches from the egg sac, ripping away and dragging torn cartilage and tissue behind it.

NOTE: *In all filmed versions of* Aliens, *Ripley races through sub-level 3 while holding Newt and fleeing from the pursuing Alien Queen. The two humans then reach the safety of a mesh-enclosed freight elevator, which takes them to the relative safety of an upper landing platform inside the explosion-wracked atmosphere processor. But Ripley and Newt are soon again threatened by the Queen, since the gigantic Xenomorph has ridden a second elevator up to the same platform.*

The identical scene in the Aliens *screenplay, however, does not let Ripley and Newt reach the safety of that elevator. Instead, they are forced to rely on a sub-level ladder*

ALIENS

Design sketch for Power Loader

and stairway, as the following script excerpt illustrates:

INT. CATACOMBS – CORRIDOR

Ripley uses the flame-thrower ahead of her, firing bursts of pulse-rifle fire down side corridors at indistinct shapes and shadows. The weapon is empty when she reaches the freight elevators. A mass of debris, falling down the shaft from a high level, has demolished the lift cage she descended in. She slams the control for the other cage and hears the sound of the lift motor's whine as it

begins its slow descent from several levels up. An enraged screech echoes in the corridor. Ripley sees a silhouette moving in the smoke...The Queen. Her last cartridge is reading zeros. The grenades are gone. Ripley drops the weapon and looks up the shaft to the descending lift...then at the approaching figure. The elevator won't be in time. She runs to a ladder set in the wall as a horrendous screech beats in her ears. She scrambles up the rungs.

INT. SECOND LEVEL

A miniature version of the Narcissus shuttlecraft, aboard which a hibernating Ripley is found at the beginning of Aliens

Ripley struggles up through a narrow hatch, Newt clinging to her. She dives aside as a powerful black arm shoots up through the opening, its razor claws slamming into the grille floor inches from her.

Looking down through the grille she sees the great horrifying jaws directly below her, wet and leering. She scrambles up, running, as the grille floor lifts and buckles behind her with the titanic force of the creature below. It hurls itself with insane ferocity against the metal, pacing her from below as she runs.

INT. STAIRWELL

Ripley reaches an open grid emergency stairwell and sprints upward. It rocks and shudders with the station's death throes.

INT. CORRIDOR – ELEVATORS

The lift reaches bottom, the doors rolling open. The Queen turns and freezes, as if contemplating the open lift cage.

INT. STAIRWELL

ALIENS

Ripley stumbles, smashing her knees against the metal stairs. As she rises she hears the lift motors start up. Looking down through the latticework of the station she sees the lift cage start ominously upwards.

EXT. LANDING PLATFORM

Ripley, with Newt still clinging to her, slams through the door opening on to the platform. Through wind-whipped streamers of smoke she sees...THE SHIP IS GONE.

                    RIPLEY
    BISHOP!

Her shouts become inarticulate screams of hatred, outrage at the final betrayal. She scans the sky. Nothing.

28 RIPLEY SUITS UP
(NOT IN THE *THEATRICAL CUT* OR *SPECIAL EDITION*)
A) SCENE 193
B) After: Scene 192 / The alien hits a moment later.
NOTE: *In all filmic versions of* Aliens, *once the Alien Queen tears Bishop in half aboard the* Sulaco, *the enormous creature chases Ripley to an open doorway. Ripley then manages to activate the door itself. This slams shut in the Queen's face, leaving Ripley secure on the other side of a thick metal barrier. Now comes a short shot of Ripley standing in a darkened chamber on the other side of that door, looking at something we can't see.*

This object – plus Ripley's interaction with it – are revealed by the final following Aliens *script extract, which describes a short scene that does not appear in any filmed version of* Aliens:

INT. DARK CHAMBER

[After slamming the door in the Queen's face], Ripley moves ferret-quick among dark, unrecognisable machines.

VARIOUS ANGLES: very tight on what she is doing...her feet going into stirrup-like mechanisms. Velcro straps fastened over them. Fingers stabbing buttons in a sequence. Her hand closing on a complex grip-control. The hum of powerful motors. The whine of hydraulics.

A few moments later, it is revealed that Ripley has been strapping herself into a Power Loader – the same device she will use to push the Alien Queen into an airlock and, finally, into the silent glacial emptiness of outer space.

THE END

The APC, driven by an adrenalin-fuelled Ripley, destroys everything in its path

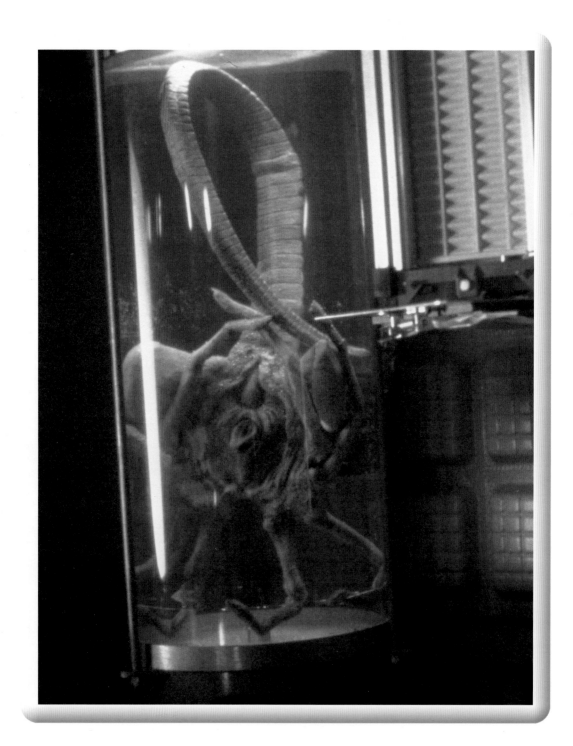

HOMEMADE

SAUSAGE

HOMEMADE SAUSAGE

CHRIS CARTER AND
JAMES PEISKER

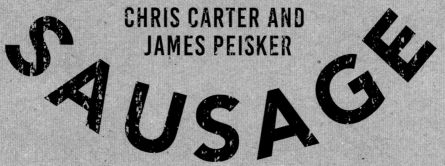

RECIPES AND TECHNIQUES TO
GRIND, STUFF, AND TWIST
ARTISANAL SAUSAGE
AT HOME

QUARRY

Quarto is the authority on a wide range of topics.

Quarto educates, entertains and enriches the lives of
our readers—enthusiasts and lovers of hands-on living.

www.quartoknows.com

© 2016 Quarto Publishing Group USA Inc.

First published in the United States of
America in 2016 by
Quarry Books, an imprint of
Quarto Publishing Group USA Inc.
100 Cummings Center
Suite 406-L
Beverly, Massachusetts 01915-6101
Telephone: (978) 282-9590
Fax: (978) 283-2742
QuartoKnows.com
Visit our blogs at QuartoKnows.com

MIX
Paper from
responsible sources
FSC® C104723

10 9 8 7 6 5

ISBN: 978-1-63159-073-3

Digital edition published in 2016
eISBN: 978-1-62788-818-9

Library of Congress Cataloging-in-
Publication Data available.

Writer: Maddie Teren
Design: Burge Agency
Photography: Andrea Behrends
                    Photography
Styling: Hannah Messinger

Printed in China

TO OUR ENDLESSLY
SUPPORTIVE WIVES,
FAMILY, AND
FRIENDS.

CONTENTS

CHAPTER 1
GRIND

CHAPTER 2
STUFF

THE CLASSICS

THE OUTLAWS

HOMEMADE SAUSAGE

PREFACE

SAUSAGE /saw-sij/ – *noun*
Highly seasoned minced meat, usually pork or beef, traditionally stuffed into the casings of prepared animal intestine or made into a small flat cake.
—*Merriam-Webster's Dictionary*

with each farmer from whom our meat is sourced, and we take great pride in all of the products that we sell.

Although butchering is the foundation of our business, what we do isn't quite so cut-and-dried. Our skills extend further than just the butcher block. They extend to the sausage stuffer. And beyond.

When we started out, Porter Road Butcher was intended to be a small neighborhood butcher shop run by just two of us: co-owners Chris Carter and James Peisker. As a business powered solely by two men, we weren't left with much room to be creative. So we stuck to the classics when it came to making sausage: breakfast sausage, kielbasa, bratwurst, Italian, chorizo, and Andouille.

Along the way, however, business took off, and then for some strange reason people wanted to work for us. Even stranger was that we hired them . . . and then shortly after that, hired some more. So we were left with more hands in the cutting room, and more brains in the kitchen, and therefore more and more sausages in the case.

Since those early days, our sausage repertoire has expanded to include a large number of links, in addition to pâtés, bologna, and our own version of pepperoni.

Although our sausages mainly revolve around **meat**, ingredients such as lentils, beans, and mushrooms can add meatiness to a meat-free link. In addition, duck, rabbit, deer, and other less common proteins can add an interesting flavor profile. Don't be afraid to experiment and push the boundaries after nailing the basics.

As both professional chefs and men who have plenty of knowledge about meat, we have created a slew of sausages that taste just the way they should (perfect), because perfection is what we strive for every day.

The purpose of this book is to give you the general knowledge and know-how for making sausages at home, either using the recipes we've provided or employing your own imagination. There is no limit to what you can create!

Porter Road Butcher is Nashville's only source for local, pasture-raised, hormone- and antibiotic-free meat that is cut to order before your eyes. As a whole animal butcher shop, we work closely

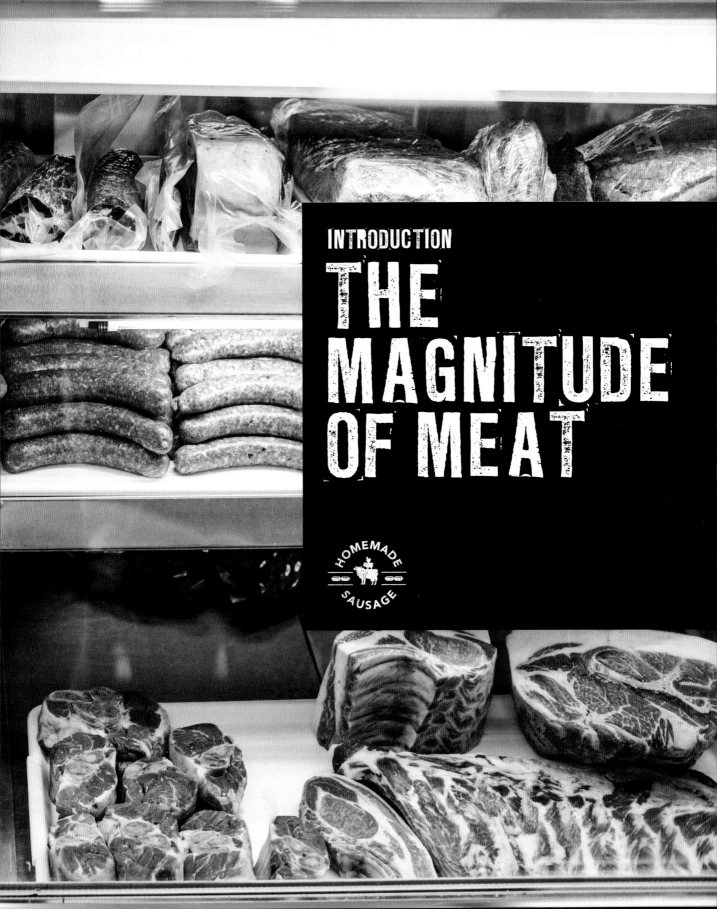

INTRODUCTION
THE MAGNITUDE OF MEAT

HOMEMADE SAUSAGE

Today our knowledge of food and our efficiency of sausage preparation are a far cry from what the Greeks and Romans were working with way back when, but strong and steady remains the foundation of this culinary staple: **meat**.

QUALITY IS KEY

By definition, the main, and most important ingredient in sausage is meat. So while this makes *any* cut or kind of meat eligible, remember that a high quality main ingredient produces a high quality final product: cooks are only as good as their starting ingredient.

A lot of people tell us, "I hate liver," when we urge them to taste our liver pâté, but what they really mean (but don't know they mean) is "I hate commodity liver." Ninety-nine percent of the time, when we offer customers a sample of *our* pâté that was made with liver from happy animals, their eyes widen, and they change their tune.

This is a flawless example of why finding excellent quality meat that comes from happy animals is paramount to making an excellent quality—and most importantly, delicious—sausage.

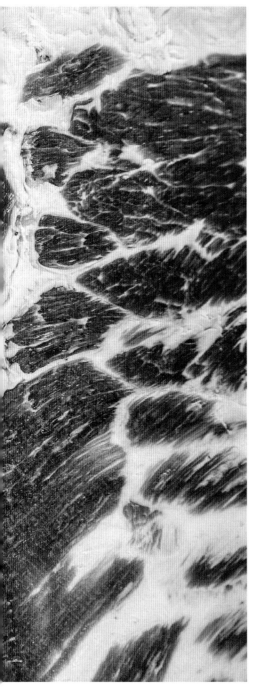

Dating back to Ancient Greece and Rome, sausage served as a way to use up what would have otherwise been discarded meat. By salting, or *curing* the meat, grinding it together with spices and vegetables, and stuffing it into the intestine of an animal, the Greeks and Romans were able to preserve meat and reduce waste— plus make something delicious.

SAUSAGE AS SUSTAINABILITY

In its foundation, sausage was about finding a way to employ every part of the animal instead of wasting it. From salami to loose sausage, pâté, and sausage links, making sausage all boils down to waste reduction and utilization.

Many people think of sausage simply as meat that is ground with spices, stuffed into casings, and then twisted into separate links, but unfortunately, those people are mistaken. Sure, sausage links are likely the most common and familiar form, but bologna, pepperoni, pâté, loose (unstuffed) sausage, and spreadable sausage all fit in to the family as well. Even a meatball is a quickly prepared sausage that home chefs make daily.

FINDING A FARMER

Serving as the foundation of your product, high quality meat is ideal. No matter where you are in the world, the best meat comes from local, responsible, and trustworthy farmers who respect their animals.

So finding a reliable and responsible butcher shop, market, or farmer is probably the most important preliminary step to making sausage.

Animals who are given natural, drug-free lives; who are given real, GMO-free, organic food; and who roam freely on pastures as they were intended, offer the tastiest meat. By eating natural and wholesome food themselves, the animals are healthier and taste closer to what they *should* taste like: delicious.

Responsible farmers give their animals full access to the outdoors, instead of locking them up in a pen lacking access to grass, fresh air, or sunlight. They don't pump them with steroids or hormones, they don't cause the animals to live in a constant state of fear and adrenaline, and they don't make them live in horrendous and unsanitary conditions. All of which means their meat is healthier, fresher, and best of all, tastier.

At Porter Road Butcher, we exclusively sell responsibly-raised, free-range, steroid- and hormone-free meat because of the quality of taste, and also because of the quality of nutrients. Animals that were raised in concentrated animal feeding operations (CAFO)—the commodity meat that you find at supermarkets—on the other hand, tend to be less colorful, less flavorful, and less nutritious.

What's more, commodity meat is often previously frozen, which leads to poorer quality. Because muscles (meat) contain ample amounts of water, water turns into ice if the meat is frozen. In turn, the ice crystals cut into the muscle fibers and loosen the muscle. Then when the meat is eventually thawed out, much of that water leaks out onto your counter or cutting board, providing you with a dry, flavorless piece of meat. No thanks.

As the foundation of our business, we've formed strong relationships with each of our farmers, ensuring that we know exactly where our meat comes from, and that the products we sell to our customers meet our high standards. Large-scale supermarkets and groceries neither have the same relationships with their suppliers, nor afford their customers the same opportunity.

Although local butcher shops like ours aren't readily available everywhere, good farmers' markets and small local grocery stores are great options for finding local and free-range beef, pork, chicken, and lamb, among other regional meats. Asking sustainable or farm-to-table restaurants where they source their meat is also an easy way to locate trusted farmers. We're willing to bet there's a good one near you.

MAKING THE CHOICE

Once you've made the choice to shop local and buy a product you can trust, then comes the selection: choosing which cut of meat is best.

In commercial sausage-making, large corporations generally stay true to the ancient idea that sausage should be made with *leftovers*: They use the buttholes, snouts, ears, testicles, and discarded scraps to fill those tubular casings and yes, they reduce waste by doing so.

Sure, that tastes fine. It even tastes *good*! But when making the stuff yourself, why not choose something better? For example, try an entire pork shoulder or a beef chuck roll in place of already ground meat, made up of God-only-knows-what. Not only does selecting a larger whole piece of meat give you more culinary control, but it also provides you with a consistent product.

Let's take a look at pork sausage, for example. In lieu of buying ground pork, which is a pre-packaged product that comes from upwards of *thousands* of hogs and employs all of the previously mentioned parts of the pig on one Styrofoam tray, use one large piece of pork instead. Dice it into cubes, and then grind it for a great finished product.

The bigger the piece of meat you start with, the more control you have over the end result because you can monitor what goes in and what stays out.

FAT IS YOUR FRIEND

In sausage-making (and cooking in general—but we won't go all the way into that for the sake of time and space), fat should not be feared. Fat is delicious, and it is a vital ingredient that adds both structure and flavor to sausage.

In general, there are two different kinds of fat on an animal: back fat and lower body fat. Lower body fat is a supple and soft fat that can be heated, rendered down, and turned into tallow (beef) and lard (pork), which are mostly used in cooking and baking, respectively.

Back fat, however, is not "greasy" like lower body fat, which has a higher water content and therefore melts easily. Back fat has a lower water concentration, which makes it thicker and more resistant to heat, and thus perfect for adding more substance to a sausage link. Those little chunks of fat also make sausage taste even more delicious and incredibly juicy.

For our sausages, we generally use the ratio of 70 percent meat to 30 percent fat. Usually, we just eyeball the ratio, so feel free to do the same. Proportions don't have to be exact.

Depending on the cut of meat you choose, you may be left with enough fat to satisfy the proper ratio in your sausage. If you find yourself lacking enough fat, however, you can buy back fat from your local butcher shop or farmer, and then dice it up and mix it in with the rest of the ingredients. In making chicken sausages, we substitute good, rich, European-style butter for animal fat.

So don't fear fat! Befriend it, instead.

GOOD FATS VS. BAD FATS

As we learn more about food every single day, we learn how various items are produced, what benefits they offer, and the problems they can potentially cause. In turn, conflicting information arises and causes confusion for consumers:

Kale is the ultimate "super food." vs. eating too much kale will cause cancer.

Red wine is fattening, filled with sugar, and bad for your liver vs. one glass of red wine each night is beneficial to your overall health.

Increased intake of carrots will reduce your risk of cardiovascular disease and improve your eye strength vs. adding too many carrots to your diet will cause your skin to turn orange.

And who could forget the age-old favorite:

Eating fat will make you fat vs. fat is good in moderation.

We're not doctors, we don't have Ph.D.s, and we certainly didn't spend an additional four years in a university wearing lab coats and peering into microscopes. But we did learn a thing or two at culinary school, and we have been known to read books from time to time. So here's what we know about fat.

Although certain fats *can* make you fat if consumed in excess, not all fats are bad. Fat is *necessary* for a healthy and functioning body. Plus, there are many different kinds of fats and the body must maintain a balance of "good" and "bad."

Most commonly discussed are the omega-3s and omega-6s fatty acids. Omega-3s are the "good" fats that are frequently sourced from seafood, such as salmon. A less commonly known but equally delicious source, omega-3s are also available in high levels from grass-fed beef.

Omega-6s, on the other hand, are the "bad" fats that come from foods such as French fries and ice cream, but they are still essential to maintaining a proper and balanced diet; they are needed for building healthy cells and the proper functioning of your brain and nerves.

Our bodies cannot produce these fats on their own, so humans must get them from food. Plant-based oils, such as corn oil, contain high levels of omega-6s, which is why CAFO animals—which feed mostly on corn— are much higher in omega-6s, which partially contributes to red meat getting a bad rap for being bad for your health. Contrarily, grass-fed animals have a high level of omega-3s, making them a healthier alternative to grain-fed (like CAFO animals) or grain-finished meat (animals that feed on grass for the majority of their lives and finish their lives eating grains such as corn).

As humans, we need a *balance* of 3s and 6s, which is why we follow the motto, "everything in moderation." The ideal ratio is 1:1 or 1:2, omega-3s:omega-6s.

CHAPTER 1
GRIND

NAILING THE BASICS

Like many labor-intensive exploits that take place in the kitchen, when it comes to making sausage, plenty of prep work is involved. Pay careful attention if you want to present a beautiful and delicious product. We believe the following four rules are the most important things to keep in mind when making sausage.

- Pick the best meat; quality meat makes quality sausage.

- Always use fresh ingredients; they make a difference.

- Use the right tools.

- Employ proper technique.

PICK THE BEST MEAT

Meat is the foundation of a sausage—or at least, in *this* book it is. So why would you pick anything *other* than excellent?

First and foremost, look for a local or regional product that is free of hormones and steroids and was given free range or was pasture raised. That will provide you with quality meat that has better flavor and texture.

Second, use your senses: look, touch, and smell.

LOOK

Take a look at the color of the meat you've selected. The darker the piece of meat, the more developed the muscles are, and the more flavorful the meat will be. Take chicken, for example. Thighs and legs are darker, juicier, and much more fatty and delicious than its dryer competitor, the breast. Furthermore, meat with a higher fat content provides additional moisture in cooking, which is delicious and ideal for sausage.

TOUCH

Pick up the piece of meat and feel it, even if it's packaged. An ideal product is one that is fresh and not previously or currently frozen. So take a look, read the

> **NOTE**
> Because of the omega-3s in grass-fed beef, it can sometimes give off somewhat of a fishy smell! This doesn`t mean that it is bad (unless it has an unusually rank and off-putting smell), but instead that it`s a good and healthy piece of meat.

package, and find out whether the meat you've chosen has been in the freezer. Then feel the meat: You want it to be firm, but not hard. It should have some give, but not be soft or wiggly like jelly. Think about how *your* muscles feel.

SMELL

Go on, give the meat a sniff. One of the best ways to check the freshness of a meat product is to smell it. If it smells even slightly off or has any sort of off-putting odor, pick a different piece. Of course, good, aged beef will give off a stronger and earthier odor, but your nose will naturally distinguish the difference between a sweetly strong beefy smell from a rank piece of meat.

Once you've selected your piece of meat, all you need to do is dice it up and toss it into the grinder.

Of course, if you don't have (or don't want to buy) a meat grinder or if you are uncertain about grinding meat yourself, find trusted local butchers who choose responsible farmers for sourcing their animals, and ask them to grind it for you. But really, grinding meat is easy and fun. Give it a go!

ALWAYS USE FRESH INGREDIENTS

Fresh herbs, local vegetables, whole spices, dairy from happy cows, and eggs from happy chickens will make a big difference in your final product. Yes, it might cost you a little more up front, but the return on that investment will be so incredible, you'll forget all about your down payment. So go on and invest in the best.

Plenty of online debate exists regarding the appropriateness of dried herbs versus fresh, and the fight for the dried variety has been a strong and valiant one. But when it all boils down, fresh herbs provide a more potent, full, and longer lasting flavor that you won't get from dried herbs. The oils that fresh herbs release and the richness of flavor they provide is far superior to what the flaky, dried kind will put out, so do it right and go fresh. We promise you'll taste the difference.

Just like herbs, spices are much better fresh as well—meaning freshly ground. Certain recipes of ours do call for ground spices, but we always start with the spice in its truest form and then grind it ourselves, using a spice grinder. This method provides fuller, stronger, richer flavors, unlike pre-ground spices that have been sitting on the shelves and releasing their delicious fumes into the nostrils of unassuming passersby. Plus, the larger grind and the non-uniformity of the ground pieces will provide for better texture and bigger bursts of flavor.

USE THE RIGHT TOOLS

Making sausage doesn't require an extensive amount of tools, but there are a few essential items you'll need to get the job done properly. The best and most important tool, however, is one that you already have: your hands. Your hands are by far your most valuable instruments in the kitchen—particularly in the realm of sausage. So don't be afraid to get your hands into the meat of the mix.

SCALE

That being said, a scale is critical in making sure all of your ingredients are measured properly, providing you with a consistent product every time. A small and inexpensive digital scale is suitable for measuring spices and herbs, and a packing scale could be used to measure larger ingredients such as meat.

We weigh our spices and herbs to ensure an accurate reading instead of using measurements with a tablespoon or teaspoon. As James always likes to say, "a pound [454 g] of bowling balls and a pound [454 g] of feathers weigh the same amount" but the mass of the two are much different. A tablespoon of bowling balls and a tablespoon of feathers are quite distinctive!

MEAT GRINDER

Beginning with a large piece of meat, dicing it down, and then grinding it yourself is your best bet for consistency and quality. But even so, how much cooler is it to go from points A to Z totally on your own? No matter which kind of a grinder you have or how mighty your machinery, grinders are crucial to making a sausage that will have a chewy and consistent texture.

A meat grinder can cost anywhere from $50 to $500, but the most important factor to consider is maintaining a sharp blade. When the blade becomes dull, it slows down the grinding process and adds heat to the meat as it continually and slowly pulverizes the same spot. That slow and hot pulverization will deteriorate the emulsification—meaning the equal distribution of ingredients (particularly the fat) and the overall structure—of the sausage.

Avid sausage makers might invest in pricier machinery that will last a lifetime, while fair-weather sausage makers could simply buy the attachments for their electric mixer. It's up to you.

SPICE GRINDER

For better flavor in your sausage, a spice grinder is a crucial tool. Ground spices will suffice, but whole spices are generally less expensive and taste better, too. A coffee grinder will work in place of a spice grinder as well, but be sure to wipe it out thoroughly to remove any stray coffee grinds before using it for your spices.

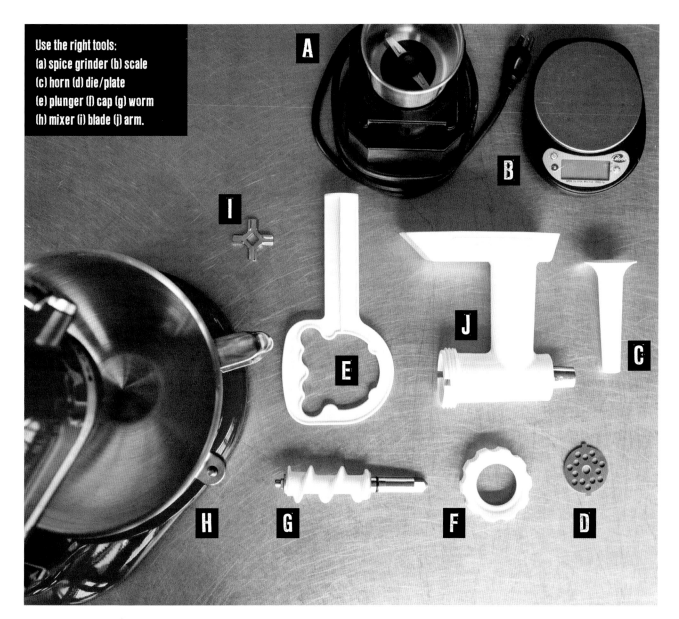

Use the right tools:
(a) spice grinder (b) scale
(c) horn (d) die/plate
(e) plunger (f) cap (g) worm
(h) mixer (i) blade (j) arm.

NOTE
Make sure your scale uses both metric and standard systems of measurement, so you can use recipes from throughout the world.

STUFFER

If you intend to exclusively make loose, unstuffed sausage, then a sausage stuffer is obviously of no use to you; you can excavate this tool from your box.

On the other hand, if you're a link-lover ready to whip up some weenies, a stuffer is essential for stuffing the meat into its casing.

Both horizontal and vertical stuffers exist, but we prefer and recommend the vertical, stainless steel canister-style stuffer. They can be a little pricey, but a decent one won't completely break the bank; they usually cost between $50 and $200. Again, for the electric mixer–equipped there is also a stuffing attachment, which works in conjunction with the grinding attachment. These are best used for smaller batches, and they require quite a bit of muscle power.

An interesting note about casings: There is no such thing as an organic casing. All casings come from commodity pork, which means there is no way for sausages to be 100 percent organic. It`s something we would like to change, but at this point in time beggars can`t be choosers, and we choose to eat Bacon Jalapeño Bratwursts, just as they are. What can you do?

CASINGS

When you make sausage links, consider these factors when selecting a casing: the ingredients in the sausage, the grind (or coarseness) of the meat, and the desired use for the sausage. At Porter Road Butcher, hog casings are our most common casing of choice, but we do employ smaller sheep casings for hot dogs, and we use easily peelable synthetic casings for larger, smoother sausages such as bologna and mortadella.

You can buy many different types and sizes of casings, but we will stick with just two main varieties here: natural casings and synthetic casings.

NATURAL CASINGS are generally preferable when making "dinner sausages," as in sausages that you'll be eating whole, like a hotdog or bratwurst. Although it makes some people a little squeamish to hear it, natural casings are, in fact, the intestines of an animal. Once cleaned and lubricated, the intestines can stretch and twist without breaking, which makes them perfect for stuffing and twisting into sausage links.

Casings must always be used fresh, and they should never, ever be frozen. If frozen, casings will crack and therefore won't be able to hold stuffing. If you find yourself with excess casings after making a batch of sausage, instead of freezing them, simply cover them with salt and stick them into the refrigerator to keep them fresh and ready for your next sausage-making adventure! Just try to use them within the next couple of months so they are still fresh and good.

SYNTHETIC CASINGS are made from things like cellulose and other derivatives of vegetable matter. They are rubbery in appearance and not recommended for eating. We generally use these for large sausages such as bologna and mortadella. It would be pretty frightening if any pig had an intestine that was 6 inches (15 cm) in diameter . . .

POKER

A seemingly simple tool that's very important, pokers are three-pronged devices used to poke tiny holes into the sausage casing, allowing liquid and steam to escape while it is cooked, thus preventing your sausage from bursting open. You could use a thumb-tack or sewing needle as an excellent substitute.

Sausages that are going to be smoked should not be poked. As the sausage heats up in the smoker, the fat will leach out of those holes and drip out, leaving you with a shriveled, fat-less, moisture-less sausage link. So don't poke 'em!

SMOKER

Again, not *all* sausages require smoking. In fact, there are some varieties that we *never* smoke! But smoking your sausage is another great way to add flavor and further impress your dinner guests.

LEARN THE TECHNIQUE

Many steps make up the road toward delicious and flavorful sausages, and the journey traveled can often look intimidating—but it shouldn't! More so, it should look like a sweet African safari on which you are about to embark: very exciting, a little bit scary, but overall fun. By following our step-by-step instructions, you'll be cranking out all sorts of sausages in no time.

STEP 1: SANITIZE

The first step in making sausage, sanitization is crucial to ensuring your sausage avoids contamination. Particularly in a home kitchen, germs and contaminants thrive all over: on the counter, in the sink, and on improperly cleaned kitchen tools, to name a few. Make sure your workspace, tools, and most importantly, your hands, are all clean before you do anything. Constantly wash your hands and keep your workstation clean throughout the entire process to avoid cross-contamination.

STEP 2: CHILL GRINDING AND MIXING EQUIPMENT

One of the most important things to remember while making sausage is to keep everything cold. If the meat becomes too warm, it won't grind properly, which will ruin the emulsification (structure) and prevent both liquid and fat from absorbing into the meat. *That* leads you to a dry, crumbly, and less flavorful sausage and *that* leads to sadness.

Refrigerate the equipment you'll be using to grind and mix your sausage for at least 30 minutes to allow it to properly chill.

STEP 3: WEIGH AND PREPARE INGREDIENTS

Use your digital scale to accurately measure out all of your ingredients. Keep wet ingredients separate from dry ingredients until it's time to mix. Wash and thoroughly dry herbs before using and weighing them.

Trim your meat *before* you weigh it; any sinews, bone fragments, or silver skin you remove will affect the weight. When weighing meat, create an ideal fat-to-lean ratio of 70 percent meat to 30 percent fat. Once the meat is trimmed, cleaned, and weighed, dice it into 1- to 2-inch (2.5 to 5 cm) cubes, small enough to fit into the hole of your grinder. Return meat to the refrigerator after it's been measured to keep it very cold.

STEP 4: MISE EN PLACE

Literally, that means "to put into place."
Before you begin grinding or mixing,
gather all of your essential items and
have them available and ready for use:
grinding tools, mixing tools, ingredients,
and so on. Have everything you need at
your workstation, and eliminate anything
that is unnecessary. The best part?
Having all of the ingredients measured
out and tools by your side makes you feel
like you're hosting your own television
cooking show. And that feels great.

STEP 5: MIX MEAT AND SEASONINGS

Using your hands, combine the diced meat and other ingredients in a large bowl or container. Remember: your hands are your best tools in the kitchen! Make sure the seasoning is distributed as evenly as possible. Return the meat to the fridge.

STEP 6: GRIND SEASONED MEAT

Assemble your cleaned and chilled grinder, turn it on, and slowly add meat into the feed tube. Be careful to not overload or overfill the grinder. Add the meat slowly, piece by piece, so the elbow doesn't overfill. If you notice any smearing or clogging on the die, turn off the grinder and clean out the die. Smearing could also come as a result of the meat's temperature, so check it out to make sure it's still chilled.

This is also a time in which you could grind the meat again, if you are going for a sausage that is firmer and less crumbly. The more you grind the meat, the finer the texture will become and the firmer the sausage will be as well. Once the seasoned meat has been ground, you have the option to add liquid for more flavor or moisture.

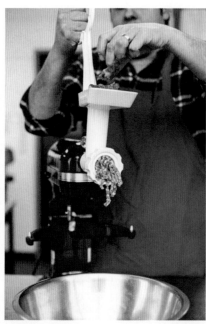

NOTE
The majority of our recipes use a medium die for grinding, but check the specifications on each recipe before you begin.

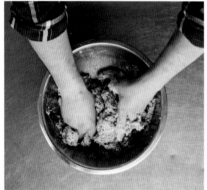

STEP 7: MIX

Using either your hands (preferable) or
your electric mixer with a paddle
attachment, mix the ground meat and
ingredients together. The more you mix,
the firmer the bite of your sausage will
become. Most sausages need anywhere
from 2 to 4 minutes of mixing. You will
know when your sausage is thoroughly
mixed if it sticks to your palm when you
hold some in your hand and then turn
your hand palm-side down.

   This could be the end of the road! If
you are making loose, unstuffed sausage,
then you've arrived at your final
destination. On the other hand, if you will
be stuffing your sausage into links, return
your ground meat to the fridge to chill.

STEP 8: CLEAN YOUR CASINGS

When using natural casings (recommended), soak them in water and find one end of the intestine. Hold one end of the casing up to the nozzle of your sink and, supporting the rest of the casing with one hand, carefully rinse the inside of the casing. Do this several times with each casing to make sure they are thoroughly cleaned and to check for holes. If you find any holes in your casings, cut those sections out.

Once the casings have been thoroughly cleaned, allow them to rest in water while you assemble your stuffing equipment. You can allow the casings to rest in water in a sealed container for up to one week. If you don't use all of your clean casings, just repack them in salt and keep them in the refrigerator, but remember: *Never freeze casings.*

If you are using synthetic casings, simply soak them in water until they are rehydrated.

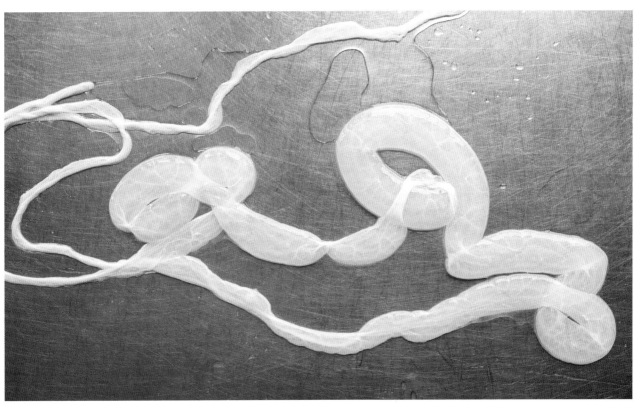

STEP 9: IT`S TIME TO STUFF!

Here's where the fun really begins!

Assemble your stuffer or stuffing attachment and fill the sausage canister with the chilled, ground, and seasoned meat. Press down and compact the meat to eliminate any air pockets.

Lubricate the feeder tube with water and slide the casing onto the tube. Once the casing is entirely scrunched onto the feeder tube, pull 2 inches (5 cm) of casing off the tip of the tube. Grasp the casing end with one hand and begin cranking with the other hand.

Once you can see meat begin to make its way out of the tube, pinch off the end of the casing so the meat is forced to expand inside of it as you slowly pull away, keeping a grip on the casing. Be sure both the casing and the counter on which the sausage will fall are very wet and lubricated to prevent any ripping or sticking.

When about 3 to 4 inches (7.6 to 10 cm) of sausage have made their way into the casing, let go of the end and use one hand to feed the casing off of the tube while the sausage is being cranked out with your other hand.

As you are doing this, be mindful about filling the casing. You want to find that sweet spot where the casing is filled with meat and a little amount of air remains, but not so full that it will bust when you begin twisting.

Once all of the meat has been stuffed into the casing, leave 6 inches (15 cm) of empty casing on the end and cut off any excess to reserve for future use.

NOTE
Casing can last in the fridge for 1 week soaking in water.

Fill the sausage canister with the chilled, ground, and seasoned meat. Press down and compact the meat to eliminate any air pockets.

Lubricate the feeder tube with water and slide the casing onto the tube.

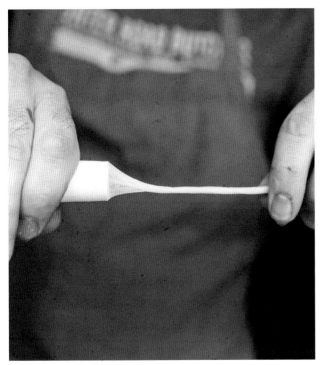

Once the casing is entirely scrunched onto the feeder tube, pull 2 inches (5 cm) of casing off the tip of the tube.

Grasp the casing end with one hand and begin cranking with the other hand.

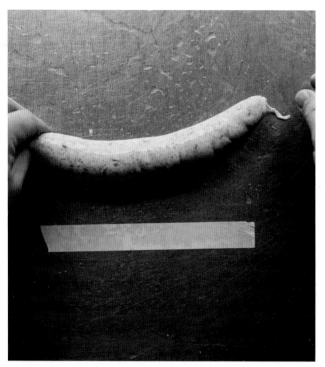

Measure the desired length of the sausage and mark your workspace with either a piece of tape or marker, ensuring consistency in the length of your links.

Then, keeping a hold on the pinched spot, slide one hand down to the beginning mark and pinch off the next length. Now, twist! Pick up the sausage, holding onto the two pinched spots, and swing it like a jump rope.

When you get to the end, tie it off with a simple knot.

Use a sausage poker to poke each sausage three times, or where air bubbles are visible. These tiny holes will allow the liquid to release while the sausages cook and prevent them from exploding.

STEP 10: TIE OFF AND TWIST

Tie off one end of the sausage, and twist making a simple knot.

Measure the desired length of the sausage and mark your workspace with either a piece of tape or marker, ensuring consistency in the length of your links. Starting from the tied-off end, use one hand to pinch at the appropriate length. Then, keeping a hold on the pinched spot, slide your other hand down to the beginning mark and pinch off the next length. Now, twist! Pick up the sausage, holding onto the two pinched spots and swing it like a jump rope. Repeat the process until no sausage remains. When you get to the end, tie it off with a simple knot.

Use a sausage poker to poke each sausage three times, or where air bubbles are visible. These tiny holes will allow the liquid to release while the sausages cook and prevent them from exploding.

As mentioned earlier, do not poke the sausages if you are planning to smoke them.

For best results, refrigerate the sausages overnight, uncovered, to dry out the casing. This will make the sausage slightly firmer to the touch and add ease for cooking. Snip the sausages at the twists to make them into separate links, or leave as a whole rope of links like those you might have seen in cartoons.

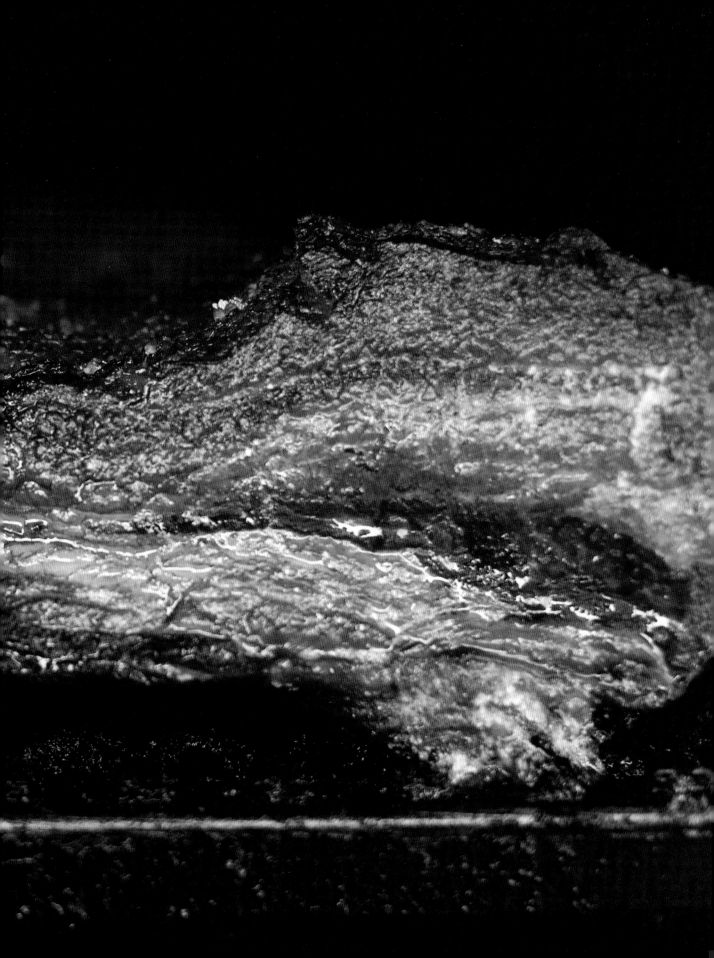

CHAPTER 2

STUFF

Making sausage doesn`t have to be an exact science. Instead it should feel more like a science experiment. Let`s say you`re getting bored of using pork as a main protein. Use lamb or beef or even give chicken a try. Just remember about the fat-to-meat ratio and compensate for lean (a.k.a. less fatty) meat when you substitute. In each recipe, we`ve offered the actual number of diameter that we use for grinding meat here in our shop, but as a home sausage chef, don`t feel the need to follow every recipe so exactly. Any medium-sized die will do if the recipe calls for it (even if it`s not exactly $1/32$), and any large hog casing will work just fine in a recipe that necessitates it.

HOMEMADE SAUSAGE

THE CLASSICS

Simply put, these sausages are classics. They're the ones that people count on at the grocery store, the ones that they eat week after week, and the ones that are recognizable, comfortable, and familiarly delicious. These sausages have likely made appearances on your dinner table at least one time before, they've been strong contenders for the grill at your family's backyard barbecue, and they might appear as a mere ingredient in one of your most famous recipes. These sausages are tried, and they are true.

When we initially opened the doors to our first shop in East Nashville back in 2011, these were the sausages that we selected as the residents of our display case. Our goal was to lure customers in using items they knew and trusted. Then, and only then, could we begin to steer them off the straight and narrow toward more unfamiliar territory. Because of the foundation that these sausages laid for our business, they hold special spots in our hearts, and we will always think of them as classics.

Breakfast Sausage

HOMEMADE
SAUSAGE

Our famous breakfast sausage is notoriously delicious due to its bold flavor, hint of sweetness, and tantalizing texture. (It's got whole, toasted fennel seeds suspended throughout.) It's amazing! Although we created our own version of this recipe, the idea came from the popular store-bought breakfast sausage that is readily available all over the United States. To uncover the secret recipe, James took a trip to the grocery store on a Sunday afternoon with a pad of paper and a marker in hand, and took notes on the information on back of the package. Then he walked right back out of the store. After a few rounds of trial and error, we landed on this perfect blend!

YIELD: 5 POUNDS (2.27 KG)/ 75 LINKS
DIE: 3/16 (MEDIUM)

1½ ounces (43 g) fennel seed

5 pounds (2.27 kg) pork

1½ ounces (43 g) salt

⅞ ounce (25 g) fresh ginger

¾ ounce (21 g) fresh sage

¼ ounce (7 g) red pepper flakes

⅓ ounce (9 g) brown sugar

⅓ ounce (9 g) ground black pepper

24–26 mm sheep casings (optional)

METHOD

1. In a large skillet over medium heat, toast the fennel until slightly golden and fragrant. Set aside to cool.

2. Dice the pork into small, 1-inch (2.5 cm) cubes.

3. In a large bowl, mix all of the other ingredients together with your hands until they are equally distributed.

4. Grind the mixture two times through a grinder on a medium die.

5. After each run through the grinder, use your hands to mix the ingredients together and fully emulsify the loose sausage. (The mixture should be sticky and well combined and the sausage should stick to your hand when it's turned upside down.)

6. Form the sausage into patties or keep it loose.

7. If you're stuffing the sausage into links, add the loose sausage mixture to the stuffer; pack it down to remove all air pockets.

8. Stuff the sausage into sheep casings and twist links 15 to 1 pound (455 g). (Generally, each sausage should be around 2 inches [5 cm] long.)

9. Lightly poke each sausage link with a poking tool about 2 times.

10. Put the twisted links in the refrigerator, uncovered, and allow them to set overnight to dry out the casings.

11. Snip the sausages at the seams to separate into links.

Kielbasa

HOMEMADE SAUSAGE

A traditional, fresh, Polish sausage, Kielbasa is incredibly flavorful and is near and dear to the hearts of true Polish folks—particularly those who are no longer living in a country where it is readily available. As it just so happens, our East Nashville neighbors, the owners of a small, family-owned dry-cleaning business, are Polish in origin. Therefore, we knew they would be perfect taste buds on which to test our Kielbasa. When we thought we had it right, we gave the family a couple of links to take home and sample, and the response we received was overwhelmingly positive. So overjoyed with finding a taste of home here in Nashville, the grandmother came back to the shop the next day just to give each one of us a "grandma mouth kiss," as we like to call it. After an experience like that, we knew we got it right.

YIELD: 5 POUNDS (2.27 KG)/ 10 LINKS
DIE: 3/16 (MEDIUM)

5 pounds (2.27 kg) pork

1½ ounces (43 g) salt

2⅓ ounces (66 g) garlic

⅔ ounce (19 g) fresh oregano

⅓ ounce (9 g) black pepper

29–32 mm hog casings

METHOD

1. Dice the pork into small, 1-inch (2.5 cm) cubes.

2. In a large bowl, mix all of the ingredients together with your hands until they are equally distributed.

3. Grind the mixture two times through a grinder on a medium die.

4. After each run through the grinder, use your hands to mix the ingredients together and fully emulsify the loose sausage. (The mixture should be sticky and well combined and the sausage should stick to your hand when it's turned upside down.)

5. Add the loose sausage mixture to the stuffer; pack down to remove all air pockets.

6. Stuff the sausage into the hog casings and twist links 2 to 1 pound (455 g). (Generally, each sausage should be around 8 to 9 inches [20 to 33 cm] long.)

7. Lightly poke each sausage link with a poking tool 3 to 5 times.

8. Put the twisted links in the refrigerator, uncovered, and chill overnight to dry out the casings.

9. Snip the sausages at the seams to separate them into links.

Italian Sausage:

Sweet or Spicy

Italian sausage is one of our favorite sausages to make for two main reasons. First, it is incredibly beautiful, and second, it is extremely versatile. When the ingredients are all mixed together, beautiful and bright colors emerge. There's vibrant green from the fresh herbs, a sharp contrasting red from the paprika and cayenne, and nice, bold flecks of dark black, deep red, and bright yellow from the various peppers. Plus, it's such an adaptable sausage when it comes to cooking that it works extremely well in a variety of arenas. We often like to leave it unstuffed so it can be browned and mixed into a pasta sauce, added into savory breakfast pinwheels, or even crumbled into a soup. Mangia!

YIELD: 5 POUNDS (2.27 KG)/ 15 LINKS
DIE: 3/16 (MEDIUM)

5 pounds (2.27 kg) pork

1½ ounces (43 g) salt

1⅛ ounces (32 g) sugar

½ ounce (14 g) fennel seed

¼ ounce (7 g) coriander

⅞ ounces (25 g) paprika

Pinch of cayenne

⅞ ounces (25 g) fresh oregano

⅞ ounces (25 g) fresh basil

½ ounce (14 g) red pepper flakes

¼ ounce (7 g) black pepper

29–32 mm hog casings

METHOD

1. Dice the pork into small, 1-inch (2.5 cm) cubes.

2. In a large bowl, mix all of the ingredients together with your hands until they are equally distributed.

3. Grind the mixture two times through a grinder on a medium die.

4. After each run through the grinder, use your hands to mix the ingredients together and fully emulsify the loose sausage. (The mixture should be sticky and well combined and should stick to your hand when it's turned upside down.)

5. Add the loose sausage mixture to the stuffer; pack it down to remove all air pockets.

6. Stuff the sausage into the hog casings and twist links 3 to 1 pound [455 g]. (Generally, each sausage should be 5 to 6 inches [13 to 15 cm] long.)

7. Lightly poke each sausage link with a poking tool 3 or 4 times.

8. Put the twisted links in the refrigerator, uncovered, and chill overnight to dry out the casings.

9. Snip the sausages at the seams to separate them into links.

Chorizo

HOMEMADE SAUSAGE

"Chorizo" is somewhat of a loaded term because the word means different things to different people. From Portugal, to Mexico, to Spain and beyond, this sausage has incredible variance from culture to culture. Traditional Mexican chorizo is sold fresh, meaning raw and uncooked, and it incorporates plenty of ancho chile and cumin into the ingredient list. Spanish chorizo, on the other hand, is dry cured and eaten more like a salumi, alongside cheese or even on its own, with a strong presence of paprika. What we've come up with for this recipe is like a mixture of the two. We took our favorite elements from both Mexican and Spanish chorizo and combined them into one to make a fresh chorizo that is truly unique to us.

YIELD: 5 POUNDS (2.27 KG)/ 15 LINKS
DIE: 3/16 (MEDIUM)

5 pounds (2.27 kg) pork

1½ ounces (43 g) salt

½ ounce (14 g) ancho chile powder

¼ ounce (7 g) paprika

¼ ounce (7 g) cayenne pepper

⅓ ounce (9 g) cumin

Pinch of fresh black pepper

⅝ ounce (18 g) garlic

¼ ounce (7 g) fresh oregano

29–32 mm hog casings

METHOD

1. Dice the pork into small, 1-inch (2.5 cm) cubes.

2. In a large bowl, mix all of the ingredients together with your hands until they are equally distributed.

3. Grind the mixture two times through a grinder on a medium die.

4. After each run through the grinder, use your hands to mix the ingredients together and fully emulsify the loose sausage. (The mixture should be sticky and well combined. The sausage should stick to your hand when it's turned upside down.)

5. Add the loose sausage mixture to the stuffer; pack it down to remove all air pockets.

6. Stuff the sausage into the hog casings and twist links 3 to 1 pound (455 g). (Generally, each sausage should be 5 to 6 inches [13 to 15 cm] long.)

7. Lightly poke each sausage link with a poking tool 3 or 4 times.

8. Put the twisted links in the refrigerator, uncovered, and chill overnight to dry out the casings.

9. Snip the sausages at the seams to separate them into links.

Sage Sausage

HOMEMADE SAUSAGE

When we opened our doors for the first time in November of 2011, Thanksgiving was just around the corner. We knew exactly what to do to get new customers in the door and to keep them coming back again, and again, and even again, so we gave the people what they wanted: classic Thanksgiving dinner sausage. When word got out about the incredible deliciousness of our Sage Sausage, a very trendy, local coffee shop asked us to make it for them to sell at breakfast, and we graciously obliged. Through both the coffee shop's support, and our customers' excellent taste in meat, Sage Sausage gained instant fame in Nashville. To this day, it is still one of our top-sellers during the holiday season, and we particularly like adding it to cornbread dressing or in the middle of a freshly baked biscuit.

YIELD: 5 POUNDS (2.27 KG)/ 15 LINKS
DIE: 3/16 (MEDIUM)

5 pounds (2.27 kg) pork

1½ ounces (43 g) salt

1½ ounces (43 g) fresh sage

1¾ ounces (50 g) fresh ginger

¾ ounces (21 g) garlic

1¾ ounces (50 g) fennel bulb

¼ ounce (7 g) black pepper

⅛ ounce (4 g) red pepper flakes

29–32 mm hog casings (optional)

METHOD

1. Dice the pork into small, 1-inch (2.5 cm) cubes.

2. In a large bowl, mix all of the ingredients together with your hands until they are equally distributed.

3. Grind the mixture two times through a grinder on a medium die.

4. After each run through the grinder, use your hands to mix the ingredients together and fully emulsify the loose sausage. (The mixture should be sticky and well combined, and should stick to your hand when it's turned upside down.)

5. Add the loose sausage mixture to the stuffer; pack it down to remove all air pockets.

6. Stuff the sausage into the hog casings and twist the links 3 to 1 pound (455 g). (Generally, each sausage should be 5 to 6 inches [13 to 15 cm] long.)

7. Lightly poke each sausage link with a poking tool 3 or 4 times.

8. Put the twisted links in the refrigerator, uncovered, and chill overnight to dry out the casings.

9. Snip the sausages at the seams to separate them into links.

British Bangers

HOMEMADE SAUSAGE

Necessitating a little creativity in the kitchen, World War I brought on food and meat rations that were enforced across Great Britain, leaving every family with less than they were accustomed to. In an effort to keep some sense of normalcy at mealtime and to keep their families feeling full, home chefs elected to make sausages with their small portions of rationed meat and stretched out the portions by adding bread and cereals to the mix. When the sausages were cooked, they were simply put in a cast-iron pot and set on top of a big, hot fire. As they finished and were ready to be eaten, they would hiss and pop and bang around in the pot—hence the name, British Bangers.

YIELD: 5 POUNDS (2.27 KG)/ 15 LINKS
DIE: 3/16 (MEDIUM)

5 pounds (2.27 kg) pork

1 ounce (28 g) white pepper

⅜ ounce (12.25 g) salt

¼ ounce (7 g) ground ginger

⅛ ounce (4 g) chopped fresh sage

¼ ounce (7 g) ground nutmeg

5½ ounces (156 g) dried breadcrumbs

29–32 mm hog casings

METHOD

1. Dice the pork into small, 1-inch (2.5 cm) cubes.

2. In a large bowl, mix all of the ingredients together with your hands until they are equally distributed.

3. Grind the mixture two times through a grinder on a medium die.

4. After each run through the grinder, use your hands to mix the ingredients together and fully emulsify the loose sausage. (The mixture should be sticky and well combined, and should stick to your hand when it's turned upside down.)

5. Add the loose sausage mixture to the stuffer; pack it down to remove all air pockets.

6. Stuff the sausage into the hog casings and twist the links 3 to 1 pound (455 g). (Generally, each sausage should be 5 to 6 inches [13 to 15 cm] long.)

7. Lightly poke each sausage link with a poking tool 3 or 4 times.

8. Put the twisted links in the refrigerator, uncovered, and chill overnight to dry out the casings.

9. Snip the sausages at the seams to separate them into links.

NOTE:
Pork stock is best if it`s made at home from raw pork bones and fresh ingredients. Homemade pork stock has great health benefits and a wonderful gelatinous texture unparalleled by store-bought brands. If you don`t have time to make pork stock, however, the store-bought variety will suffice.

Irish Bangers

HOMEMADE SAUSAGE

"We like Irish Bangers because they are sausages that are similar to British Bangers except they are way better because they have lots of herbs in them, which make them taste good. British Bangers are good, too, but they are more bland and easy to mask with other ingredients in a dish. Irish Bangers, on the other hand, are really, really delicious on their own, or as a classic 'Bangers and Mash' dish, served with some mashed taters."—Chris Carter

YIELD: 5 POUNDS (2.27 KG)/ 15 LINKS
DIE: 3/16 (MEDIUM)

5 pounds (2.27 kg) pork

⅓ ounce (9 g) fresh thyme

⅓ ounce (9 g) fresh rosemary

⅓ ounce (9 g) fresh basil

2 eggs

8 cloves garlic

⅓ ounce (9 g) fresh oregano

⅛ ounce (4 g) salt

¼ ounce (7 g) freshly ground black pepper

6 ounces (168 g) breadcrumbs

1 cup (235 ml) pork stock (See note at left.)

29–32 mm hog casings

METHOD

1. Dice the pork into small, 1-inch (2.5 cm) cubes.

2. In a large bowl, mix all of the other ingredients, except for the stock, together with your hands until they are equally distributed.

3. Grind the mixture two times through a grinder on a medium die.

4. After the first run through the grinder, use your hands to emulsify the mixture and fully combine the ingredients.

5. After the second grind, add the stock to the mixture, and then using your hands, mix the ingredients again thoroughly, until the mixture becomes sticky and fully combined. (The sausage should stick to your hand when it's turned upside down.)

6. Add the loose sausage mixture to the stuffer; pack it down to remove all air pockets.

7. Stuff the sausage into the hog casings and twist the links 3 to 1 pound (455 g). (Generally, each sausage should be 5 to 6 inches [13 to 15 cm] long.)

8. Lightly poke each sausage link with a poking tool 3 or 4 times.

9. Put the twisted links in the refrigerator, uncovered, and chill overnight to dry out the casings.

10. Snip the sausages at the seams to separate them into links.

Garlic and Parsley

HOMEMADE SAUSAGE

We've reiterated time and time again the importance of good quality meat and fresh ingredients when it comes to making sausages, and our Garlic and Parsley Sausage is a perfect example of why this rings true. It's almost like a "poster sausage" for using quality components. The recipe for Garlic and Parsley uses a few simple ingredients, all of which are likely to be sitting around your house already, but the end result is something fantastic. This simple sausage link proves that by putting in the effort on the front end, not much work is needed to enhance the flavors. Simply letting the ingredients speak for themselves is the best way to show off the deliciousness.

YIELD: 5 POUNDS (2.27 KG)/ 15 LINKS
DIE: 3/16 (MEDIUM)

5 pounds (2.27 kg) pork

1 ounce (28 g) salt

¼ ounce (8 g) freshly ground black pepper

1½ ounces (40.5 g) garlic

1 ounce (30 g) fresh parsley

Pinch of red pepper flakes

Pinch of lemon zest

29–32 mm hog casings

METHOD

1. Dice the pork into small, 1-inch (2.5 cm) cubes.

2. In a large bowl, mix all of the other ingredients together with your hands until they are equally distributed.

3. Grind the mixture two times through a grinder on a medium die.

4. After each run through the grinder, use your hands to mix the ingredients together and fully emulsify the loose sausage. (The mixture should be sticky and well combined, and should stick to your hand when it's turned upside down.)

5. Add the loose sausage mixture to the stuffer; pack it down to remove all of the air pockets.

6. Stuff the sausage into the hog casings and twist the links 3 to 1 pound (455 g). (Generally, each sausage should be 5 to 6 inches [13 to 15 cm] long.)

7. Lightly poke each sausage link with a poking tool 3 or 4 times.

8. Put the twisted links in the refrigerator, uncovered, and chill overnight to dry out the casings.

9. Snip the sausages at the seams to separate them into links.

THE OUTLAWS

Unlike the Classics, the sausages with which you are at least a little bit familiar, the Outlaws are sausages that you might never have heard of, or simply never thought to classify as sausages. This group of sausages makes up somewhat of a motley crew. Their origins vary, their frameworks differ vastly, and even their method of creation differs here and there.

The flavors and textures in the Outlaws are incredible. Some are new, and all are exciting, which is why we would never call them "the losers" or anything else that is similarly derogatory. Outlaws are law breakers, rule benders, and ones who fearlessly step outside the lines. They might be a little off the beaten path, but they're definitely worth the adventure. Take a walk on the wild side, and give one of these sausages a shot!

Kimchi Sausage

Kimchi is traditionally a Korean dish made of spicy-sour, fermented vegetables. It can be made by slicing or chopping cabbage, radish, or cucumber, layering the vegetables with plenty of bold spices, and then putting them into a clay pot and burying it in the ground for at least a month to ferment. Our customer and friend Alan Powel is a farmer who ferments kimchi in large batches for us to use. When he first brought it to us, we didn't necessarily know what *else* to do with a giant batch of fermented and spiced cabbage, so we decided to make a sausage out of it! That's what we call utilization, friends. It took us a handful of tries, a bunch of tweaking, and even a deconstruction of the kimchi to get the recipe just right, but now it is one of our favorites.

YIELD: 5 POUNDS (2.27 KG)/ 75 LINKS
DIE: 3/16 (MEDIUM)

5 pounds (2.27 kg) pork

1 cup (240 g) kimchi paste

1 tablespoon (15 ml) soy sauce

⅓ ounce (9 g) salt

⅓ ounce (9 g) black pepper

5½ ounces (156 g) roughly chopped cabbage

29–32 mm hog casings

METHOD

1. Dice the pork into small, 1-inch (2.5 cm) cubes.

2. In a large bowl, mix all of the other ingredients together with your hands until they are equally distributed.

3. Grind the mixture two times through a grinder on a medium die.

4. After each run through the grinder, use your hands to mix the ingredients together and fully emulsify the loose sausage. (The mixture should be sticky and well combined, and should stick to your hand when it's turned upside down.)

5. Add the loose sausage mixture to the stuffer; pack it down to remove all of the air pockets.

6. Stuff the sausage into the hog casings and twist the links 3 to 1 pound (455 g). (Generally, each sausage should be 5 to 6 inches [13 to 15 cm] long.)

7. Lightly poke each sausage link with a poking tool 3 or 4 times.

8. Put the twisted links in the refrigerator, uncovered, and chill overnight to dry out the casings.

9. Snip the sausages at the seams to separate them into links.

Potato Sausage

When James told fellow St. Louis chef Kevin Nashan that he and his new business partner were planning to open a butcher shop in Nashville, the James Beard–celebrated chef Nashan was eager to offer help. He handed over a 2-inch (5 cm) thick stack of papers, each one stamped with a recipe that he'd collected throughout his successful career. Having spent plenty of time abroad immersed in various cultures, and having apprenticed with countless famous chefs, Nashan had learned a thing or two in his day, and he was eager to pass along some knowledge. Potato Sausage was the first recipe we tried out of his stack of hundreds, and nearly three years later, we still love it.

YIELD: 4 POUNDS (1.8 KG)/ 12 LINKS
DIE: 3/16 (MEDIUM)

1½ pounds (680 kg) potatoes

4 pounds (1.8 kg) pork

1 ounce (28 g) salt

¼ ounce (7 g) black pepper

⅛ ounce (4 g) red pepper flakes

½ ounce (14 g) sugar

2 cloves garlic

½ cup (120 ml) white wine

29–32 mm hog casings

METHOD

1. Add the potatoes to a stockpot and cover them with cool water by 2 inches (5 cm). Bring to a boil and boil the potatoes until tender, about 15 minutes. Drain and cool. Pinch one end of a potato with all five of your fingers to pull the skin off. Dice the potato into small cubes. Repeat with the remaining potatoes and set aside. Meanwhile, as the potatoes are boiling, dice the pork into small, 1-inch (2.5 cm) cubes. Return it to the refrigerator to keep cool.

2. In a large bowl, mix all of the ingredients, except for the wine and potatoes, together with your hands.

3. Grind the mixed ingredients two times through a grinder on a medium die.

4. After each run through the grinder, use your hands to mix the ingredients together and fully emulsify the loose sausage. (The mixture should be sticky and well combined, and should stick to your hand when it's turned upside down.)

5. Add the wine and potatoes and use your hands to incorporate them. Mix the ingredients thoroughly until they are evenly blended.

6. Add the loose sausage mixture into the stuffing canister; pack it down to remove any air pockets.

7. Stuff the sausage into the hog casings and twist the links 3 to 1 pound (455 g). (Generally, each sausage should be 5 to 6 inches [13 to 15 cm] long.)

8. Lightly poke each sausage link with a poking tool 3 or 4 times.

9. Put the twisted links in the refrigerator, uncovered, and chill overnight to dry out the casings.

10. Snip the sausage at the seams to separate it into links.

Beef Bologna

HOMEMADE SAUSAGE

As whole animal butchers, we've learned that every part of the animal can be put to use somewhere and somehow, because throwing meat away is like throwing money into the trash—it hurts. When breaking down beef, for example, we extract all of the prime cuts first; then we dice down the rest of the meat and turn it into ground beef; and finally, we roast the bones and use them for stock and render down the fat to make into tallow. But what about those fatty pieces of trim that are pushed to the side during the breakdown of the beef, you ask? Well, we make it into bologna, of course! Fry up a piece of this in a pan and smear a little yellow mustard on some good, white bread, and it tastes like nostalgia.

YIELD: 10 POUNDS (4.5 KG)/1 LOG
DIE: 1/8 (SMALL)

10 pounds (4.5 kg) fatty beef

2 ounces (56 g) salt

1 ounce (28 g) pink salt

½ ounce (14 g) black pepper

½ ounce (14 g) white pepper

½ ounce (14 g) nutmeg

⅓ ounce (10 g) coriander

Pinch of dried bay leaves

½ ounce (16 g) garlic

Synthetic casings

METHOD

1. Dice the fatty beef into 1-inch (2.5 cm) cubes.

2. In a bowl, mix the salts together to create a cure. In a large bowl, toss the beef in the salt mixture, covering each piece. Put the beef in the fridge and cure it for two days.

3. Remove beef from the fridge and using your hands, mix it together with in a bowl with the remaining ingredients.

4. Grind the mixed ingredients four times through a grinder on a small die. Keep the mixture very cold during the grinding process. If the meat begins to lose its chill, return it to the refrigerator before continuing to grind it.

5. Using the largest sausage horn available on your sausage stuffer, stuff the ground meat into a bologna casing and tie it off at the end.

6. Create a large water bath, big enough to submerge the entire bologna roll, and bring the water temperature up to 150°F (70°C). *Note: A circulator is a tool that will help to maintain the temperature of the water and is vital for this style of cooking.*

Cook the bologna for 6 hours or until the internal temperature reaches 150°F (70°C). Or fill a slow cooker full of water and set it to the highest setting. Submerge the bologna roll in the water, taking care to tie the ends tightly to prevent water from seeping inside. After 2 hours, insert a thermometer into the center of the bologna to read the temperature. Continue checking the bologna every hour until the internal temperature reaches 150°F (70°C). Remove it from the water and put it directly into an ice bath (a large bowl of ice water) to stop the cooking process.

7. Let the bologna cool completely before removing the casing and/or slicing it.

Cotechino

HOMEMADE SAUSAGE

Pronounced koh-te-KEEN-oh, this Italian-in-origin sausage is a common mealtime staple at New Year's and served alongside lentils, which promise money and prosperity in the New Year. Dating as far back as the 1500s, incorporating the skin of the hog into this sausage was thought of as a great way to use scraps and reduce waste. Fortunately, because the skin is so gelatinous, and because we grind it on a larger diameter than the actual pork meat, the larger hunks of gelatinous skin add a great chewy texture and a good supply of fat to the sausage. That's why this sausage is so succulent and tasty. Who *wouldn't* want to ring in the New Year with something as good as this?

YIELD: 4 POUNDS (1.8 KG)/8 LINKS
DIE FOR PORK MEAT: 3/16 (MEDIUM)
DIE FOR PORK SKIN: 3/8 (LARGE)

4 pounds (1.8 kg) pork

1 pound (453 g) pork skin

2 ounces (56 g) salt

¼ ounce (7 g) black pepper

Pinch of coriander

Pinch of cloves

Pinch of cayenne

Pinch of allspice

³⁄₈ ounce (11 g) sugar

Pinch of nutmeg

29–32 mm hog casings

METHOD

1. Dice the pork into small, 1-inch (2.5 cm) cubes.

2. Separately, dice the pork skin into small, 1-inch (2.5 cm) pieces.

3. In a large bowl, mix all of the ingredients, except for the pork skin, together with your hands.

4. Run the pork skin through a grinder once, using a large die. Set aside.

5. Grind the mixed ingredients two times through a grinder on a medium die.

6. After each run through the grinder, use your hands to mix the ingredients together and fully emulsify the loose sausage. (The mixture should be sticky and well combined, and should stick to your hand when it's turned upside down.)

7. Add the ground pork skin and use your hands to incorporate it. Mix the ingredients thoroughly until they are evenly blended.

8. Add the loose sausage mixture into the stuffing canister; pack it down to remove any air pockets.

9. Stuff the sausage into the hog casings and twist the links 3 to 1 pound (453 g). (Generally, each sausage should be 5 to 6 inches [13 to 15 cm] long.)

10. Lightly poke each sausage link with a poking tool 3 or 4 times.

11. Put the twisted links in the refrigerator, uncovered, and chill overnight to dry out the casings.

12. Snip the sausages at the seams to separate them into links.

Chicken and Herb Sausage

HOMEMADE
SAUSAGE

Because chicken is naturally a very lean animal in comparison to say, pork, it doesn't leave a whole lot of fat for us to incorporate into sausage. As a way to integrate fat back into the meat and aid in emulsification, moisture, and deliciousness, we add butter. After all, butter makes everything better. One of our favorite things about Chicken and Herb Sausage is its deceptive nature. Because people think of chicken as a lean and healthy choice for meat, Chicken and Herb Sausage automatically falls into that category as well. Little do they know that part of the reason this link is so good is because of the buttery deliciousness that is mixed throughout. Oopsie!

YIELD: 5 POUNDS (2.27 KG)/ 15 LINKS
DIE: 3/16 (MEDIUM)

4½ pounds (2 kg) chicken, preferably boneless, skinless thighs

½ pound (227 g) butter

1½ ounces (43 g) salt

¼ ounce (7 g) black pepper

⅜ ounce (11 g) parsley

⅜ ounce (11 g) fresh chives

¼ ounce (7 g) fresh tarragon

¼ ounce (7 g) fresh oregano

¾ ounce (21 g) garlic

29–32 mm hog casings

METHOD

1. Dice the chicken into small, 1-inch (2.5 cm) cubes.

2. Cube the butter into small, ½-inch (1.25 cm) cubes.

3. In a large bowl, mix all of the ingredients together with your hands until they are equally distributed.

4. Grind the mixture two times through a grinder on a medium die.

5. After each run through the grinder, use your hands to mix the ingredients together and fully emulsify the loose sausage. (The mixture should be sticky and well combined, and should stick to your hand when it's turned upside down.)

6. Add the loose sausage mixture to the stuffer; pack it down to remove all the air pockets.

7. Stuff the sausage into the hog casings and twist the links 3 to 1 pound (455 g). (Generally, each sausage should be 5 to 6 inches [13 to 15 cm] long.)

8. Lightly poke each sausage link with a poking tool 3 or 4 times.

9. Put the twisted links in the refrigerator, uncovered, and chill overnight to dry out the casings.

10. Snip the sausages at the seams to separate them into links.

Asian Sausage

After being hired at the shop and working as a counter clerk for a couple weeks, Chad Curtis quickly became the number one fan of our PRB Beef Jerky. Since the job of marinating and dehydrating meat fell to him, the list of ingredients that made up said delicious jerky was soon memorized and when he was promoted to sausage maker, an idea was born. Chad knew that the Asian-style flavors that made up the jerky would translate to a dynamite sausage, so he ran his idea past the rest of the team, and together they came up with a trial batch. After changing some of the ingredients from the powdered variety to fresh and adjusting salt levels, the Asian Sausage was officially born and further became a staff favorite. This sausage goes wonderfully with rice, mixed with vegetables in a stir-fry, or crumbled and stuffed into a lettuce wrap.

YIELD: 5 POUNDS (2.27 KG)/ 15 LINKS
DIE: 3/16 (MEDIUM)

5 pounds (2.27 kg) pork

¾ ounce (21 g) salt

⅞ ounce (25 g) fresh ginger

¾ ounce (21 g) garlic

⅓ ounce (9 g) wasabi powder

1⅛ ounces (32 g) sugar

1⅛ ounces (32 g) sesame seeds

¼ ounce (7 g) red pepper flakes

2¼ ounces (64 g) scallions

4½ ounces (118 ml) soy sauce

29–32 mm hog casings

METHOD

1. Dice the pork into small, 1-inch (2.5 cm) cubes.

2. In a large bowl, mix all of the ingredients, except for the scallions and soy sauce, together with your hands until they are equally distributed.

3. Grind the mixture through a grinder one time on medium die. Add the soy sauce and mix into the meat with your hands until it is emulsified.

4. Grind the mixture again through a grinder on a medium die. Add the scallions, mix the ingredients together with your hands until the scallions are evenly distributed and the mixture is emulsified. (The mixture should be sticky and well combined, and should stick to your hand when it's turned upside down.)

5. Add the loose sausage mixture to the stuffer; pack it down to remove all of the air pockets.

6. Stuff the sausage into the hog casings and twist links 3 to 1 pound (455 g). (Generally, each sausage should be 5 to 6 inches [13 to 15 cm] long.)

7. Lightly poke each sausage link with a poking tool 3 or 4 times.

8. Put the twisted links in the refrigerator, uncovered, and chill overnight to dry out the casings.

9. Snip the sausages at the seams to separate them into links.

THE WURST

Contrary to how it may sound, "The Wurst" are most certainly not the *worst* of the sausages in our repertoire. Who would actually qualify a group like that in a book for other people to read? Conversely, these sausages are some of the best-selling and best tasting links that we`ve got up our sleeves.

While the presence of "wurst" in each name hints at a group of similar products with only slight variation, the variance among this group is quite pleasantly distinct. The South African Boerewors are beef-based, un-twisted sausages that are presented in a long, curving coil, the Currywurst are slightly sweet and cinnamon-scented and would make for an excellent Christmastime addition, and even though neither of us comes from the northern Midwest, we've been told that our Bratwursts blow anything from Milwaukee out of the water. Just sayin'... We hope you agree that ours are the best wursts ever.

When master chef and charcuterie genius Brian Polcyn traveled to Nashville to teach a class about charcuterie and sausages, we jumped at the opportunity to attend. Already hugging his James Beard–nominated book *Charcuterie* near and dear to our hearts, we were thrilled with the opportunity to learn firsthand about technique and spend the day with a culinary stud. We have since adopted his bratwurst recipe as our own, and our customers have absolutely fallen in love with it, calling it the best bratwurst they've ever had. What's more, we've even *improved* the recipe by using our farm fresh pork, free-range local eggs, and incredibly rich, locally made cream. We're certain that it's those simple tweaks that make our bratwurst stand out among the rest.

YIELD: 5 POUNDS (2.27 KG)/ 15 LINKS
DIE: 3/16 (MEDIUM)

5 pounds (2.27 kg) pork

1¾ ounces (50 g) salt

¼ ounce (7 g) white pepper

¼ ounce (7 g) ground ginger

¼ ounce (7 g) nutmeg

2 eggs

1 cup (236 ml) cream

29–32 mm hog casings

NOTE:
We also used this recipe for a cooking competition, but substituted smoked duck for pork. These Smoked Duck Bratwursts were amazing! Maybe one of the best wurst ever.

METHOD

1. Dice the pork into small, 1-inch (2.5 cm) cubes.

2. In a large bowl, mix all of the ingredients except for the eggs and cream together with your hands until they are equally distributed.

3. Grind the mixture two times through a grinder on a medium die.

4. After each run through the grinder, use your hands to mix the ingredients together and fully emulsify the loose sausage. (The mixture should be sticky and well combined, and should stick to your hand when it's turned upside down.)

5. Using your hands, add the cream and eggs. Mix the ingredients thoroughly, until the mixture becomes sticky and emulsified. (The sausage should stick to your hand when it's turned upside down.)

6. Add the loose sausage mixture to the stuffer; pack it down to remove all of the air pockets.

7. Stuff the sausage into the hog casings and twist links 3 to 1 pound (455 g). (Generally, each sausage should be 5 to 6 inches [13 to 15 cm] long.)

8. Lightly poke each sausage link with a poking tool 3 or 4 times.

9. Put the twisted links in the refrigerator, uncovered, and chill overnight to dry out the casings.

10. Snip the sausages at the seams to separate them into links.

Hot Brat[wurst]

It was summertime of 2012, when we realized that people had become familiar with our sausages and our products. "Maybe y'all ought to try doing something kind of fun," they implored, "like something spicy!" Talk about fun: a hot bratwurst. Because Chris is a weenie when it comes to spicy food, we waited until he was sunbathing by the pool to play around with spicing things up in the sausage department. Fortunately, the addition of cayenne pepper and red pepper flakes added just enough heat to jazz up our sausage selection, but not so much as to take Chris out. "I mean I *can* eat it," he says, "I'm just sweating the whole time I do." We'd call that a success.

YIELD: 5 POUNDS (2.27 KG)/ 15 LINKS
DIE: 3/16 (MEDIUM)

5 pounds (2.27 kg) pork

1¾ ounces (50 g) salt

¼ ounce (7 g) white pepper

¼ ounce (7 g) ground ginger

¼ ounce (7 g) nutmeg

Pinch of cayenne

½ ounce (14 g) red pepper flakes

2 eggs

1 cup (235 ml) cream

29–32 mm hog casings

METHOD

1. Dice the pork into small, 1-inch (2.5 cm) cubes.

2. In a large bowl, mix all of the ingredients except for the eggs and cream together with your hands until they are equally distributed.

3. Grind the mixture two times through a grinder on a medium die.

4. After each run through the grinder, use your hands to mix the ingredients together and fully emulsify the loose sausage.

5. After the second grind, add the cream and eggs. Mix the ingredients very thoroughly, until the mixture becomes sticky and emulsified. (The sausage should stick to your hand when it's turned upside down.)

6. Add the loose sausage mixture to the stuffer; pack it down to remove all of the air pockets.

7. Stuff the sausage into the hog casings and twist links 3 to 1 pound (455 g). (Generally, each sausage should be 5 to 6 inches [13 to 15 cm] long.)

8. Lightly poke each sausage link with a poking tool 3 or 4 times.

9. Put the twisted links in the refrigerator, uncovered, and chill overnight to dry out the casings.

10. Snip the sausage at the seams to separate them into links.

Winterwurst

HOMEMADE SAUSAGE

When the holidays roll around, everyone at the shop gets in the spirit. Chris's grandmother spends almost a whole day decking our halls with boughs of holly, Nashville gets transported back in time with our yearly revival of the traditional holiday Spiced Round, and we subsequently find ourselves longing for those spicy-sweet flavors in all of our December food. Cue the Winterwurst. In an effort to create a sausage that sings of the season, this Porter Road Butcher original variation is spiced with clove and allspice, giving it those familiar flavors that evoke Christmas so clearly.

YIELD: 5 POUNDS (2.27 KG)/ 15 LINKS
DIE: 3/16 (MEDIUM)

5 pounds (2.27 kg) pork

1½ ounces (42 g) salt

½ ounce (15 g) black pepper

⅓ ounce (9 g) coriander

¼ ounce (7 g) clove

¾ ounce (21 g) fresh oregano

¾ ounce (21 g) fresh parsley

¼ ounce (7 g) allspice

29–32 mm hog casings

METHOD

1. Dice the pork into small, 1-inch (2.5 cm) cubes.

2. In a large bowl, mix all of the ingredients together with your hands until they are equally distributed.

3. Grind the mixture two times through a grinder on a medium die.

4. After each run through the grinder, use your hands to mix the ingredients together and fully emulsify the loose sausage. (The mixture should be sticky and well combined, and should stick to your hand when it's turned upside down.)

5. Add the loose sausage mixture to the stuffer; pack it down to remove all of the air pockets.

6. Stuff the sausage into the hog casings and twist links 3 to 1 pound (455 g). (Generally, each sausage should be 5 to 6 inches [13 to 15 cm] long.)

7. Lightly poke each sausage link with a poking tool 3 or 4 times.

8. Put the twisted links in the refrigerator, uncovered, and chill overnight to dry out the casings.

9. Snip the sausages at the seams to separate them into links.

Currywurst

Created more than 100 years ago, Currywurst is an iconic food of German pop culture, and it is still served to this day as a favorite German street food. The dish is unapologetically uncomplicated, and it consists of just three main ingredients: a steamed and/or fried pork sausage and some variation of ketchup, which is mixed with curry powder. Our Currywurst is quite a bit different from the German street food sweetheart, because we mix garam masala into the pork and leave any sort of saucy tomatoes out of the equation. This Currywurst sausage has a beautiful balance of sweet and savory, and it tastes great straight off of the grill or out of the oven.

YIELD: 5 POUNDS (2.27 KG)/ 15 LINKS
DIE: 3/16 (MEDIUM)

5 pounds (2.27 kg) pork

7 ounces (198 g) salt

¼ ounce (7 g) white pepper

¼ ounce (7 g) ground ginger

¼ ounce (7 g) ground nutmeg

⅓ ounce (9 g) garam masala

2 eggs

1 cup (235 ml) cream

29–32 mm hog casings

METHOD

1. Cut the pork into small, 1-inch (2.5 cm) cubes.

2. In a large bowl, mix all of the ingredients except for the eggs and cream with your hands until they are equally distributed.

3. Grind the mixture two times through a grinder on a medium die.

4. After each run through the grinder, use your hands to mix the ingredients together and fully emulsify the loose sausage. (The mixture should be sticky and well combined, and should stick to your hand when it's turned upside down.)

5. Using your hands, add the cream and eggs. Mix the ingredients very thoroughly, until the mixture becomes sticky and emulsified; the sausage should stick to your hand when it's turned upside down.

6. Add the loose sausage mixture to the stuffer; pack it down to remove all of the air pockets.

7. Stuff the sausage into the hog casings and twist links 3 to 1 pound (455 g). (Generally, each sausage should be 5 to 6 inches [13 to 15 cm] long.)

8. Lightly poke each sausage link with a poking tool 3 or 4 times.

9. Put the twisted links in the refrigerator, uncovered, and chill overnight to dry out the casings.

10. Snip the sausage at the seams to separate them into links.

Knackwursts

Admittedly, Knackwursts are not familiar sausages to customers who frequent our shop because veal is something that we (almost) never ever carry. But when Hatcher Family Dairy Farm—the folks who provide us with our delicious local milk—had a dairy cow that calved a male, they knew what to do with him. They decided to finish the male calf on both pasture and on his mother's milk, the most humane way possible, and then sell him to us. So when we got this very special kind of meat into our shop, we knew we had to seize the opportunity to do something great and traditional: Knackwursts.

YIELD: 4 POUNDS (1.8 KG)/ 12 LINKS
DIE: 3/16 (MEDIUM)

4 pounds (1.8 kg) veal

⅝ ounce (18 g) salt

⅛ ounce (4 g) pink salt

¼ ounce (7 g) black pepper

Pinch of nutmeg

⅛ ounce (4 g) paprika

Pinch of coriander

Pinch of allspice

1 ounce (28 g) milk powder

29–32 mm hog casings

METHOD

1. Cut the veal into small, 1-inch (2.5 cm) cubes.

2. In a large bowl, mix all of the ingredients together with your hands until they are equally distributed.

3. Grind the mixture two times through a grinder on a medium die.

4. After each run through the grinder, use your hands to mix the ingredients together and fully emulsify the loose sausage. (The sausage should stick to your hand when it is turned upside down.)

5. Add the loose sausage mixture to the stuffer; pack it down to remove all of the air pockets.

6. Stuff the sausage into the hog casings and twist links 3 to 1 pound (455 g). (Generally, each sausage should be 5 to 6 inches [13 to 15 cm] long.)

7. Lightly poke each sausage link with a poking tool 3 or 4 times.

8. Put the twisted links in the refrigerator, uncovered, and chill overnight to dry out the casings.

9. Snip the sausages at the seams to separate them into links.

Bacon Jalapeño Bratwurst

HOMEMADE
SAUSAGE

When our friends from Old School Farm (OSF) showed up at our shop in the summer of 2014 with mountains of jalapeños, we came up with a fantastic idea that would use both our unsightly bacon ends and their excess spicy pepper crop. Always up for some good old-fashioned bartering, we explained our plan to OSF. We got to take every last jalapeño off of their hands at little to no cost, and in exchange they received Bacon Jalapeño Bratwursts and Porter Road Butcher hamburgers for their Friday Night Farm Dances. So they were able to enjoy the fruits of their bounty after all! We all shook hands, and the deal was done. Bacon Jalapeño Bratwursts have been a fan favorite ever since.

YIELD: 5 POUNDS (2.27 KG)
15 LINKS
DIE: 3/16 (MEDIUM)

3.75 pounds (1.7 kg) pork

1.25 pounds (567 g) bacon

1½ ounces (43 g) salt

¼ ounce (7 g) white pepper

¼ ounce (7 g) powdered ginger

¼ ounce (7 g) ground nutmeg

1¾ ounces (50 g) jalapeños

1 cup (235 ml) cream

2 eggs

2 ounces (55 g) scallions, sliced

29–32 mm hog casings

METHOD

1. Dice the pork and bacon into small, 1-inch (2.5 cm) cubes.

2. In a large bowl, mix all of the ingredients together, except for the eggs, cream, and scallions, until they are equally distributed.

3. Grind the mixture two times through a grinder on a medium die.

4. After each run through the grinder, use your hands to mix the ingredients together and fully emulsify the loose sausage.

5. Following the second grind, use your hands to add the cream, eggs, and scallions. Mix the ingredients thoroughly, until the mixture becomes sticky and emulsified. (The sausage should stick to your hand when it's turned upside down.)

6. Stuff the sausage into the hog casings and twist links 3 to 1 pound. (Generally, each sausage should be 5 to 6 inches [13 to 15 cm] long.)

7. Lightly poke each sausage link with a poking tool 3 or 4 times.

8. Put the twisted links in the refrigerator, uncovered, and chill overnight to dry out the casings.

9. Snip the sausages at the seams to separate them into links.

South African Boerewors

HOMEMADE SAUSAGE

Sausage is one of those foods that for many people is extremely nostalgic. Because it is often born as the love child of leftover yet traditional scraps of food, sausage holds memories and stories. With so many fond flavors in one bite, this makes sausage into a crown jewel of flavor. This recipe for Boerewors came to us from a customer who had recently relocated to Nashville from South Africa and was desperate for a taste of home—for a taste of tradition. Her butcher in South Africa actually sent her the recipe, and she brought it to us, hopeful that we would be able to grant her wish. We did, and we loved it. And so did she.

**YIELD: 4 POUNDS (1.8 KG)/
1 SPIRAL LINK
DIE: 3/16 (MEDIUM)**

3 pounds (1.4 kg) beef

1 pound (455 g) pork fat

1¾ ounces (50 g) salt

⅛ ounce (4 g) black pepper

1⅛ ounces (32 g) coriander

Pinch of ground cloves

Pinch of nutmeg

29–32 mm hog casings

METHOD

1. In a large bowl, mix all of the ingredients together with your hands until they are evenly distributed.

2. Grind the mixture two times through a grinder on a medium die.

3. Using your hands, mix the ingredients again thoroughly until they become sticky and emulsified. (The sausage should stick to your hand when it's turned upside down.)

4. Add the loose sausage mixture to the stuffer; pack it down to remove all of the air pockets.

5. Stuff the sausage into the hog casings and do not twist. Instead, spiral it into one tight coil.

6. Lightly poke the entire spiral roughly every 3 inches (7.5 cm), starting from the center of the spiral and working all the way to the end.

7. Put the sausage spiral into the refrigerator, uncovered, and chill overnight to dry out the casings.

THE LITTLE LAMBS

Because lambs are significantly smaller animals than hogs, and because pork is usually the main protein that we use for making sausages, when it comes to lamb sausage, our repertoire of original lamb sausage recipes is also significantly smaller. The four recipes that we have listed here are all very different, but each one is incredibly flavorful and robust. Because people can be fearful of the gamier, sweeter, and overall stronger flavor of lamb in comparison to the well-known and familiar pork flavor, that fear *can* then prevent them from trying lamb sausages, but we`re here to tell you that it shouldn`t.

The sweet flavor of lamb, mixed with the compilation of incredibly robust ingredients used here, make these sausages true standouts—in the best meaning of the word.

Lamb Merguez

HOMEMADE SAUSAGE

Lamb Merguez is a traditional North African sausage that is heavily seasoned, oftentimes spicy, and always rich in flavor. These sausages are particularly popular in Morocco, and they are commonly served with traditional fare such as couscous, white beans, or vegetables. With such a rich and hearty flavor profile, however, Merguez is equally delicious served all by itself; it can win over the audience without much support from the chorus line. Absent in our Merguez is the traditional North African spice, harissa, which makes our version milder in heat, but still full in flavor. If you're a heat lover, however, feel free to bring on the harissa in your recipe!

YIELD: 5 POUNDS (2.27 KG)/ 15 LINKS
DIE: 3/16 (MEDIUM)

5 pounds (2.27 kg) lamb

1½ ounces (43 g) salt

¼ ounce (7 g) black pepper

⅓ ounce (9 g) red pepper flakes

½ ounce (14 g) sweet paprika

¼ ounce (7 g) cumin

⅝ ounce (18 g) garlic

½ ounce (14 g) fresh oregano

Pinch of fresh thyme

⅝ ounce (18 g) scallions

29–32 mm hog casings

METHOD

1. In a large bowl, mix all of the ingredients together with your hands until they are equally distributed.

2. Grind the mixture two times through a grinder on a medium die.

3. Using your hands, mix the ingredients again thoroughly until the mixture becomes sticky and emulsified. (The sausage should stick to your hand when it's turned upside down.)

4. Add the loose sausage mixture to a stuffer; pack it down to remove all of the air pockets.

5. Stuff the sausage into the hog casings and twist links 3 to 1 pound (455 g). (Generally, each sausage should be 5 to 6 inches [13 to 15 cm] long.)

6. Lightly poke each sausage link with a poking tool 3 or 4 times.

7. Put the twisted links in the refrigerator, uncovered, and chill overnight to dry out the casings.

8. Snip the sausages at the seams to separate them into links.

Lamb Diablo

HOMEMADE SAUSAGE

It was a Wednesday afternoon in October, when we had broken down two lambs and were left with plenty of meat that was ready to be ground, stuffed, and twisted into Lamb Merguez sausage links . . . until we realized we were short on ingredients. With the absence of oregano, Merguez sausage was taken off the table, but time was working against us as we brainstormed ideas for a new lamb sausage. James proposed a spicy lamb sausage—to excite the taste buds of those who love the heat—and his idea paid off. After we sold out of the first batch, people began inquiring for more, and soon Lamb Diablo became a steadfast staple sausage.

YIELD: 5 POUNDS (2.27 KG)/ 15 LINKS
DIE: 3/16 (MEDIUM)

5 pounds (2.27 kg) lamb, cut into 1-inch (2.5 cm) cubes

1¾ ounces (50 g) salt

⅓ ounce (10 g) black pepper

1 ounce (28 g) garlic

13 ounces (364 g) chopped onion

½ cup (120 g) sambal (chili paste)

29–32 mm hog casings

METHOD

1. In a large bowl, mix all of the ingredients together with your hands until they are equally distributed.

2. Grind the mixture two times through a grinder on a medium die.

3. Using your hands, mix the ingredients again thoroughly until the mixture becomes sticky and emulsified. (The sausage should stick to your hand when it's turned upside down.)

4. Add the loose sausage mixture to the stuffer; pack it down to remove all of the air pockets.

5. Stuff the sausage into the hog casings and twist links 3 to 1 pound (455 g). (Generally, each sausage should be 5 to 6 inches [13 to 15 cm] long.)

6. Lightly poke each sausage link with a poking tool 3 or 4 times.

7. Put the twisted links in the refrigerator, uncovered, and chill overnight to dry out the casings.

8. Snip the sausages at the seams to separate them into links.

Lamb Chumichurri

HOMEMADE SAUSAGE

Chimichurri is one of our favorite things. You could say we have an obsession with it. It's flavorful, fresh-tasting, and best of all, versatile. With fresh herbs as the foundation of this sauce, chimichurri works well on steak, would easily jazz up a side of sad-looking vegetables, and could even be used to make a quick and easy, light pasta sauce. The only thing we don't like about chimichurri is all the chopping. That's why putting it into a sausage makes so much sense. The grinder does all the chopping for you. This sausage is great on the grill, *and* with a side of chimichurri.

YIELD: 5 POUNDS (2.27 KG)/ 15 LINKS
DIE: 3/16 (MEDIUM)

5 pounds (2.27 kg) lamb

1½ ounces (43 g) salt

¼ ounce (7 g) black pepper

⅛ ounce (4 g) red pepper flakes

⅞ ounce (25 g) garlic

⅞ ounce (25 g) fresh oregano

1¾ ounces (50 g) fresh parsley

29–32 mm hog casings

METHOD

1. In a large bowl, mix all of the ingredients together with your hands until they are equally distributed.

2. Grind the mixture two times through a grinder on a medium die.

3. Using your hands, mix the ingredients again thoroughly until the mixture becomes sticky and emulsified. (The sausage should stick to your hand when it's turned upside down.)

4. Add the loose sausage mixture to the stuffer; pack it down to remove all of the air pockets.

5. Stuff the sausage into the hog casings and twist links 3 to 1 pound (455 g). (Generally, each sausage should be 5 to 6 inches [13 to 15 cm] long.)

6. Lightly poke each sausage link with a poking tool 3 or 4 times.

7. Put the twisted links in the refrigerator, uncovered, and chill overnight to dry out the casings.

8. Snip the sausages at the seams to separate them into links.

Lambdouille

Lamb is harder to sell than other types of meat because it has a stronger, sweeter, and somewhat earthier flavor. We've come to find that people either love it or seriously do not. Once the main cuts like loin chops, rack of lamb, and leg of lamb have sold out, we either have to work hard to sell what's left or figure out what to do with the meat before it goes bad. Itching for something new to play around with and tired of the same ole Merguez that we often employ for lamb, the guys at the East Nashville shop came up with this smoky, lamb-centric version of the Louisiana classic Andouille, and we've got to say: it's delicious. The play-on-words certainly doesn't hurt, either.

YIELD: 5 POUNDS (2.27 KG)/ 15 LINKS
DIE: 3/8 (LARGE)

5 pounds (2.27 g) lamb

1½ ounces (43 g) salt

Pinch of pink salt

Pinch of ground white pepper

⅓ ounce (9 g) cumin

1 ounce (28 g) ancho chile powder

Pinch of cayenne

¼ ounce (7 g) paprika

2 ounces (56 g) milk powder

¼ cup (60 ml) ice water

Pinch of sliced scallions

29–32 mm hog casings

METHOD

1. In a large bowl, mix all of the ingredients, except for the water and scallions, together with your hands until they are equally distributed.

2. Grind the mixture once a through grinder on a large die.

3. Using your hands, add the scallions and mix into the once-ground mixture. Once it is completely combined, run the mixture through the grinder one more time on the same medium die.

4. Add the ice water to the mixture and then use your hands to incorporate the water into ground sausage mix. Combine it thoroughly, until the mixture becomes sticky and emulsified.

5. Add the loose sausage mixture to the stuffer; pack it down to remove all of the air pockets.

6. Stuff the sausage into the hog casings and twist links 3 to 1 pound (455 g). (Generally, each sausage should be 5 to 6 inches [13 to 15 cm] long.) Do not poke.

7. Put the twisted links in the refrigerator, uncovered, and chill overnight to dry out the casings.

8. Smoke the sausages at 225°F (107°C) for 1 hour, or until the internal temperature is 150°F (65°C).

9. Cool the sausages completely and then snip them at the seams to separate them into links.

In the sausage world, however, smokers are coveted, glorified, and overall desirable and delicious. In the sausage world, "smokers" aren't classified as people who smoke; they are classified as sausages that are smoked by people.

In reality, any sausage in the whole entire world could be thrown on the smoker and given that extra layer of rich, woody, delicious flavor. For that matter, almost any consumable product could be afforded said opportunity, but the following three links are our go-tos when it comes to the smoker—meaning, they are always smoked, and they are never served fresh. These sausages emerge from the clouds with slightly taught skin and beautiful char marks that get our mouths watering and our nostrils flaring.

THE SMOKERS

Ah, the smokers. In today's modern and health-conscious age, smoking—and consequently people who smoke—are often frowned upon because of the damage done to their lungs and speedy deterioration of their health.

Sure, we like to stick to tradition when it comes to food, but on the other hand, it can also be fun to step out, take the road less traveled, and try something new every now and again. Any Louisiana native will immediately notice one major difference in our Andouille: i'ts noticeably smaller size, as opposed to the horseshoe-shaped full pound (455 g) link they're used to back home. The flavors however, do come closer to the classic Cajun link. Our Andouille can be used in a variety of ways to add some incredible smoke and richness to any dish.

YIELD: 5 POUNDS (2.27 KG)/ 15 LINKS
DIE: 3/8 (LARGE)

5 pounds (2.27 kg) pork

1½ ounces (43 g) salt

¼ ounce (7 g) pink salt

Pinch of ground white pepper

¼ ounce (7 g) cumin

⅞ ounce (25 g) ancho chile powder

Pinch of cayenne

¼ ounce (7 g) paprika

2 ounces (57 g) milk powder

¼ cup (60 ml) ice water

Pinch of sliced scallions

29–32 mm hog casings

METHOD

1. In a large bowl, mix all of the ingredients, except for the water and scallions, together with your hands until they are equally distributed.

2. Grind the mixture once through a grinder on a large die.

3. Using your hands, add the scallions and mix them into the once-ground mixture. Once completely combined, grind the mixture through the grinder one more time on the same large die.

4. Add the ice water to the mixture and then use your hands to incorporate the water into the ground sausage mix. Combine it thoroughly, until the mixture becomes sticky and emulsified.

5. Add the loose sausage mixture to the stuffer; pack it down to remove all of the air pockets.

6. Stuff the sausage into the hog casings and twist links 3 to 1 pound (455 g). (Generally, each sausage should be 5 to 6 inches [13 to 15 cm] long. Do not poke.

7. Put the twisted links in the refrigerator, uncovered, and chill overnight to dry out the casings.

8. Smoke the sausages at 225°F (107°C) for 1 hour, or until the internal temperature is 150°F (65°C).

9. Cool the sausages completely and then snip them at the seams to separate them into links.

Summer Sausage

HOMEMADE SAUSAGE

The first time that we decided to make Summer Sausage just so happened to fall on a pretty big day of the year: Super Bowl Sunday, which, oddly enough, is not in the summer. Because we had to order special casings for this particular type of sausage, we chose to go all out in light of the event and ordered football-shaped casings, laces and all. When we stuffed and then smoked the sausages and they came out looking like footballs, we were sure they would sell out quickly, and we were right—despite the fact that one of our employees accidentally labeled them "Surper Bowl Sausages" in our case. This smoky sausage pairs well with cheese and crackers, plenty of good beer, and of course, football.

YIELD: 5 POUNDS (2.27 KG)/ 5 LINKS
DIE: 1/8 (SMALL)

5 pounds (2.27 kg) beef

1 ounce (28 g) mustard

2 ounces (57 g) garlic

⅓ ounce (9 g) coriander

⅛ ounce (4 g) red pepper flakes

⅛ ounce (4 g) black pepper

2 42–45 mm large hog casings

METHOD

1. Dice the beef into small, 1-inch (2.5 cm) cubes.

2. In a large bowl, mix all of the ingredients together with your hands until they are equally distributed.

3. Grind the mixed ingredients four times through a grinder on a small die. Keep the mixture *very* cold during the grinding process; if the meat begins to lose its chill, return it to the refrigerator before continuing to grind.

4. Add the loose sausage mixture to the stuffer; pack it down to remove all of the air pockets.

5. Stuff the ground meat into a large hog casing and tie it off at the end. Twist into five 1-pound (455 g) links. Do not poke the links. The links should be around 12 inches (30.5 cm) in length.

6. Put the sausage in the fridge, uncovered, overnight to allow the sausage to set and the casings to dry out.

7. Smoke the sausages at 225°F (107°C) for 1½ to 2 hours.

8. Cool the sausages completely. Slice thinly and use as a topping for pizza or sandwich meat.

Porteroni

HOMEMADE SAUSAGE

Porteroni is our version of a classic pepperoni, and it's pretty much as simple as that. Although pepperoni is traditionally cured meat, our Porteroni is semi-cured and then smoked, giving it a similar consistency to that of pepperoni, and just as long of a shelf life. Pepperoni is usually made from a mixture of beef and pork—serving as a way to use up scraps of animals and turning it into one of our favorite pizza toppings—but for Porteroni we stick to purely beef. Try it on top of a pizza, as a filling for calzone, or even in an omelet! It brings a bold flavor to everything it touches.

YIELD: 5 POUNDS (2.27 KG)/ 5 LINKS
DIE: 1/8 (SMALL)

5 pounds (2.27 kg) fatty beef

1 ounce (28 g) salt

½ ounce (14 g) pink salt

¾ ounce (21 g) sugar

½ ounce (14 g) red pepper flakes

½ ounce (14 g) hot paprika

½ ounce (14 g) sweet paprika

¼ ounce (7 g) cayenne

¾ ounce (21 g) fennel seed, toasted and ground

¾ ounce (21 g) garlic

2 42–45 mm large hog casings

METHOD

1. Dice the fatty beef into 1-inch (2.5 cm) cubes.

2. In a bowl, mix the salt and pink salt together to create a cure.

3. In a large bowl, toss the fatty beef in the salt mixture, covering each piece. Put the beef in the fridge and cure it for two days.

4. Remove the beef from the fridge and using your hands, mix it together with the remaining ingredients.

5. Grind the mixed ingredients four times through a grinder on a small die. Keep the mixture very cold during the grinding process; if the meat begins to lose its chill, return it to the refrigerator before continuing to grind.

6. Add the loose sausage mixture to the stuffer; pack it down to remove all of the air pockets.

7. Stuff the ground meat into a large hog casing and tie it off at the end. Twist it into five 1-pound (455 g) links. Do not poke the links. The links should be around 12 inches (30 cm) in length.

8. Put the sausage in the fridge, uncovered, overnight to allow the sausage to set and the casings to dry out.

9. Smoke the sausages at 225°F (107°C) for 1½ to 2 hours.

10. Allow the sausages to cool completely. Slice thinly and use as a topping for pizza or sandwich meat.

As a butcher shop that was born in Tennessee, our Southern pride is no different than any other Southern soul's and we display our pride through our food—sausage included. These sausages show that they are Southern through the ingredients they require and the memories they evoke.

Whether it's "Rocky Top" that's your anthem, "Georgia on my Mind" that brings you right back home, or "Sweet Home Alabama" that gets your toe a-tappin', any Southerner from any of our hot and humid states will feel a little more at home with the following recipes.

THE SOUTHERNERS

If you took a survey of the southern half of the United States, you would likely find a wide variation in culture across the board. You would notice a difference in the local accents, a difference in the traditional food, a difference in the favored music, and even a difference in the common entertainment, which would vary from city to city, and state to state. But if there`s one thing that southerners all have in common, it`s their pride for being just that: Southern.

Louisiana Hot Links

HOMEMADE
SAUSAGE

Back in Porter Road Butcher's early days, we noticed an influx of customers hailing from New Orleans who continually patronized our shop. Coming from a land where fresh sausages and local butchers weren't the same kind of novelty that ours was (and still is) in Nashville, they expected to find products in our case similar to those they would find in the meat markets from their homeland. And though we did have a mean Andouille to offer them, we received quite a few inquiries for spicy Louisiana links. So we obliged. Hey, it's always fun to have an excuse to experiment! We found the list of ingredients on a grocery store reconnaissance, and soon our New Orleans native customers left the shop with a giant smile on their faces and fire in their eyes and bellies.

YIELD: 5 POUNDS (2.27 KG)/ 15 LINKS
DIE: 3/16 (MEDIUM)

5 pounds (2.27 kg) pork

1½ ounces (43 g) salt

¼ ounce (7 g) black pepper

⅛ ounce (4 g) cayenne pepper

½ ounce (14 g) red pepper flakes

⅞ ounce (25 g) hot paprika

¼ ounce (7 g) garlic powder

Pinch of allspice

Pinch of dried bay leaves

½ ounce (14 g) mustard seed

29–32 mm hog casings

METHOD

1. In a large bowl, mix all of the ingredients together with your hands until they are equally distributed.

2. Grind the mixture two times through a grinder on a medium die.

3. Using your hands, mix the ingredients again thoroughly until they become sticky and emulsified. (The sausage should stick to your hand when it's turned upside down.)

4. Add the loose sausage mixture to the stuffer; pack it down to remove all of the air pockets.

5. Stuff the sausage into the hog casings and twist links 3 to 1 pound (455 g). (Generally, each sausage should be 5 to 6 inches [13 to 15 cm] long.)

6. Lightly poke each sausage link with a poking tool 3 or 4 times.

7. Put the twisted links in the refrigerator, uncovered, and chill overnight to dry out the casings.

8. Snip the sausage at the seams to separate them into links.

Memphis Sausage

HOMEMADE SAUSAGE

Back in his college days, Chris Carter was known among his group of friends for being a whiz on the barbecue. He was skilled with cooking and grilling meat, and he and his friend's original barbecue rub was loved by all who were fortunate to have a taste. Many years later when said friend, Chris Hudgens, was hired on as one of Porter Road Butcher's first employees, Hudge immediately felt nostalgic to be working in the kitchen with his old barbecuing friend Carter, and even more so to be using that same BBQ rub in the shop. With the title of "sausage maker" handed to him after a few short months, Hudge couldn't hold in his longing for Memphis BBQ much longer, and thus decided to pay tribute to his hometown with a Memphis-style BBQ Sausage.
This link is one of our bestsellers during the summer months. It's perfect for grilling and easily brings that big, bold, savory-sweet BBQ flavor to the party without all of the fuss.

YIELD: 5 POUNDS (2.27 KG)/ 5 LINKS
DIE: 3/16 (MEDIUM)

5 pounds (2.27 kg) pork

⅓ ounce (9 g) fresh black pepper

⅓ ounce (9 g) white pepper

1½ ounces (43 g) salt

2½ ounces (71 g) brown sugar

¾ ounce (21 g) smoked paprika

¼ ounce (7 g) red pepper flakes

3⅓ ounces (94 g) scallions

¼ ounce (7 g) garlic

¼ ounce (7 g) ancho chile powder

1 ounce (30 ml) bourbon

1 ounce (28 g) mustard

½ ounce (14 g) honey

½ ounce (14 g) tomato paste

29–32 mm hog casings

METHOD

1. In a large bowl, add all of the ingredients except for the bourbon, mustard, honey, and tomato paste. Mix them together with your hands until they are equally distributed.

2. Grind the mixture two times through a grinder on a medium die.

3. Add the wet ingredients (bourbon, mustard, honey, and tomato paste) to the ground mixture and mix thoroughly, until the mixture becomes sticky and emulsified. (The sausage should stick to your hand when it's turned upside down.)

4. Add the loose sausage mixture to the stuffer; pack it down to remove all of the air pockets.

5. Stuff the sausage into the hog casings and twist links 3 to 1 pound (455 g). (Generally, each sausage should be 5 to 6 inches [13 to 15 cm] long.)

6. Put the twisted links in the refrigerator, uncovered, and chill overnight to dry out the casings.

7. Snip the sausage at the seams to separate them into links.

Boudin

Similar to chorizo, Boudin is a sausage that can't firmly connect its name to one specific product or list of ingredients. The components that make up this sausage differ based upon the prefix or suffix that accompanies it, as well as the place of origin. Boudin noir, dark and red in appearance, is a "blood sausage" that actually necessitates pork blood in an effort to make the sausage rich, moist, and velvety in texture. Boudin blanc, on the other hand, eliminates blood from the equation and only uses white meat like chicken or other poultry. Our Boudin, unlike either of the formerly mentioned French-style Boudin sausages, has more Cajun tendencies, incorporating rice, pork liver, and hot sauce to bring out those beloved Louisiana flavors.

YIELD: 4 POUNDS (1.8 KG)/12 LINKS
DIE: 3/16 (MEDIUM)

4 pounds (1.8 kg) pork

1 pound (455 g) pork liver

2 onions, roughly chopped

½ head celery, roughly chopped

½ red bell pepper, roughly chopped

10 cloves garlic, roughly chopped

¼ cup (60 ml) Worcestershire sauce

¾ cup (175 ml) hot sauce

3 bay leaves

1½ teaspoons gumbo file powder

1 tablespoon (5.3 g) cayenne pepper

½ cup (120 g) Creole mustard

8 cups (½ gallon, [1.9 L]) pork stock

4 cups (780 g) medium-grain rice

3⅓ ounces (100 g) scallions

1¼ ounces (35 g) fresh parsley

29–32 mm hog casings

METHOD

1. Separately cut the pork and pork liver into small, 1-inch (2.5 cm) cubes.

2. Over medium-high heat, brown the pork in a large stockpot. Once browned, add the onion, celery, bell pepper, and garlic and cook until translucent.

3. Add the cubed pork livers and sauté until browned.

4. Add the remaining ingredients, except for the rice, scallions, and parsley, and simmer over low heat for 4 hours.

5. Using a colander or large strainer, strain the meat mixture from the cooking liquid. Be sure to reserve the cooking liquid—do *not* throw it out!

6. Set the mixture aside and cool it completely in the refrigerator overnight.

7. Meanwhile, bring the cooking liquid to a boil in a large pot with a lid. Add the rice to the liquid and reduce the heat to low. Replace the lid on the pot and cook the rice for 15 to 20 minutes, or according to the package instructions. Strain the excess cooking liquid (if any) and discard. Set aside the rice and let it cool completely overnight.

8. In the morning, add the rice to a large bowl and set it below the mouth of the grinder. Grind the cooled meat mixture once on a medium die, allowing it to fall into the bowl with the rice.

9. Using your hands, mix the rice and ground meat together until they are integrated. Finally, mix in the parsley and scallions with your hands until evenly distributed.

10. Add the loose sausage mixture to the stuffer; pack it down to remove all of the air pockets.

11. Stuff the sausage into the hog casings and twist links 3 to 1 pound (455 g). (Generally, each sausage should be 5 to 6 inches [13 to 15 cm] long.)

12. Lightly poke each sausage link 3 or 4 times with a poking tool.

13. Put the twisted links in the refrigerator, uncovered, and chill overnight to dry out the casings.

14. Snip the sausages at the seams to separate them into links.

Tennessee Mortadella

HOMEMADE SAUSAGE

One reason we love Tennessee Mortadella is because of the juxtaposition of cultures that makes our brains spin as we try to make sense of it. Mortadella is the Italian grandfather of what we know in America as that uniform, circular, and bubblegum pink lunchmeat called "baloney." Originating in Bologna, Italy, mortadella shares a skeleton with bologna, but it has undergone far less cosmetic-corrective surgery. mortadella is known for ingredients like chunks of fat, bright green pistachios, or even whole, un-ground spices that are suspended throughout the cylindrical meat, giving it beautiful texture and color. The lunchmeat now associated with the American south, on the other hand, is so overly processed, it looks perfectly smooth and lacks any inconsistencies. For this Tennessee-skewed version of Italian Mortadella, we crossed *back* over the pond to add some Southern flair: Tennessee whiskey and chunks of jowl bacon. Yeehaw!

YIELD: 10 POUNDS (4.5 KG)/1 LOG
DIE: 1/8 (SMALL)

10 pounds (4.5 kg) fatty beef

2 ounces (57 g) salt

1 ounce (28 g) pink salt

1⅛ ounces (32 g) black pepper

½ ounce (14 g) white pepper

½ ounce (14 g) mustard powder

½ ounce (14 g) garlic

12.8 ounces (363 ml) Tennessee whiskey

1½ pounds (680 ml) jowl bacon, unsliced

4.84 x 27-inch (12.3 x 68.5 cm) synthetic, fibrous casing

METHOD

1. Dice the fatty beef into 1-inch (2.5 cm) cubes.

2. Mix the salts together to create a cure.

3. In a large bowl, toss the fatty beef in the salt mixture, covering each piece. Put the beef in the fridge and let it cure for two days.

4. Remove the beef from the fridge and using your hands, mix it together with the remaining ingredients, except for the whiskey and jowl bacon.

5. Grind the mixed ingredients four times through a grinder on a small die. Keep the mixture *very* cold during the grinding process; if the meat begins to lose its chill, return it to the refrigerator before continuing to grind.

6. Before grinding the meat for the fourth time, add the whiskey to it, and incorporate it with your hands. Grind it through a small die for the fourth time, allowing the whiskey to aid in emulsifying the meat.

7. Dice the jowl bacon into roughly 1-inch (2.5 cm) cubes. Using your hands, incorporate it into the ground meat until it is evenly distributed. (This will allow large hunks of bacon to appear when the meat is later sliced, adding texture and visual interest.)

8. Using the largest sausage horn available, stuff the ground meat into a synthetic mortadella (or bologna) casing and tie it off at the end.

9. Create a water bath big enough to submerge the entire mortadella roll, and bring the water temperature up to 150°F (65°C). *Note: A circulator is a tool that helps maintain the temperature of the water and is vital for this style of cooking.*

Cook the mortadella for 6 hours, or until the internal temperature reaches 150°F (65°C). Or fill a slow cooker full of water and set it to the highest setting. Submerge the mortadella in the water, taking care to tie the ends tightly to prevent water from seeping inside. After 2 hours, insert a thermometer into the center of the mortadella. Continue checking the mortadella every hour, until the internal temperature reaches 150°F (65°C). Remove it from the water and put it directly into an ice bath (a large bowl of ice water) to stop the cooking process.

10. Allow the mortadella to cool completely before removing the casing and/or slicing.

Nashville Hot Chicken Sausage

HOMEMADE
SAUSAGE

Nashville has become somewhat of a food festival mecca over the past decade or so, but no food festival holds a candle to the East Nashville Hot Chicken Festival, which takes place every year on the Fourth of July. In preparation for our first ever Hot Chicken Festival back in 2012, we created this sausage to rival our "real" hot chicken competitors, such as Prince's, Hattie B's, and Bolton's. Even though we had beer on hand for the duration of the festival, nothing could quite tame our taste buds after feasting on a few of these fiery sausages. Word to the wise: beer is horrible for neutralizing a spicy mouth. Drinking milk or eating a piece of white bread is the most effective way to go.

YIELD: 5 POUNDS (2.27 KG)/ 15 LINKS
DIE: 3/16 (MEDIUM)

4½ pounds (2 kg) boneless, skinless chicken thighs, quartered

½ pound (227 g) butter, ½-inch (1.3 cm) dice, frozen

1½ ounces (43 g) salt

¼ ounce (7 g) freshly ground black pepper

⅛ ounce (4 g) cayenne pepper

½ ounce (14 g) red pepper flakes

⅞ ounce (25 g) hot paprika

¼ ounce (7 g) garlic powder

Pinch of allspice

Pinch of dried bay leaves

½ ounce (14 g) mustard seed

29–32 mm hog casings

METHOD

1. Cut the chicken into small, 1-inch (2.5 cm) cubes.

2. Separately, cut the butter into roughly 1-inch (2.5 cm) cubes. Keep both the chicken and the butter very cold.

3. In a large bowl, mix all of the ingredients together with your hands until they are equally distributed.

4. Grind the mixture two times through a grinder on a medium die.

5. Using your hands, mix the ingredients again, very thoroughly, until it becomes sticky and emulsified. (The sausage should stick to your hand when it's turned upside down.)

6. Add the loose sausage mixture to the stuffer; pack it down to remove all of the air pockets.

7. Stuff the sausage into the hog casings and twist links 3 to 1 pound (455 g). (Generally, each sausage should be 5 to 6 inches [13 to 15 cm] long.)

8. Put the twisted links in the refrigerator, uncovered, and chill overnight to dry out the casings.

9. Snip the sausages at the seams to separate them into links.

10. Do not poke the sausages. Smoke the sausages at 225°F (107°C) for 1 hour, or until an internal temperature of 165°F (74°C).

THE NOT-QUITE-SAUSAGE

Most definitions qualify sausage as ground meat mixed with spices, and then stuffed into some sort of cylindrical casing, but the qualifications for being both stuffed and cylindrical need not always apply. Pâté, chilled and spreadable meats often made from animal offal and fat, might not be the first thing that comes to mind at the mention of sausage, but at their foundation fit all of the *truly necessary* requirements. Pâté was born as a way of using what would otherwise be discarded meat, it necessitates fat as an ingredient, and vegetables, spices, and herbs are usually mixed in to add flavor and flair.

The difference? Pâté does not come in a casing. Pâté is cooked in a terrine, in a water bath, at a lower heat, and is then pressed and chilled before being eaten. Pâté is not usually grilled, sautéed, or broiled; but simply spread on crackers or toast and enjoyed with cheese. So while pâté still lives in the brotherhood of sausage, in reality the two are closer to cousins than first-of-kin.

Tennessee Pâté

PÂTÉ SPICE

Before you start, all three of our pâté recipes call for "Pâté Spice," which is a mixture of spices that we always keep on hand.

¼ ounce (7 g) ground cloves

¼ ounce (7 g) ground nutmeg

¼ ounce (7 g) ground ginger

¼ ounce (7 g) ground coriander

⅜ ounce (11 g) ground cinnamon

Pinch of white pepper

In a small bowl, combine all of the ingredients. Store in a container with a lid in a cool, dry place at room temperature. Bon appétit!

The not-quite-sausages we've selected for this book go in descending order of boldness to ease in any of you pâté rookies slowly. We like to call our Tennessee Pâté, "pâté for beginners," because it contains no liver at all, but it still introduces the flavor, look, and consistency of a traditional pâté. Lacking that iron-y, and what some people consider to be undesirable flavor, we think this Southern version of the French favorite is pretty awesome.

YIELD: 5 POUNDS (2.27 KG)
2 PÂTÉ LOAVES
DIE: 3/16 (MEDIUM)

5 pounds (2.27 kg) pork

¼ cup (75 g) salt

¼ ounce (7 g) black pepper

⅜ ounce (11 g) pink salt

¼ ounce (7 g) Pâté Spice (see recipe at left)

2 ounces (57 g) fresh parsley

Pinch of fresh thyme

1¾ ounces (50 g) garlic

5¼ ounces (149 g) chopped onion

¼ cup (31 g) flour

4 eggs

1 cup (235 ml) cream

½ cup (118 ml) Tennessee whiskey, such as Jack Daniels

METHOD

1. Dice the pork into small, 1-inch (2.5 cm) cubes.

2. Mix all of the ingredients together, except for the eggs, cream, and whiskey.

3. Put the pork and spice mixture into the freezer until they are very cold, about 30 minutes.

4. Once the pork and spice mixture is thoroughly chilled, grind the pork mixture two times through a grinder on a medium die.

5. Add the eggs, cream, and whiskey, and mix everything together thoroughly with your hands.

6. Line a pâté terrine with oven-safe plastic wrap (available at most restaurant supply stores: try Darnell Wrap), leaving at least 6 inches (15 cm) of excess plastic wrap on all four sides. To receive a finished product that looks beautiful and clean, first fill your plastic-wrapped terrine with water and use the weight of the water to press the plastic wrap to the edges of the terrine. The bottom and the edges should be smooth, with as few wrinkles as possible. Pour out the water.

7. Now press the meat mixture into the terrine. *Note: It can be helpful to hit the bottom of the terrine on the counter or floor, being mindful to not hit it too hard that it breaks or cracks, which will help pack the meat into the terrine.*

8. Once the terrine is filled and the meat packed down, use your hands to smooth out the top, again creating an even layer. Then cover the top of the meat with the excess plastic wrap and fold the edges of the wrap in, around the other sides of the loaf.

9. Put the terrine into a larger, ovenproof vessel (such as a Dutch oven or deep casserole dish—something that is deep enough so that the terrine does not peek out over the top), and fill the vessel with water to create a water bath. The water level should almost reach the top edge of the terrine, but the top should still be dry and open to the heat of the oven.

10. Cook at 325°F (170°C) degrees for 1½ hours, or until the internal temperature reaches 150°F (65°C).

11. Carefully remove the water bath and terrine from the oven together. Then carefully remove the terrine from the water bath and discard the water.

12. Using bricks or other heavy objects, press the terrine at room temperature for 1 hour.

13. Finally, move the terrine to the refrigerator and continue to press it overnight.

Country Pâté

You're getting there, you fearless pâté pioneer, you. You're getting close to "the real thing." Our Country Pâté has a liver-to-meat ratio of only 1:4, meaning the presence of liver is far inferior to that of the meat, thus this pâté has inserted itself as the middleman between a pâté pupil and a pâté purist. If you liked the Tennessee Pâté and you're ready to take your taste buds to the next level, this recipe will slowly introduce the flavor of pork liver to your palate. Said to be the strongest in flavor out of commonly consumed animal liver, pork liver isn't something that many people are comfortable diving right into. So, good for you for taking the first step! We know you're going to love it.

**YIELD: 5 POUNDS (2.27 KG)/
2 PÂTÉ LOAVES
DIE: 3/16 (MEDIUM)**

1 pound (455 g) pork liver

1 small onion, chopped

½ cup (120 ml) whiskey

4 pounds (1.8 kg) pork

¼ cup (75 g) salt

2 teaspoons pink salt

2 tablespoons (13 g) black pepper

2 tablespoons (14 g) Pâté Spice (see page 104)

2 tablespoons (5 g) fresh thyme

6 cloves garlic

2 tablespoons (8 g) fresh parsley

2 tablespoons (15 g) flour

½ cup (120 ml) cream

4 eggs

METHOD

1. In a sauté pan over very high heat, quickly sear the liver until brown. *Note: Do not cook the liver. Only sear it on high heat. If the liver is cooked for a long period of time, it will take on an undesirable, grainy consistency instead of its traditional smooth mouth feel.*

2. Add the onion and cook it until it's translucent.

3. Being mindful of the flame, deglaze the pan with the whiskey.

4. Put the mixture in the freezer to cool, about 30 minutes.

5. Remove it from the freezer and add all of the remaining ingredients, except for the flour, cream, and eggs. Using your hands, combine the mixture thoroughly.

6. Add the flour, cream, and eggs and thoroughly combine with your hands.

7. Using a medium die, run the mixture through a grinder twice, using your hands to further emulsify and combine the mixture after each grinder run.

8. Line a pâté terrine with oven-safe plastic wrap (available at most restaurant supply stores: try Darnell Wrap), leaving at least 6 inches (15 cm) of excess plastic wrap on all four sides. To receive a finished product that looks beautiful and clean, fill a plastic-wrapped terrine with water and use the weight of the water to press the plastic wrap to the edges of the terrine. The bottom and the edges should be smooth, with as few wrinkles as possible. Pour out the water.

9. Press the meat mixture into the terrine. *Note: It can be helpful to hit the bottom of the terrine on the counter or floor, being mindful to not hit it too hard that you break or crack it, which will help pack the meat into the terrine.*

10. Once the terrine is filled and the meat is packed down, use your hands to smooth out the top, again creating an even layer. Then cover the top of the meat with the excess plastic wrap and fold the edges of the wrap in, around the other sides of the loaf.

11. Once the meat is sealed in the plastic wrap, put the terrine into a larger, ovenproof vessel (like a Dutch oven or a deep casserole dish—something that is deep enough so that the terrine does not peek out over the top), and fill the vessel with water to create a water bath. The water level should almost reach the top edge of the terrine, but the top should still be dry and open to the heat of the oven.

12. Cook at 325°F (163°C) for 1½ hours, or until an internal temperature of 150°F (65°C).

13. Carefully remove the water bath and terrine from the oven together. Then carefully remove the terrine from the water bath and discard the water.

14. Using bricks or other heavy objects, press the terrine at room temperature for 1 hour.

15. Finally, refrigerate the terrine and continue to press it overnight.

Pork Liver and Bacon Pâté

HOMEMADE SAUSAGE

Liver has a rich, iron-y taste that should be appreciated and celebrated rather than feared and avoided. The depth of flavor from this pork liver and bacon pâté is something to behold and love—plus, there's bacon in it! Nobody can be afraid of bacon. The creamy, smooth texture of the pâté makes it feel like butter as it melts onto your tongue, leaving a sweet pork and smoky bacon taste in its wake. Pork Liver and Bacon Pâté pairs perfectly with something simple like a cracker or good piece of toast. A dollop of fig jam or a smear of mustard is also sure to make your taste buds happy.

YIELD: 5 POUNDS (2.27 KG)/ 2 PÂTÉ LOAVES
DIE: 1/8 (SMALL)

4 pounds (1.8 kg) pork liver

1 pound (455 g) bacon ends

½ pound (228 g) pork back fat

¼ cup (75 g) salt

2 teaspoons pink salt

2 tablespoons (13 g) black pepper

2 tablespoons (14 g) Pâté Spice
(see page 104)

2 tablespoons (8 g) fresh parsley

2 tablespoons (5 g) fresh thyme

1 medium onion, roughly chopped

6 cloves garlic

1 cup (235 ml) whiskey

2 tablespoons (15 g) flour

½ cup (118 ml) cream

4 eggs

METHOD

1. Separately, cut the liver, bacon, and back fat into small, 1-inch (2.5 cm) pieces.

2. Using your hands, mix the liver, back fat, spices, and herbs thoroughly and then place in the freezer to cool.

3. Meanwhile, in a sauté pan over medium-high heat, cook the bacon until golden brown.

4. Add the onion and garlic to the pan with the bacon, and cook until it is translucent.

5. Being mindful of the flames, carefully deglaze the pan with the whiskey.

6. Add the bacon-and-onion mixture to the liver mixture from freezer. Mix well.

7. Return the mixture to the freezer and allow it to cool completely, about 30 minutes.

8. Once the mixture has cooled, grind it four times on a small die.

9. Using your hands, mix in the flour, cream, and eggs until thoroughly combined and incorporated.

10. Line a pâté terrine with oven-safe plastic wrap (available at most restaurant supply stores: try Darnell Wrap), leaving at least 6 inches (15 cm) of excess plastic wrap on all four sides. To receive a finished product that looks beautiful and clean, fill a plastic-wrapped terrine with water and use the weight of the water to press the plastic wrap to the edges of the terrine. The bottom and the edges should be smooth, with as few wrinkles as possible. Pour out the water.

11. Press the meat mixture into the terrine. *Note: It can be helpful to hit the bottom of the terrine on the counter or floor, being mindful to not hit it too hard that it breaks or cracks. This will help pack the meat into the terrine.*

12. Once the terrine is filled and the meat packed down, use your hands to smooth out the top, again creating an even layer. Then cover the top of the meat with the excess plastic wrap and fold the edges of the wrap in, around the other sides of the loaf.

13. Once the meat is sealed in the plastic wrap, put the terrine into a larger, ovenproof vessel (like a Dutch oven or a deep casserole dish—something that is deep enough so that the terrine does not peek out over the top), and fill the vessel with water to create a water bath. The water level should almost reach the top edge of the terrine, but the top should still be dry and open to the heat of the oven.

14. Cook at 325°F (170°C) degrees for 1½ hours, or until an internal temperature of 150°F (66°C).

15. Carefully remove the water bath and terrine from the oven together. Then carefully remove the terrine from the water bath and discard the water.

16. Using bricks or other heavy objects, press the terrine at room temperature for 1 hour.

17. Finally, move it to the refrigerator and continue to press it overnight.

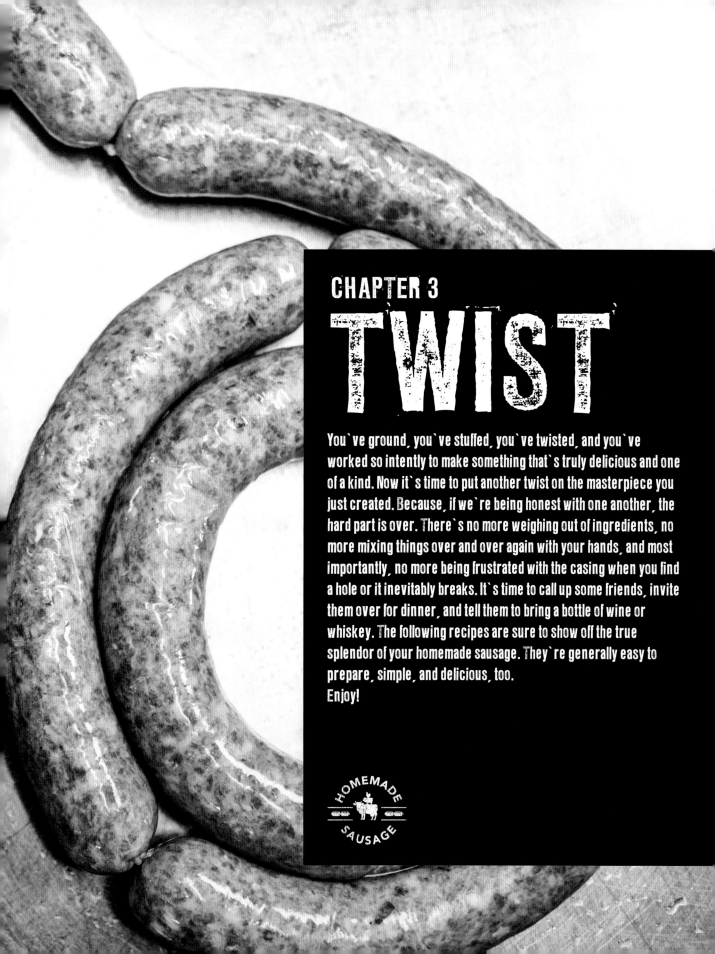

CHAPTER 3
TWIST

You`ve ground, you`ve stuffed, you`ve twisted, and you`ve worked so intently to make something that`s truly delicious and one of a kind. Now it`s time to put another twist on the masterpiece you just created. Because, if we`re being honest with one another, the hard part is over. There`s no more weighing out of ingredients, no more mixing things over and over again with your hands, and most importantly, no more being frustrated with the casing when you find a hole or it inevitably breaks. It`s time to call up some friends, invite them over for dinner, and tell them to bring a bottle of wine or whiskey. The following recipes are sure to show off the true splendor of your homemade sausage. They`re generally easy to prepare, simple, and delicious, too.

Enjoy!

HOMEMADE SAUSAGE

The Best Breakfast

HOMEMADE
SAUSAGE

Sausage Biscuit

This sausage biscuit is one we sell for breakfast at our West Nashville shop six days a week through the drive-through window, and it is consistently one of our customers' favorites. The sausage is filled with fresh ingredients and robust spices; the biscuits come out of the oven golden-crisp on top and warm and fluffy in the middle; and the drizzle of local honey acts like the glue that holds everything together: no slipping and sliding around, plus an extra dose of sweetness to balance the savory sausage and biscuit. Oftentimes we'll add a fried egg or some local Cheddar cheese on top, but the good simplicity of a biscuit, sausage, and drizzle of honey does just the trick for us in the early morning. Who are we kidding? It does the trick for us any time of the day.

YIELD: 12 SANDWICHES

FOR THE BISCUITS

¼ pound (115 g) cold butter, plus extra melted for brushing

4 cups (480 g) unbleached all-purpose flour

1 tablespoon (14 g) baking powder

1 tablespoon (18 g) salt

1 cup (235 ml) buttermilk

FOR THE BISCUIT SANDWICHES:

2½ pounds (1.1 kg) loose Breakfast Sausage (see page 53)

Local honey

METHOD

1. Make the biscuits: Dice the butter into ½-inch (1 cm) cubes. Return it to the fridge.

2. In a large bowl, mix the flour, baking powder and salt together.

3. Cut the cold butter into flour mixture, mixing it with your hands until the butter is broken down into pebble-sized pieces.

4. Add the buttermilk and, using your hands, mix by folding the mixture over and over again, until you begin to notice flaky layers. Only mix until the flour and buttermilk are combined. Don't be afraid of large chunks of butter that are likely to remain in the dough. That's a good thing!

5. Using your hands, spread out the dough on a floured surface to a 1-inch (2.5 cm) thick patty. Using a 3-inch (7.6 cm) diameter ring mold, cut out biscuits and transfer them to a baking sheet. Once filled, put the baking sheet into the refrigerator, uncovered, to cool for at least 30 minutes or up to 12 hours or freeze for later use.

6. Make the biscuit sandwiches: Using ¼ pound (115 g) of sausage at a time, pat the sausage into a disc that's roughly ¼-inch (0.6 cm) thick. Transfer to a baking sheet and continue until you've formed 12 sausage patties.

7. Preheat the oven to 350°F (180°C). Bake the biscuits for 20 minutes, rotating every 5 minutes to ensure even cooking.

8. Add the sausage to the oven when 10 minutes remain on the biscuits, while you do your second rotation.

9. When 5 minutes remain, brush the top of the biscuits with melted butter.

10. Make sure the biscuits are golden and the sausage is browned before removing them from the oven.

11. Using a serrated knife, slice each biscuit in half. Drizzle honey on the bottom half and then place a sausage patty on top of the honey. Replace the top half of the biscuit and enjoy.

Very Southern

HOMEMADE SAUSAGE

Mortadella and Pimento Cheese Sandwich

As elementary as a bologna cheese sandwich may sound, it's difficult to dispute the deliciousness of such a nostalgic childhood lunchtime staple. So why not bring it back, but make it better than ever? Kick that square of processed yellow to the curb, and instead invite a classic Southern cheesy spread to join the fun. Amp up the flavor of regular ole bologna by adding some smoky bacon and sweet, smooth whiskey to your pink deli meat. Then get things almost as hot as Alabama on the Fourth of July by frying it up and squishing it between two toasted buns. You're going to feel so much Southern love, you'll be licking your lips for some sweet tea and tapping your toe to bring on the banjo music.

YIELD: 4 SANDWICHES

FOR THE PIMENTO CHEESE

Makes 2 cups (500 g)

1 cup (115 g) shredded Cheddar cheese

1 cup (115 g) shredded Colby cheese

½ cup (115 g) mayonnaise

¼ cup (45 g) diced pimentos or roasted red peppers

2 tablespoons (18 g) pickled jalapeños, diced

2 tablespoons (30 ml) pickled jalapeño juice

Salt and pepper, to taste

4¼ inch (11 cm) slices Tennessee Mortadella (see page 100)

4 burger buns, slice in half

Melted butter, for toasting

METHOD

1. Preheat the oven to 350°F (180°C).

2. Heat a large skillet over medium-high heat.

3. Make the pimento cheese: Mix all of the pimento cheese ingredients together in a large bowl. Set aside.

4. Make the sandwiches: Butter both the sliced side of your burger bun and the outside. Set both sides of the bun, face down, on the center rack of the oven to toast for 3 minutes.

5. Meanwhile, add sliced bologna to the hot skillet and fry it on both sides until browned around the edges, about 2 minutes per side.

6. Spread pimento cheese on the top half of the toasted bun, put fried bologna on the bottom half, and press both sides together. Enjoy!

Irish "Bangers 'n Mash"

HOMEMADE SAUSAGE

with Onion Gravy

At its simplest, bangers and mash is just that—sausage and mashed potatoes—but it doesn't have to be. To the uneducated plebeians with whom you might be caught eating, this meal seems like a very simple and unchallenging dish to prepare, but with a couple of easy tweaks, bangers 'n mash will go from drab to fabulous. For this recipe we added richness and flavor to our potatoes with a sizeable pad of butter and some silky cream, and we upped the classiness by running the potatoes through a ricer, making them perfectly smooth. Finally, the addition of traditional onion gravy topped off with a sprinkle of chives gives these freshly homemade Irish Bangers and Mash the right amount of flare for some newfound fancy friends.

YIELD: 4 SERVINGS

4 Irish Bangers (see page 63)

Minced fresh chives

FOR MASH

3 medium Russet potatoes

1 tablespoon (18 g) salt

¼ cup (56 g) butter

¼ cup (60 ml) cream

Salt and pepper, to taste

FOR GRAVY

2 tablespoons (28 g) butter, divided

1 small onion, minced

1 teaspoon fresh thyme, minced

2 tablespoons (15 g) flour

2 cups (475 ml) beef stock

Salt and pepper, to taste

METHOD

1. Preheat the oven to 350°F (180°C).

2. Make the mash: Peel the potatoes.

3. Add the potatoes to a large stockpot and add 1 tablespoon (18 g) salt. Fill the pot with water until the potatoes are covered by 2 inches (5 cm).

4. Bring the water to a boil. Boil the potatoes for 10 to 15 minutes until they are knife tender.

5. Put the Irish Bangers onto a sheet tray and cook them in the oven for 12 to 15 minutes, until they reach the desired doneness.

6. Make the gravy: In a small stockpot over medium heat, add the butter and the onion. Sweat the onion until translucent. Add the thyme and simmer until aromatic. Sprinkle the flour over the onion mixture and cook for 1 minute, stirring occasionally. Slowly whisk in the stock, being sure to continue to whisk with each addition. Cook on low heat until it reaches the desired thickness. Season with salt and pepper.

7. Strain the potatoes through a colander and put them in a stockpot. Put the potatoes in the oven for 5 minutes. Remove and rice the potatoes in a food mill.

8. To the hot stockpot, add ¼ cup (56 g) butter and ¼ cup (60 ml) cream, and allow the butter to melt.

9. Return the potatoes to the pot with the butter and cream. Using a large spoon or spatula, mix the potatoes with the butter and cream, and then add salt and pepper to taste. (Make sure to not over-mix the potatoes or they will become gummy.)

10. Serve the sausages and mashed potatoes both drizzled with onion gravy and garnished with chives.

Italian Cotechino and Lentils

HOMEMADE SAUSAGE

It seemed fortuitous that we chose to clean out our large freezer just four days before New Year's Eve in 2014. While digging through the frozen depths of Meat Mountain, we discovered frostbitten meatballs, made space for upwards of 40 giant turkeys, and best of all, got our hands on a long lost, admittedly forgotten, vacuum-sealed package of pig skin—not a football. Cotechino and lentils might sound like an odd dish to enjoy at such a festive time as the New Year, but the beauty of this dish is that every element promises all sorts of success for the year to come. Pigs, fat as they are, are said to represent prosperity (not weight gain), and lentils are coin-shaped, which signify money. Pair your meal with a bottle of chilled Italian Prosecco, and your New Year's Eve holds the promise of prosperity, wealth, and lots of bubbles and fun.

YIELD: 4 SERVINGS

1 tablespoon (15 ml) grapeseed or vegetable oil

1 small onion, small dice

1 medium carrot, small dice

4 cloves garlic, minced

1 teaspoon fresh thyme

1 cup (192 g) green lentils, rinsed

2 cups (475 ml) pork or chicken stock

2 pounds (910 g) Cotechino (see page 71), in 4 links

FOR THE SALAD

1 teaspoon Dijon mustard

1 whole lemon, juice only

1 tablespoon (15 ml) olive oil

1 fennel bulb, very thinly sliced

1 small red onion, very thinly sliced

1 bunch of fresh parsley, washed and picked

Salt and pepper, to taste

METHOD

1. Preheat the oven to 350°F (180°C).

2. In a medium pot, heat the oil over high heat. Sauté the onion and carrot for 2 minutes, and then add the garlic. Cook for 1 minute more, and then add the thyme, lentils, and stock.

3. Reduce the heat to low and cover the pot with a lid. Cook for 5 minutes, turn off the heat, and then let sit for 20 minutes, allowing the water to fully absorb.

4. Place the Cotechino on a baking sheet with a lip. Roast for 15 minutes in the oven, until golden brown.

5. Make the salad: In a medium-sized bowl, whisk the mustard, lemon juice, and olive oil together. Add the fennel, red onion, and parsley, and toss. Season with salt and pepper. Set aside.

6. Once the lentils and sausage are done cooking, scoop ½ cup (96 g) of the lentils into a shallow bowl. Place one Cotechino link on top, and garnish with a quarter of the salad mixture.

Game Day Gumbo

HOMEMADE SAUSAGE

As guys, we are pretty much required to both love sports and love watching them regularly, but for us the best reason for watching sports or making a big deal about any particular game is that it gives us license to eat good food and drink good beer. What better way is there to spend a weekend than drinking an ice cold beer while cooking a batch of gumbo, and then drinking an ice cold beer while eating a bowl of gumbo? The oven-based, dark-hued roux, paired with our smoky Andouille sausage, imparts some incredible depth and richness to this hearty concoction, and makes it even more perfect for a cool fall day in the peak of football season. It almost makes us want to root for the New Orleans Saints.

YIELD: 8 SERVINGS

½ cup (60 g) flour

½ cup (112 g) butter

1 pound (455 g) Andouille, sliced into coins (see page 90)

1 pound (455) chicken, diced (preferably boneless skinless thighs)

1 large onion, small dice

2 ribs of celery, small dice

2 red bell peppers, small dice

8 cloves of garlic, minced

½ pound (225 g) okra, sliced

1 can (15 ounces [420 g]) diced tomatoes

1 teaspoon fresh thyme

4 bay leaves

1 tablespoon (7 g) gumbo file powder

Dash of cayenne pepper

Dash of smoked paprika

Salt and pepper, to taste

2 quarts (2 L) chicken stock

1 pound (455 g) shrimp, peeled and deveined

METHOD

1. Preheat the oven to 300°F (150°C).

2. In a bowl, mix the flour and butter together and put in a Pyrex dish or small casserole. Bake in the oven until the color reaches a very dark brown. (This could take anywhere from 30 minutes to 2 hours, depending on how dark you want it. This is your roux. It should be near chestnut in color.)

3. Heat a large stockpot over medium-high heat. Add the sausage and cook for 2 minutes. Add the chicken and cook until both the chicken and sausage are golden brown. Remove from the pot and reserve for later. Do not discard any rendered fat from the sausage and chicken.

4. Add the onion, celery, bell peppers, and garlic to the pot with the rendered fat and sauté until softened.

5. Add the roux and all of the remaining ingredients to the stockpot, except for the browned meat and shrimp.

6. Turn the heat down to low. Simmer for 1 hour over low heat, stirring occasionally to prevent sticking on the bottom.

7. Add the chicken, sausage, and shrimp and cook for an additional 15 minutes.

8. Serve as is or over rice.

Nashville Hot Chicken Pasta

HOMEMADE
SAUSAGE

"Hot Chicken" is an especially spicy variety of fried chicken that has gained notoriety across the world as Nashville's culinary claim-to-fame. Although the origin of this fiery fowl is not easily determined, what is undisputable is the way the bird is served. Chicken is breaded and deep-fried, tossed in a fire-red and cayenne-heavy sauce, served on a piece of white toast, and then stabbed with a pickle chip. In creating and cooking with our Nashville Hot Chicken Sausage, however, we like to employ a little more creativity. We substitute the pasta for white bread, garnish with parsley instead of pickles, and add cream, alcohol, and a bit of smoke to fire up your taste buds.

YIELD: 4 SERVINGS

2 links Nashville Hot Chicken Sausage, smoked, sliced into coins (see page 102)

1 red bell pepper, diced

1 medium onion, diced

2 ribs of celery, diced

1 cup (235 ml) sherry

1 pound (455 g) bow tie pasta

1 cup (235 ml) heavy cream

1 bunch of fresh parsley, chopped

METHOD

1. In a sauté pan over medium-high heat, brown the sausage until golden and crispy around the edges.

2. Meanwhile, fill a large pot with water and bring it to a boil.

3. Add the bell pepper, onion, and celery to the pan with the sausage and sauté, stirring occasionally, until browned.

4. Deglaze the pan with the sherry. Bring the heat up and allow the liquid to reduce by half.

5. When the water has come to a rolling boil, add the pasta and cook until al dente, about 9 minutes or according to the package instructions.

6. Add the cream to the sausage and vegetable mixture and again allow the liquid to reduce by half.

7. Drain the pasta and immediately add it to the sauté pan to toss with the chicken sausage mixture. Portion a quarter of the pasta onto each plate and garnish it with fresh parsley.

Easy Chorizo Torta

HOMEMADE SAUSAGE

Unlike the star of this recipe, the chorizo, a chorizo torta generally calls to mind the *same* image for all people who know and love this easy and delicious sandwich. The prep time is minimal, the ingredients are common, and the combination of hot, red chorizo and cool, green avocado will be both a delight to your eyes and to your tongue. This is one of our favorite sandwiches to make in the shop as a treat for a staff meal when there's something good to celebrate. *¡Ole!*

YIELD: 4 SERVINGS

1 pound (455 g) unstuffed Chorizo (see page 59)

4 large hot dog or hoagie rolls

1 head iceberg lettuce, shredded

1 tomato, sliced

1 avocado, peeled, pitted, and sliced

1 cup (230 g) sour cream

METHOD

1. Preheat the oven to 375°F (190°C).

2. Heat a large sauté pan over medium-high heat. Add the chorizo to the pan and brown, stirring occasionally.

3. Slice the buns in half, butter both halves, and toast them in the oven for 5 minutes.

4. Remove the buns from the oven and top each with a quarter of the browned chorizo. Top each sandwich with lettuce, tomato, avocado, and sour cream.

Moroccan Merguez

HOMEMADE SAUSAGE

with Couscous and Cucumber Yogurt

Hailing from a part of the world where bold flavors and strong spices are beloved, it makes sense that merguez would be such a good complement to something like light and fluffy couscous. With an appearance like rice but a composition closer to pasta and a flavor that sits somewhere in between, couscous adds wonderful texture and visual interest, and it also acts as a fire extinguisher for the heat of the spicy sausage. Cucumber yogurt sauce further cools the palate and incorporates some delightful creaminess into the dish, making this meal one for the books. You'll be sure to impress guests with this simple to make, but jaw-droppingly flavorful composition. Note: The sauce can be made up to 24 hours in advance.

YIELD: 4 SERVINGS

1 teaspoon olive oil

1 medium onion

1 large carrot

4 cups (946 ml) chicken stock

4 Merguez links (see page 84)

2 cups (350 g) dry Israeli couscous

1 tablespoon (4 g) fresh parsley, chopped

½ of an English cucumber, peeled

½ cup (115 g) plain, whole-fat or Greek yogurt

Salt and pepper, to taste

METHOD

1. Preheat the oven to 350°F (180°C).

2. In a large saucepan over low heat, add the oil, onion, and carrot and sweat for 3 to 5 minutes, until softened. Add the stock to the pan and bring it to a boil.

3. Add the merguez links to a sheet tray and roast in the oven for 12 to 15 minutes, or until desired doneness.

4. Once the chicken stock is boiling, add the couscous, stir to combine, and immediately turn off the heat. Cover the pot with a lid and let sit for 15 minutes. Fluff with a fork. Add the parsley and mix.

5. Cut the cucumber in half, lengthwise. Using a spoon, scoop out the soft flesh and set it aside. Dice the leftover firm flesh of the cucumber into small pieces. Set it aside.

6. In a small bowl, mix the cucumber components into the yogurt. Season the dressing with salt and pepper.

7. Remove the merguez from the oven and let rest for 5 minutes. Plate a quarter of the couscous in a shallow bowl. Slice the merguez on a diagonal into ¾-inch (1.9 cm) pieces and lay out on top of the couscous. Top with a dollop of the cucumber sauce.

Fried Boudin Balls

HOMEMADE SAUSAGE

with Spicy Remoulade Dipping Sauce

People from Louisiana swear by Boudin, no matter the variety. Every individual worships his or her own special recipe and will promise you that theirs indeed reigns supreme. And though nobody can necessarily agree on which combination of ingredients is the best, they all agree that making Boudin Balls is the best way to eat it. Because what part of a fried ball of sausage dipped into a creamy and tangy sauce sounds bad? Cat's got our tongue . . .

YIELD: 18 PIECES

1 pound (455 g) unstuffed Boudin (see page 98)

2 cups (240 g) flour

2 eggs

1 cup (235 ml) milk

2 cups (230 g) breadcrumbs

1 quart (1 L) lard or vegetable oil

REMOULADE

1 cup (225 g) mayonnaise

2 tablespoons (30 g) pickle relish

12 dashes hot sauce

METHOD

1. With cold, clean hands, roll the Boudin into quarter-size balls.

2. Set up three medium-sized bowls. Fill the first one with flour. In the second bowl, whisk together the eggs and milk until they are well mixed. Put the breadcrumbs into the third bowl.

3. Roll the Boudin balls in the flour until they are fully coated. Then roll the floured balls in the egg mixture, and finally cover the balls with breadcrumbs and set them aside. Repeat the process until all of the Boudin is used.

4. In a small bowl, mix the mayonnaise, pickle relish, and hot sauce together for the remoulade. Set it aside.

5. In a Dutch oven or deep cast-iron skillet, heat the lard to 350°F (180°C).

6. Working in batches of five, gently place the Boudin balls in the hot lard and fry until they are golden brown, about 4 to 5 minutes. If the fat is too shallow to cover an entire ball, turn the balls once the immersed side is golden.

7. Using a slotted spoon, remove the golden Boudin balls from the oil and set them aside on a paper towel.

8. Dip the fried Boudin balls in the spicy remoulade and enjoy!

Beer-Braised Bratwurst

HOMEMADE
SAUSAGE

with Yellow Mustard and Sauerkraut

Braising bratwursts in beer is a great way to add even more moisture and flavor to these already-perfect links, but the down side is that after doing so they look kind of like a giant, dead worm. Yikes. To make them flavorful *and* appealing to the eye—don't forget, you eat with your eyes first—we suggest two important things: good beer and a hot pan. Instead of grabbing a whole case of the light stuff, choose a six-pack of something flavorful, hearty, and delicious. You get to drink two of the six anyway. Finally, use a screaming hot pan to brown both sides of the brat to give it some color and curb-appeal; the moisture from the beer will keep it from sticking.

YIELD: 4 SERVINGS

6-pack of your favorite local pale ale, such as Yazoo Pale Ale from Nashville

4 Bratwursts (see page 75)

4 large hot dog buns

Yellow mustard

Sauerkraut

METHOD

1. Pour 4 of the beers into a large stockpot, turn the heat to high, and bring the beer to a boil. Enjoy the two other beers by drinking them.

2. Add the bratwursts and bring the beer to a simmer. (Make sure the beer doesn't re-boil or the bratwursts may burst.)

3. Separately, heat a large sauté pan over high heat.

4. Once the bratwursts float, remove them from the beer and add them to the hot pan. Sear the bratwursts on both sides until golden.

5. Toast the buns.

6. Put the bratwursts in the buns, spread one half of the bun with the mustard, and top the brat with more mustard and sauerkraut.

YIELD: 4 SERVINGS

4 Currywurst links (see page 78)

FOR BRAISED CABBAGE

1 small head of red cabbage, cored and shredded

2 ounces (59 ml) red wine

1 ounce (29.6 ml) apple cider vinegar

1 tablespoon (20 g) honey

FOR SPÄTZLE

1 cup (120 g) flour

1 teaspoon salt

½ teaspoon ground white pepper

½ teaspoon ground nutmeg

2 large eggs, whisked

¼ cup (60 ml) milk

¼ cup (56 g) butter

2 tablespoons (8 g) fresh parsley

2 tablespoons (6 g) fresh chives

2 tablespoons (8 g) fresh tarragon

Salt and pepper, to taste

Roasted Currywurst

HOMEMADE SAUSAGE

with Spätzle and Braised Cabbage

With "curry" at the forefront of the word, *currywurst* might call forth to mind the vibrant flavors and traditional dishes of India, due to the country's love for and common use of curry in its cuisine. This version of currywurst, however, originates from a different country entirely. The "wurst" portion of this sausage hails from Germany and therefore pairs well with those tiny little spätzle dumplings and braised red cabbage. Best of all, this recipe for spätzle hails straight from the lion's mouth: James' German mother-in-law.

METHOD

1. Preheat the oven to 350°F (180°C).

2. Make the braised cabbage: In a medium-sized pot, add all of the ingredients for the cabbage and mix. Simmer, covered, over medium-low heat for 45 minutes, or until the cabbage is tender.

3. Fill a medium stockpot with water and bring it to a boil.

4. Make the spätzle: In a bowl, mix the flour, salt, pepper, nutmeg, eggs, and milk together with a spatula until just combined. (Be sure not to overwork.)

5. Scrape the dough onto a perforated pan or into a colander with holes no smaller than the diameter of a #2 pencil. Working directly over the pot of boiling water, scrape the dough with a spatula until little balls of the dough fall through into the boiling water below. Continue scraping the dough until all of it has gone through. (If you don't have an appropriate colander or perforated pan, you can alternatively use a large zipper-lock bag. Simply scrape all of the dough into a bottom corner of the bag and twist the top like you would a pastry bag. Snip a small hole in the corner of the bag and carefully squeeze out small ribbons of dough (no longer than 1 inch [2.5 cm]) into the pot of boiling water. You'll want to move quickly so as to allow the spätzle to cook more or less at the same rate, since the bag method is much slower.)

6. Boil the spätzle until it floats to the top of the water. Using a slotted spoon, remove the spätzle and set it aside to cool in a colander, allowing any remaining water to drain off.

7. Put the currywurst on a sheet tray and roast it in the oven for 12 to 15 minutes, or until it reaches the desired level of doneness.

8. In a large sauté pan over medium-high heat, melt the butter. Add the spätzle and sauté until it begins to color, about 1 to 2 minutes. Add the herbs and toss to combine.

9. On each of four plates, place one-fourth of the spätzle and top with one roasted currywurst and braised cabbage.

Grilled Kielbasa

HOMEMADE SAUSAGE

with Roasted Potatoes and Chimichurri

Originating in Argentina, chimichurri is a fresh, herb-and-garlic-flavored sauce that makes a lovely accompaniment to meat. Although many people choose to use chimichurri as a marinade for meat, we like to let the flavors of the meat be the star, and let the chimichurri take on a supporting role. By grilling the kielbasa instead of pan-frying or oven-roasting it, the sausage will get a nice crust and smoky char on the outside, flavors that go perfectly with the earthy yet bright chimichurri. Use your roasted potatoes to mop up any leftover green goodness. It's too delicious to rinse down the sink!

YIELD 4 TO 6 SERVINGS

2 tablespoons (30 ml) grapeseed oil

2 pounds (910 g) Fingerling potatoes

Salt and pepper, to taste

4 Kielbasa links (see page 55)

FOR CHIMICHURRI

½ cup (120 ml) grapeseed oil

½ cup (30 g) chopped fresh parsley

½ cup (32 g) chopped fresh oregano

¼ cup (40 g) chopped garlic

1 teaspoon red pepper flakes

2 tablespoons (30 ml) red wine vinegar

Salt and pepper, to taste

METHOD

1. Preheat the oven to 400°F (200°C) and preheat the grill to medium heat, around 350°F (180°C).

2. Pour the oil into a large bowl. Add the potatoes, season with salt and pepper, and mix to coat.

3. Put the potatoes onto a sheet pan with a lip, placing the cut sides face down. Roast the potatoes until they are golden, about 45 minutes.

4. Make the chimichurri: In a medium-sized bowl, mix together all of the ingredients for the chimichurri. Set it aside.

5. Grill the Kielbasa for 12 to 15 minutes until cooked through and crispy on the outside.

6. Plate the potatoes, top each plate with one kielbasa link, and garnish with ample amounts of chimichurri.

9 O'clock Italian Pasta

HOMEMADE SAUSAGE

When James gets home after a late night at work, this pasta is one of his standby go-to options. It's both quick and easy, plus it requires mostly staple ingredients, meaning he can whip it up when he walks in the door around 8:30 and have it on the table by 9—with no additional trip to the grocery store necessary. After a long, hard day at work, the last thing anybody wants to do is make special stops and then slave away in the kitchen for a good dinner. Nine O'clock Italian Pasta alleviates thinking, stressing, and worst of all, eating something sub-par. Plus, it makes us feel just a little bit Italian for eating so late in the first place!

YIELD: 4 SERVINGS

1 pound (455 g) loose Italian sausage (see page 57)

1 medium onion, diced

8 cloves garlic, minced

1 can (28 ounces, [794 g]) crushed tomatoes

1 pound (455 g) pasta, such as spaghetti

2 sprigs fresh basil, chopped

2 sprigs fresh oregano, chopped

Parmesan cheese, to taste

METHOD

1. In a medium-sized pot over medium-high heat, brown the sausage.

2. Meanwhile, bring a large pot of salted water to a boil.

3. Add the onion and garlic and sauté until they are translucent.

4. Add the crushed tomatoes and simmer for 10 minutes.

5. While the tomatoes are simmering, add the pasta to the boiling water and cook until al dente, according to the package instructions. Strain the pasta through a colander.

6. Add the herbs to the pasta sauce and mix well.

7. Put a quarter of the pasta into a shallow bowl, and ladle a quarter of the sauce on top. Grate the desired amount of fresh Parmesan on top, and serve hot.

ABOUT PORTER ROAD BUTCHER

Here at Porter Road Butcher, we are passionate about providing Nashvillians with the best product available. Our meat is both healthier and better tasting because of the natural lives that our animals lived, and even the appearance of the meat tells the story of a happy life: beautiful marbling, bright vivid color, and firm, shapely cuts.

During their lives on the farms, our cows eat grass like they were intended to do, our chickens live on a green pasture blanketed by plenty of sunshine and outfitted with protection from predators, and our pigs root and forage and play around in the mud just like they do over at Old MacDonald's Farm. Never would our animals ever come from someplace like a concrete lot. No way!

We know that happy animals are the best animals, and we therefore make sure all of our animals have had the best lives possible—with just one bad day at the end of it.

By forming relationships with our farmers, we create both bonds of trust and levels of friendship, therefore holding one another accountable for the best possible product that we can then deliver to you, our friends and customers.

Keeping in line with Porter Road Butcher's mission to provide the freshest and most natural meats available, we make our sausages, pâtés, bone stocks, prepared foods, breakfast, lunch, and even dog food completely from scratch, always using the freshest ingredients available. Because, why would we use anything less?

First and foremost, quality is the driving force behind everything that Porter Road Butcher does. As a business that is owned and operated by two culinarians, Chris Carter and James Peisker, and staffed by a bunch of food-loving employees, passion and creativity are mixed into everything we do, continually increasing the quality of our work.

As a rule, we source our animals from no farther than three hours outside of our shops, and we aim to use local produce when available. Our dairy comes from a local dairy farmer, our eggs from a local egg farmer, our cheese from a small local farm with pasture-raised animals, and our market products are sourced exclusively from the region. We will stamp our name on nothing less than excellence.

HOW IT ALL BEGAN

It was a Thursday night at one favorite Nashville restaurant, and it was the first time that Chris Carter and James Peisker met. Chris was manning the meat station and James was in charge of fish, and a conversation naturally developed as the tickets started firing and the kitchen began to heat up. Before their first night of work together was over, they had formed a funny and friendly camaraderie.

As time wore on and the two spent more time together in the kitchen, James and Chris began to realize quite a few similarities between the two of them: similar work style, similar quirky senses of humor, and similar disdain for their current jobs. One sunny afternoon, Chris was driving to work and spotted a restaurant space for sale. An idea struck him and he proposed starting a business with James. Eager for a change and hungry for more creative freedom, James hopped on board, and from that moment forward, the two were business partners.

While dreaming of their own restaurant space, Chris and James noticed an emerging trend in the culinary world and soon chose to bring said trend to Nashville: artisanal butcher shops. "Lindy and Grundy was about to cut the ribbon for their shop in Los Angeles, the Butcher & Larder had just opened their doors in Chicago, and we figured we could open up a butcher shop for a sixth of the price of what we were initially looking at, and then put that money toward our restaurant space once we had enough saved," said James.

IT MADE PERFECT SENSE.

The guys searched Nashville up and down for the right spot to plant their inaugural shop, but getting all of their ducks in a row required a lot of work—much more than they anticipated.

While they looked for brick-and-mortar, the soon-to-be Butcher Boys got the business going: farmers dropped off hogs to their commercial rent-a-kitchen downtown where they had enough space to entirely break down the animal; then they set up a booth at the Farmer's Market to sell fresh meat and sausage on the weekends.

"It was ridiculous," said Chris. "We would be breaking down an entire pig while the women in the kitchen space next to us were preparing lasagna and brownies and stuff."

Initially the two envisioned their shop settled in a small space located at the intersection of Porter Road and Greenwood Avenue in East Nashville, hence the name "Porter Road Butcher." But even though Chris lived just down the street and it was there that the boys set up their first [very primitive] office (complete with financial projections and amateur blueprints stapled to the walls) the space at Porter Road didn't work out. Disappointed, they kept looking.

While Chris worked the morning shift at neighborhood favorite spot Mitchell's Deli, James worked at neighboring Watanabe Japanese restaurant during dinner, affording them one person to be working at the butcher shop around the clock. Whether that meant trimming hedges and mowing lawns to earn extra dough, meeting with investors to squeeze out another drop of money, flexing their culinary muscles by booking catering events, or doing other manly-man work, there was no rest for the weary when it came to bringing their idea to fruition.

It was James who drove past Tom's Elite Barbecue, located on a bustling Gallatin Avenue in East Nashville, at the very moment they officially closed their

doors and put a "for rent" sign in their window. The location, he decided, was perfect and before they knew it, Chris and James were shaking hands and signing on the dotted line.

Despite the Gallatin Road location, they kept the name, "Porter Road Butcher" and ran with it. There's a certain ring to it, don't you think? Fortunately, business at the shop has taken off, despite the somewhat confusing name, and has only become stronger, bigger, and better since their doors opened in November of 2011.

In preparation for opening up their first butcher shop, Chris and James drove all over middle Tennessee to meet with famers, tour their operations, and learn about their farming practices to find the right sources for meat that they'd be proud and excited to sell.

What they ended up with was this: beef from Bethpage, Tennessee; chicken

from Ashland City, Tennessee; hogs and eggs from Summertown, Tennessee; lamb from Chattanooga; and cheese from all over the state and region.

Their operation has expanded since those early days, and they now own two butcher shops (the original in East Nashville and the newer shop in West Nashville) as well as a slaughterhouse and processing facility just an hour and a half north in Princeton, Kentucky. In an effort to continue improving the presence of their business and the quality of their products, gaining a larger audience in Nashville and acquiring the ability to control the meat from the beginning to the end were paramount in changing the face of the Nashville food industry.

And although they are growing, to this day they stand by their foundational values and the roots upon which they were grown: all local, all free-range, all truly natural, and all delicious.

ABOUT THE AUTHORS

CHRIS CARTER

Growing up in Hendersonville, Tennessee, Chris Carter was raised to love food. "It was my Granny who cooked dinner for me most of the time, and she spoiled me when it came to food," said Chris. "Dinner for the two of us could be strip steaks with eggs, plus cabbage, green beans, mashed potatoes, cauliflower, broccoli, beans. It was awesome. I think that was what got me started on liking food, but I didn't really fall in love with it until later on."

Like many other kids looking for extra spending cash, Chris's entry into the restaurant industry began in high school when he procured a job as a host and busboy for a Mexican chain restaurant. He didn't exactly enjoy his first restaurant gig as much as he would others down the road, but it was the spark that began a long string of food industry jobs and eventually a successful career.

While in college at the University of Memphis, Chris was known among his friends for his superior skills on the grill and even garnered fame among his friends for his original BBQ dry rub. Even so, his passion for food didn't run much deeper than that. It was when he was working at a liquor store and first learned about wine pairings that his ears perked up and his interest in food developed.

"I get to drink wine and eat food, and then by putting the two together make everything better?" he said. "What a great excuse."

It was then that he landed on his college major, Hospitality Management, and soon graduated with a bachelor's degree. Throughout his college years, Chris held a variety of jobs as both a bartender and a server, but he finally decided to plunge into the cooking side of things in 2006 when he attended Le Cordon Bleu College of Culinary Arts in Scottsdale, Arizona.

Living in one of the United States' wealthiest cities, high quality was something that restaurants in Scottsdale demanded and it was there that Chris came to really appreciate the value of high-quality ingredients, being able to cook with beautiful and fresh local produce as well as obscure game such as bison.

Eventually seeking a change, Chris transitioned to a more corporate environment, Flemings Steakhouse, where his previous amateur expertise on the grill really shone and became even stronger. It was there that he actually perfected the art of grilling.

"People would come in there and spend close to $100 on a steak," he said. "I couldn't afford to mess that up."

Family matters brought Chris back to Nashville in 2009 where he quickly found work in a fine dining restaurant, and after a year met James Peisker, his soon-to-be business partner.

Today Chris lives in Nashville with his wife, Kelly, and their dogs, Marley and Clark. Outside of cooking for his family and cutting meat in the shop, Chris enjoys going fishing, the Grateful Dead, and occasionally dabbling in hot yoga.

JAMES PEISKER

"I guess I always had somewhat of an interest in food. My number one favorite toy when I was little was my fast-food restaurant play set, and my grandmother always likes to remind me how I was eager to stand on a stool in the kitchen and help her bake brownies at age five. Almost three decades later, I'm still exploring the culinary world."

A St. Louis native, James Peisker landed his first official restaurant job as a host for Layton's Diner when he was just fourteen years old. He woke up before the sun every Saturday and Sunday to usher customers to their seats and pour caffeine into their cups so he could walk out the door with some extra cash. He continued working in restaurants throughout his high school career, landing positions in both the front of the house and the back, but it was at The Gatesworth in St. Louis where James' mentor Brian Hardy instilled in him the foundation of his culinary education and whet his appetite for continuously learning more about food.

At Hardy's insistence, James pushed culinary boundaries, and he eventually decided it was time to go play with the big dogs: The Culinary Institute of America in Hyde Park, New York. Although not the biggest fan of high school, James was enamored with culinary school and took it upon himself to become the "teacher's pet" of his class. In addition to heading a variety of clubs and going the extra mile in the kitchen, James spent his free time learning how to butcher animals and properly cut meat.

When he graduated from CIA and returned to St. Louis, James worked his way up to being the rounds man in the kitchen of an upscale country club, meaning he essentially worked every station in the kitchen. After a while however, he found himself hungry for novelty, ingenuity, and challenge. He landed a position at one of the city's newest and trendiest restaurants, Niche, and subsequently found his niche in the booming St. Louis culinary scene.

The pig head terrine, a very popular dish at Niche, required whole-hog butchering, which meant that James was thrown onto the butcher block with his eyes closed. He initially faked and fudged his way through the execution but soon learned the proper method to breaking down a whole hog and found that he enjoyed it. Subsequently, butchering animals and working with meat became a passion, and he was able to share his skills with a number of the restaurants in the Craft Restaurant Group.

When James moved to Nashville with his then-girlfriend in 2010 and met his eventual business partner, Chris Carter, it seemed like a no brainer that the two would work together due to their similarities: a passion for food, a love for meat, a soft spot for good whiskey, and a dedication to a high-quality kitchen.

Today James lives in Nashville with his wife, Marta, and his two dogs, Asti and Oban. He loves reading books about food and the industry, enjoys cooking for his wife and friends, and is currently training for his first full marathon.

ABOUT THE WRITER

MADDIE TEREN

Unlike most people who live in Nashville today, Maddie Teren is a native Nashvillian who was born and raised in Music City, Tennessee, and still resides there today. The daughter of a successful songwriter, her father George passed down the writing gene to his daughter, but the desire to put that skill toward music did not, unfortunately, make the generational jump. Instead of writing songs, Maddie found that she enjoyed writing about food and began her first food blog when she was studying in Barcelona during college. Her friends were certain she was going to come home 30 pounds (14 kg) heavier. She did not.

As a kid who was nearly impossible to feed, Maddie's friends and family found it ironic that she grew into someone who not only enjoyed writing about food, but that she was also a person who was willing to try almost anything—at least once. When she returned from Barcelona to her small, college town of Oxford,

Ohio, she continued writing her blog but was constantly on the hunt for exciting, interesting, and delicious food. Fortunately, back at home, Nashville was all the while growing, expanding, and morphing into a food-lover's paradise, ripe for the pickin'.

Maddie graduated from college in 2012, armed with degrees in both communication and Spanish, and initially had trouble finding a job that she felt was the right fit. So, to bide some time, earn money, and continue furthering her knowledge of food and the culinary industry, she waited tables and kept up with her blog via cooking, baking, going out to eat, and always, always writing. Eventually one thing led to another, and her work paid off.

It was in August 2013 when Maddie completed her first 200-hour yoga teacher training certification, leaving her both a new sense of clarity and confidence. She immediately joined the community at her favorite Nashville studio, Shakti Power Yoga, and as it turned out, one of the owners, Kelly, just

so happened to be married to one of the Porter Road Butcher owners, Chris. And voilá! The connection was made.

Maddie transitioned into her new role as the PR and marketing manager at Porter Road Butcher in early 2014, acting as the voice behind all of PRB's social media, email newsletters, and "Butcher Blog" posts; she plans and helps run events both big and small; and she flexes her organizational muscles to keep everybody's heads on straight. The role for which she is most fond, however, is clearly being the ghost writer for *Homemade Sausage*, translating James' and Chris' words, recipes, and humor into a real, live book!

Outside of the butcher shop, Maddie loves to be outdoors, whether it's riding her bike, swimming in any body of water, or drinking a good beer on a sunny patio. She also teaches three to five hot yoga classes per week, and practices almost every day.

ACKNOWLEDGMENTS

FROM JAMES: First, I have to thank and acknowledge my parents for always pushing me to be better, supporting me in my decisions, and allowing my dreams to come true. I am always grateful for them. Second, I wouldn't be where I am today nor would I have such a big interest in food if it weren't for my mentor, chef Brian Hardy, who got me into the world of culinary arts and turned me into a foodie. Thank you, Brian, for helping me become a real food nerd. I must also recognize the amazing Gerard Craft from Niche in St. Louis, who allowed me to learn the art of butchering and helped me expand my knowledge and skills in butchering and in cooking. Finally, I wouldn't be where I am today without my wife, Marta, who is always supportive and always says yes. Marta, thank you for calming me down when I think the world is ending and for pushing me when I'm ready to stop. As they say, behind every great man is an even greater woman.

FROM CHRIS: Well first of all, I've got to thank my mama. But to thank her for her support of me wouldn't begin to say nearly enough. I'm so grateful for you, Mom, in so many ways and I am so thankful for everything you've done for me throughout my life. I feel so lucky to have your love and guidance. Second, thank you to my dad for being constantly supportive of both my life and my passions, for giving good fatherly advice, and for having so much enthusiasm for Porter Road Butcher. Thank you to my grandmothers for constantly feeding me food—lots and lots of it—and planting the seed for my love of food at an early age. Thank you to my grandfather Ralph for being "the man" and for always acting as an outstanding role model. And of course thank you to Kelly, my pescatarian wife, who does not eat meat. Thank you Kelly for being so kind and beautiful, and for supporting me in a career in which I am constantly surrounded by something you specifically avoid. Thank you for being strong, for making me stronger, and for keeping my body limber. Thank you (most of all) for loving me.

FROM CHRIS AND JAMES: We've had a lot of mentors, supporters, and cheerleaders along the path to where we are now, but there's no way we would be where we are today—with a published book . . . whaaat!?—without our Porter Road Butcher family from the past, the present, and those who will come in the future. Thank you to Leslie Gribble and Chris "Hudge" Hudgens for being there from the beginning and helping to grow and expand with us. Thank you, Leslie, for being the very first person to jump on board, for helping to grow our business, and for always making us laugh. Thank you to Hudge for being the mastermind behind (what is probably) the majority of the sausage recipes in this book. Thank you for being a good friend, a hard worker, and one of the most valuable assets to our team. Thank you to Kathleen "Cheesie" Cotter for believing in and partnering with us early on—even before brick and mortar—and sticking with us as our cheesy sister. Thank you to our shop managers and friends, Tim "Tuna" George, Stuart "Snoodleberry" Murphy, Alex Welsch, and Wesley Adams for your hard work and for running our shops better than we could have imagined.

Thank you to every single one of our farmers for all your hard work, dedication, and long hours sweating in the sun and shivering in the snow on our behalf. Thank you for laying the foundation of our business and giving us so much pride in our products and our work.

Second to last but certainly not second to least, we have to thank Maddie Teren, a.k.a. Madam Louise the communication queen, for putting up with our constant craziness and shenanigans, for keeping us in line and on task with her amazing organization, and most importantly for being so dedicated to writing this book on our behalf. Thank you for getting up at 4:30 in the morning to drive with us to Kentucky and use that time to interview us, ask us about the history of PRB, and generally inquire about our lives. Thank you for being patient when we were slow to respond to emails and not hating us when we canceled meetings at the last minute. Without you, Maddie, *Homemade Sausage* would very likely not exist, much less have been written so appropriately and in such a timely manner; we constantly found ourselves saying, "I love writing a book!"

Finally, we wouldn't be where we are today if it weren't for the support of our amazingly loyal and carnivorous customers. We love seeing you, serving you, and feeding you. Thank you for eating local and thank you for coming back.

INDEX

NOTES

ALSO AVAILABLE

The Butcher's Apprentice
978-1-59253-776-1

The Kitchen Pantry Cookbook
978-1-59253-843-0

Lebanese Home Cooking
978-1-63159-037-5

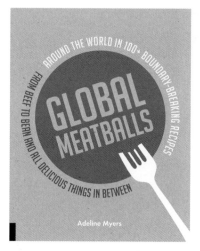

Global Meatballs
978-1-59253-954-3